A Gift of Time

A Gift of Time

A MEMOIR

~

Flora Maxwell Stuart

Birlinn

First published in 2004 by
Birlinn Limited
West Newington House
10 Newington Road
Edinburgh
EH9 1QS
www.birlinn.co.uk

Paperback ISBN 1 84158 311 1
Hardback ISBN 1 84158 337 5 (Exclusive to Traquair House)

British Library Cataloguing-in-Publication Data
A catalogue record for this book is available
from the British Library

Design: Mark Blackadder

Printed and bound by MPG Books, Bodmin

Contents

~

Preface and Acknowledgements

~

Traquair is a house steeped in romance and history and this book records a short but critical period when my late husband, Peter Maxwell Stuart, inherited it in 1962 and we went to live there.

Built in a strategic position above the River Tweed, Traquair's origins are unclear, but royal charters from the thirteenth century show that it belonged to the crown and was used by the kings of Scotland to establish their authority in the surrounding countryside where they could also indulge in their favourite sport of hunting. In the thirteenth century the building was fortified against English invasion and became one of a network of defensive towers spread along the Scottish border.

In the fifteenth century it was acquired by James III's half uncle, the Earl of Buchan, who, in 1491 gave it to his son James Stuart, the first laird of Traquair. It has remained in the hands of his descendants ever since. Before his plans for the enlargement of the house could materialise, James Stuart died fighting for his king at Flodden.

During the next two hundred years, the Stuarts of Traquair remained close to the crown and the house grew accordingly. By the time the seventh laird was granted an earldom, the building had been transformed from a three-storeyed tower to a graceful four-storeyed country house. Two-wings enclosing a courtyard were the last addition. Then time stood still. The fidelity of the Stuarts of Traquair to the Catholic faith and the Jacobite cause resulted in their exclusion from public life and forced them to live in obscurity. In 1876, when the last earl and his sister had both died childless, it passed to their second cousin, Henry Constable Maxwell, and was eventually inherited by Henry's great-grandson, my first husband, Peter.

I have written this book to describe my life before Traquair, my first impressions of the place and the changes that we had to make in order for it to become financially viable. I was lucky enough to know a whole generation who are no longer with us but from whom I learnt a wealth of information about the past.

So many different things happened each day, often unexpectedly, that it has been difficult to recount them in a coherent manner. But I want to acknowledge the many wonderful people who worked for us, often performing several functions at once, and anyone who contributed in any way to the well-being of the house.

Last, but most importantly, it has given me the chance to express my gratitude to the visitors and tourists who have unfailingly supported Traquair: visiting the house and grounds, staying the night, or choosing to get married there, and also to all those who come regularly to the Fair.

The closer I came to the present, the more difficult this book has been to write. Without the help of my agent Jenny Brown and my editor Stephanie Wolfe Murray it would not have been finished. And without my husband Robin who read it, made helpful comments and soothed my hysterics when I battled with various computers, it would not have been written at all. My grateful thanks to them all.

It gives me great pleasure to have passed Traquair on to my daughter Catherine and her husband Mark who have all the expertise and energy to deal with present-day problems. It is a great joy to think of my grandchildren, Isabella, Louis and Charlotte, growing up in the special atmosphere of this much-loved house.

Traquair, 2004   *Flora Maxwell Stuart*

Roots

~

I was born into what Roman Catholics call a 'mixed marriage.' My mother was Roman Catholic and my father began and ended his life as a Protestant. My mother, Teresa, was descended from two 'old' Catholic families of whom she was immensely proud. She considered herself to be superior to every Protestant in the kingdom, including the King and Queen. I asked her once why this was so, and she explained that her family were recusant Catholics, who had had the courage to stick to their faith. When I asked her what an 'old' family was, she said it was one that could trace its ancestry back for many generations, and the most scathing remark she could make about anyone was that 'they would not even know who their grandfather was'.

I found all this puzzling, but once my mother had established herself at the top of the social tree she was able to look down on nearly everyone else. The fact that my father, Alexander Carr-Saunders, was a Protestant did not temper her views at all. She would happily inform us that his family crest, an elephant, could not be as ancient as hers, as elephants were unknown in earlier times. My father was unperturbed by this inaccurate statement, his mind perpetually on higher matters. As long as people could converse with him at his own level he was not interested in their antecedents.

His family had produced many scholars and unusual individuals. His great-grandfather, a clergyman, had been given a temporary post in Russia and, according to family legend, had secretly married a Russian of gypsy ancestry. I enjoyed boasting about my gypsy blood, but my mother told me to keep quiet as it was all nonsense and anyway 'no one will marry you if they think it's true'.

My father, Alexander, had been brought up in a large comfortable house on the South Downs. His mother, after whom I was called, was a Scot, although she spent most of her childhood on a sugar plantation in the West Indies. The fact that he was half-Scottish was obviously of no importance to my father as he never mentioned it. His father, James Carr-Saunders, an underwriter of an insurance company, went off to the City each day. His passion was hunting, and he was said to visit the stables every evening before going into the house to greet his wife.

Alexander was fifteen years younger than his eldest sister, Florence. She was married to a naval officer who eventually became an admiral. When they were stationed abroad her two daughters were often sent to live with their grandparents. Although my father was their uncle, they were near to him in age and more like sisters.

One of these girls, Madeleine, became a woman of independent spirit and a forceful personality. My mother described her as 'thoroughly spoilt'. As a child, she convinced her parents that she was too sensitive to go to school, and after hearing Beethoven's sonata Opus 31 No 2 on a pianola she felt that she had been in touch with the composer's spirit and developed an obsession for him that lasted all her life.

When her father was appointed Commander-in-Chief of the Royal Navy East India Station, she spent two years in Bombay but, unlike her sister, she hated the social life and refused to return for the festivities to celebrate the 1911 Durbar. She chose instead to stay at home in England with her grandfather, reading and listening to Beethoven. She felt she had a calling to attach herself to a man she could admire and whose ideals she could share.

After a friendship with Axel Munthe the author of *The Story of San Michele*, (whether platonic or not we were never to know) she read *Jean Christophe*, a recently published book based on the life of Beethoven. She immediately set off for Switzerland determined to meet its author, Roman Rolland. She managed to engineer a visit to his house. At this meeting she was overwhelmed by 'the tall pale man with penetrating blue eyes' and felt as if 'we had always known one another'. Rolland mentioned that he had just written a small book on Mahatma Gandhi. She had never heard of him and asked who he was. 'He is another Christ,' Rolland told her. After more conversation he bade her goodbye and told her to take every opportunity to travel. 'Obviously dying to get rid of her' was my mother's comment.

After reading about Gandhi, Madeleine felt that at last she had found her vocation. She would go to him and assist him in 'serving the cause of oppressed India through fearless truth and non-violence'. When she wrote asking his permission to join him, he agreed on condition that she should first spend a year learning to weave and to speak the language. She duly attended weaving classes in South Kensington and studiously learnt to speak Urdu, which unfortunately she mistook for Hindi.

A year later, having sent samples of her weaving to Gandhi, she set sail for Bombay and travelled to his Sabarmati ashram. A close relationship developed. He called her Mira Behn, meaning 'daughter', and she, like all his disciples, called him Bapu, meaning 'father'.

In 1932 she accompanied Gandhi when he came to London for the Peace Conference and brought him and his small entourage to visit my parents who were living near Oxford. Gandhi made a lasting impression on both my parents. I was not yet born, but my elder brother, Edmund, was a few months old at the time, and my parents were touched by the gentle way that Gandhi held him in his arms. Gandhi stayed alone while they were eating, but the others sat down to a vegetarian lunch that they ate with relish. To my mother's amusement only Madeleine refused to eat before questioning her closely about the ingredients, even wanting to know whether the eggs had been fertilised.

My father had been a sensitive, studious child but, unlike Madeleine, had not avoided being sent to boarding school. His misery at his preparatory school was nothing compared to the purgatory he suffered at Eton. His house was notorious. Bullies had taken over and their behaviour was allowed to go unchecked. Years later he compared it to life on a convict ship. The writer Shane Leslie, who suffered with him, described the house as Liberty Hall and made use of their ordeal in his novel *The Oppidan*.

The horror of their experience bonded them for life, and when Shane was in London he occasionally dropped in on my father. On one occasion we had just moved into a new house in Brompton Square and my father had rearranged the books that lined one wall of the drawing room. Shane got up and began to scan the shelves. 'I don't see it,' he complained. 'What are you looking for?' my father asked innocently. 'My book, *The Oppidan*, where is it?' A search was begun, which ended up in my being sent down to the basement to look for it. When I eventually found it and presented it to Shane, he looked pained. With a grand gesture he took the book, announced that my father no longer deserved to own it and, asking for a pen, inscribed it with a flourish to me.

My father rarely talked about his school days except for two incidents. He was at Eton at the time of Queen Victoria's death, and the Eton boys had lined the route for the funeral. He was watching as the horses struggled to pull the heavy gun carriage bearing the coffin up the hill to Windsor until it finally become clear that the weight was too much for them. The horses had to be unharnessed and a team of Blue Jackets hastily brought in to take their place.

The other story concerned Ronald Knox, an Eton contemporary who later in life converted to Catholicism, became a priest and made a new translation of the Bible. It was the custom on Sunday evenings for an essay subject to be chalked up on a blackboard and for the older boys to send their fags to copy it down and take it back to them. One evening the question written up on the board was 'What is the oldest part of the Bible?' Ronald Knox neatly changed the 'l' to 'd', and my father remembered an entertaining evening when they all compared notes on what they considered to be the oddest part of the Bible.

When he went up to Oxford he chose to read biology, a completely new subject for him, but after reading Darwin he was convinced that this was the area where the most exciting advances would be made. He came down with a First and a high-minded ambition to improve the world in some way but was uncertain which route to take. He did not share his father's sporting tastes but had fulfilled a bargain by hunting and shooting with him in his vacations in return for then being allowed to use his generous allowance to follow his own interests. He began to collect books and pictures, and made a grand tour of the world that included walking for three weeks in the Japanese mountains.

My grandfather had been made a trustee of Miss Straton, one of the first English woman climbers. She had been obliged to marry her Swiss guide after being stranded with him several times and having to stay overnight together in mountain huts. Their marriage proved to be a happy one, so perhaps they had merely used the need for respectability as an excuse for an unconventional union. They settled in Chamonix where my father was introduced to the pleasure of climbing.

With no need to earn a living, my father furthered his education by reading for the Bar and was admitted to the Middle Temple. He then moved to the East End of London and became Subwarden of Toynbee Hall, a university settlement where Oxford graduates tried to break down class barriers and introduce education to the underprivileged. In 1912 he was elected to Stepney Borough Council. On the day the First World War broke out he was sharing a house with four friends at Wapping, and they all enlisted in the ranks of the London Scottish.

My father found himself stationed in Suez in charge of supplies. He disliked all poseurs, so was not impressed by an arrogant young Englishman, dressed as an Arab, who made a dramatic entrance followed by his escorts to collect his quota. The Englishman gave his name as T. E. Lawrence.

To pass the time my father began to work out a new theory on population and when the war was over continued to work on this project. He decided to live at Garsington outside Oxford and, believing that a farmer was 'the man who does the only job that really matters', he went into a farm partnership with Philip Morell, husband of the literary and artistic hostess Lady Ottoline Morell. They took on a manager who, not surprisingly, took them for a ride, but it introduced him to the writers and artists who frequented Garsington Hall and reinforced his interest in paintings, which continued all his life. He must have seemed a curious, introverted young man in the midst of that Bohemian group. Julian Huxley, the biologist and writer, became a lifelong friend, and his novelist brother, Aldous Huxley, used him as the model for the earnest young professor who could make no small talk in *Antic Hay*.

When my father's book *The Population Problem* was finally published in 1922, he was recognised for his original thought, and out of the blue he was offered the chair in Social Science at Liverpool University. As he disliked institutions and living in towns, the thought of being employed by a university, let alone becoming a professor, was not tempting, but he was interested in the subject and was by then in his mid-forties, so he accepted.

It was at this juncture that the unlikely meeting of my mother and father took place. My mother, Teresa Molyneux Seel, was the eldest of three girls who spent most of their lives quarrelling with each other. My grandmother, born Clare Weld Blundell, was much the youngest of a large Catholic family brought up at Ince Blundell Hall in Lancashire. A younger brother, Herbert, lived in another family property, Lulworth Castle in Dorset, and her eldest sister, Alice, married the fifteenth Lord Lovat and encouraged him to rebuild Beaufort Castle (although she later confessed that she might have 'overdone it'). Yet another sister, Annette, married George

Lane Fox, who had been heir to a large estate in Yorkshire but was disinherited for becoming a Catholic.

My grandmother, Clare, had taken it for granted that her husband would own at least a yacht and a box at the opera. When she found herself married to Edmund Molyneux Seel, a young army officer from another recusant Catholic family who could not give her such luxuries, she felt hard done by and, unreasonably, spent most of her life feeling impoverished. This unfortunate attitude rubbed off on my mother, who told us all her life how poor she was. Even as children we found it hard to sympathise when she recounted the problems of inheriting, at the age of nineteen, three houses in Kensington and the remains of her grandfather's estate in Lancashire.

My mother had grown up during the First World War when a large number of marriageable young men had been killed. She was still expected to marry, but after a lunch party at Norfolk House, where the table was surrounded by single women and the Duchess of Norfolk, tired of being besieged by her unmarried female relations, complained 'How am I supposed to find husbands for all these girls?' she made up her mind that she would take up agriculture and farm the land she had inherited at Huyton. She was among the first women to go up to Oxford University and take a degree at the School of Agriculture.

At Huyton she built up a dairy herd and began to produce tuberculin-tested milk, an innovation in those days. This she delivered personally around Liverpool, usually, she told us with annoyance, getting into trouble for arriving late. In spite of the difficulties and the financial loss she faced farming in the slump between the wars, she always looked on this as an extremely happy period of her life that ended all too soon.

She told us how she had been invited to a concert in Liverpool by an old friend but, as usual, a crisis on the farm prevented her from having anything to eat beforehand. By the interval she was starving and asked her companion to get her some sandwiches. He was a pompous young man who refused her request, saying that he could not sit next to a woman eating sandwiches at a concert. At that moment she caught sight of my father, a figure she just recognised from her time at Oxford. He was more accommodating, and her hunger was satisfied. As she thanked him, she gave him the address of her farm and told him to call in if he was passing. It was not for another year that my father's car broke down nearby and their friendship began to blossom. Their mutual interest in farming no doubt brought my parents together.

My mother's activities were a source of merriment to her relations, and the story is still recounted of how she dashed into her solicitor cousin, Frank Weld, at his Liverpool office, clutching a small bunch of wilting flowers, and asked if he could cash her a cheque in a hurry – she was on her way to Wales to get married and as usual had no ready money. The Catholic Church at that time had decreed that a 'mixed marriage' could not take place within the Liverpool diocese.

It must have been a wrench for my mother to leave her farm and an even greater change for my father, a bachelor professor of forty-six living in a well-ordered house in Liverpool, presided over by an efficient housekeeper. Her fate was sealed when my mother noticed that after dinner a new box of chocolates always appeared and she wondered why my father did not ask what had happened to the last one.

My mother respected my father for his high ideals, and he no doubt, admired her enterprise. They both had a great desire to raise a family and preferred living in the country. They soon decided to stay in Liverpool only during term-time. They had both enjoyed their years up at Oxford so they decided to look for a house in the surrounding countryside.

When she was an undergraduate at Oxford, my mother had taken a punt up the Cherwell and glimpsed from the river a house that she had never forgotten. It was a beautiful Elizabethan manor called Water Eaton. To her delight she heard that it was empty and in need of care and attention, as the family who owned it did not wish to live there. They would not sell but were prepared to grant a long lease.

Both my parents fell in love with the house, and it was

there that they created a small paradise. It was there that I spent my first eight years, which, according to the Jesuits, are the most impressionable years of one's life.

A Childhood Idyll

~

Water Eaton has lived in my memory all my life. I see it always with the eyes of a child, and it continually evokes the happiness I had there. The soft grey stone house stood as if lost in time at the end of a long drive. Its pointed finials and mullioned windows kindled images of past times. Two stone buildings, as old as the house and thought to have once been part of it, stood on either side, forming a courtyard. A flight of worn stone steps led up to the huge oak front door standing between two pillars. Low parapets ran down at either side, capped by large stone balls that would not budge however hard we pushed them.

Facing the front door across the lawns and beyond the yew trees, cut to resemble birds, was a field with a large square dovecote of the same stone as the house. Originally built to house pigeons that could be eaten during the winter months, the inside was lined with hundreds of nesting boxes. My mother filled them with white fantail pigeons who fluttered round us when we threw maize on to the lawn.

Beyond the field flowed the River Cherwell where we had our own landing stage and a punt. Expeditions in the punt were magical journeys as we glided along under weeping willows, past clumps of bulrushes. We would trail our hands in the water trying to hang on to slimy weeds.

One day, a visiting small boy and I decided to set off on our own. We got into the punt, undid the rope and began to move downstream rapidly before our escape was noticed. My chief memory is the exhilaration of freedom and then the sight of the legs of excited adults on the bank above us calling out different instructions. It was not long before the boat hit the bank, an adult got hold of the rope and we were captured and ignominiously towed back to the landing stage.

My mother was determined to carry on farming in a small way and kept little black Dexter cows that she milked by hand with the help of a cowman. She kept hens and hatched out chicks. The eggs lay in drawers in large square incubators, kept warm by oil lamps that gave an all-pervasive smell to the room. Each day the eggs had to be sprinkled with water and turned over. On the appointed date we would peer into the drawer and hear the crackling of shells as little beaks chipped holes in the eggs and eventually small damp chicks would struggle out.

The most gentle cow became mine. All their names were prefixed with 'Water', and she was called Water Lily. She stood happily munching cow cake as I was taught to wash her udder with a flannel and green household soap and to sit on a stool and lean my head against her warm, comfortable side as I clutched her teats to milk her. I gradually learnt to squirt the milk into the frothing bucket, which changed its tune as it filled up. Later, I would watch as the milk was set in flat enamel pans and see the cream being skimmed off the top. This was made into small cheeses that lay on a shelf in the dairy and had to be turned over every day.

But all the time, my security and happiness were centred on my beloved Irish nanny who reigned supreme in the nursery and was the personification of kindness and understanding. She must have been in her fifties then and had already worked for cousins, so my mother knew her well. She had long, grey hair plaited and wound round in a bun secured by numerous hairpins. Constantly troubled by corns, she wore lace-up brogue shoes with long pointed toes and nearly always a grey skirt with a cardigan and silky cream blouse. Her skin was lined but soft to touch and had a faint aroma of Ponds cold cream. My brother Edmund had his own small bedroom but I was lucky enough to sleep next to her in the large panelled nursery – she in a brass bedstead and I in a wooden cot.

Every morning I woke up to the comforting sound of her filling her chamber pot, and I squinted at her though the wooden bars as she squatted in a pale pink nightdress, her long grey hair hanging loosely down her back. A few minutes later, knowing by instinct that I was awake, she would tell me to sit up and then pass me a small celluloid beaker of fresh orange juice and a Marie biscuit. After she had boiled her kettle on a spirit stove in the corner of the room, she would get into bed again and settle down with her tea and a book.

Unless she was taking us out for a walk, Nanny always seemed to be in the nursery, which was my haven. My mother was usually busy and when she found me in the way and did not have time for me or my brother, Edmund, who was four years older, I could always be sure of a loving welcome from Nanny. She sensed immediately if I was taking refuge there only because I was in trouble and would ask me what I had done wrong. She was like God, all-seeing and all-knowing and perfectly just. I was a docile child and can never remember her ever raising her voice. Her calm presence, soft voice and contented nature must have had more influence on me than anyone else in my life.

In the winter, a coal fire burnt cheerfully in the grate, and I went off to sleep watching the shadows of the flickering flames dance on the wall. Occasionally, in the evening, Nanny would make fudge on her small stove, and I watched her drop large lumps of butter into the saucepan and was lulled to sleep by the sweet comforting smell of the melting butter and sugar and the thought of a taste of it the next day.

We children, my elder brother, Edmund, and I, and later my younger brother, Nicholas, sitting in a high chair, had our meals in the nursery dining room, a small sunny room off the main dining room served by constantly changing nursery maids – I believe only fifteen or sixteen years of age – who rarely came up to Nanny's high standards and made no impression on my life as they scarcely dared to address a word to us. The same was true of the other servants, who were mostly Austrian and kept to themselves. I never remember going into the kitchen although I do remember standing in the back kitchen and watching my mother draw a hen that had accidentally been run over. I gazed transfixed as the eggs appeared, first full-sized and shelled and then decreasing in size like Russian dolls until there was nothing but a clot of blood.

When I was three, my father was chosen to succeed William Beveridge as Director of the London School of Economics, another unsought-after position. 'The School', as he always referred to it, had been founded by the social reformers Sydney and Beatrice Webb in 1895. He was attracted by a new positive seat of learning that was unhampered by the traditions of the older universities. After staying with the Webbs and talking to Sydney till after midnight, he made up his mind to accept. It was to dominate his life for the next twenty years.

The LSE was part of London University but the only institution in Britain devoted exclusively to the teaching of the social sciences for both under- and post-graduates. It had attracted many distinguished academics to its staff and students came from all over the world. Many were politically motivated and ended up in their countries' respective governments.

My father rented a small service flat in Fetter Lane where he spent the week and where my mother would occasionally join him. Every weekend he returned by train and the house would be full of his or my mother's friends, many of them eminent academics connected to the School. To me, he remained a fairly remote figure who slept in his own bedroom adjoining a large book-lined study. He occasionally took me for a walk across the fields with a flat black metal box hanging across his back. Into this he would put wild flowers or leaves and when we returned he would sit me down next to him at his huge desk and, getting out his flower book, would carefully identify any flower or leaf he did not recognise.

My mother engaged a Froebel-trained governess and made a school-room in one of the buildings at the front of the house. Several children of the Oxford academics Frank Pakenham and Frank Taylor were driven out from north Oxford to join my brother Edmund for lessons. I watched them enviously and was occasionally allowed to join in. When it was warm, they sat at small tables and chairs outside on the lawn and after lunch, camp beds were put out for them to rest on while a story was read aloud.

The best children's books were chosen as carefully as the teacher, and later, when I learnt to read, I imagined for a long time that any adult book would be completely beyond my comprehension. I did begin to enjoy the births columns of *The Times*, however, where I experienced a thrill of horror when I read the word 'stillborn', which so often seemed to appear after a birth. We were supposed to glean our news from the *Children's Newspaper*, the most boring paper ever printed. When I first read a tabloid I could not believe that a newspaper could be so entertaining.

A small Church of England chapel stood in its own walled garden by the house. The flowerbeds were edged with neat box hedges and at Easter we searched for chocolate eggs hidden beneath them. The church was used once a month by the local parish, and I helped Nanny, who was no religious bigot, to polish the brass vases and fill them with flowers.

I rarely remember ever leaving Water Eaton, nor did Nanny, except on Sundays when we went into Oxford for Mass. When I first heard of 'days off', I asked my mother why Nanny did not have one. 'She wouldn't know what to do,' was the terse reply. She was, instead, allowed a month every summer when she would disappear to her relatives in Ireland, and I felt completely bereft until she returned with fresh butter and soda bread which she prepared in small squares for me to taste.

On the rare occasions that we were asked to children's parties in Oxford, Nanny became very anxious that we might pick up a germ. When we were ready to leave, me in my party dress and Edmund still complaining that he did not want to go, we were ordered to open our mouths and hold back our heads while she took a long brush and painted some vile-tasting pink liquid on to the back of our throats.

The War

~

The outbreak of the Second World War had, at first, little effect on our protected lives. I noticed my father bent with concentration as he tried to listen to the news on the crackling wireless and whisper anxiously to my mother. I heard her cry out in distress, 'France has fallen,' and watched his face tighten but only to mutter, 'Shh, my dear, not in front of the children.'

From time to time I picked up adult conversation and for a moment a sense of fear would grip me, but on the surface life went on as usual. My father was now too old to be called up and was occupied with the safeguarding of the LSE.

As the news worsened and the danger of bombing in Oxford became a reality, it was decided that two of the families who came to do lessons should come to live with us. Frank Taylor brought his wife and two boys, John and Julian, and Frank Pakenham, later to be Lord Longford, came with his wife Elizabeth, and their children, Antonia, Thomas and Paddy.

Each family brought its nanny so the household increased all round. Antonia, who was later to become a well-known writer, was a little older than me and became my idol. It was wonderful to have another girl to play with, and she was an imaginative, intrepid child, constantly in trouble. She wrote endless plays in which she was the queen and I was only too willing to be the lady-in-waiting and invented a string of games that kept us amused.

Three old donkeys came to take refuge with us and with

them came Miss Deering, an elderly, horsy lady with a squashed felt hat and hairy face. She had taught soldiers to ride in the First World War, and she gave us riding lessons and showed us how to groom and do exercises while sitting astride the donkeys. When Nanny objected to me returning with nails caked with donkey scurf, Miss Deering told me not to worry as horse scurf was the basic ingredient of soap. I continued to believe this for many years.

In the walled garden, beside an old summer house, was an ancient yew tree ideal for climbing. The first three branches were at an easy distance apart and then the trunk forked. A huge step was needed to get through the fork and up into the higher branches. The older children all got through with ease, but I was never able to get farther than the first branches. Time after time I watched them all disappear while I stood on the third branch imagining the delights they were experiencing above me. 'What's it like?' I would call up to Antonia, and she would describe a different world where the sky was nearly within her reach.

The first night that an air-raid siren sounded its threatening wail, we were all woken and told to get out of bed and put on our newly issued gas marks. We assembled excitedly on the ground floor, which had been chosen as the safest part of the house. The adults had brought down bedding and were trying to make the whole episode seem fun although we could sense the anxiety in their voices.

We were told to lie down and try to go to sleep. Our faces were sweaty with condensation and the smell of the new rubber of the gas masks was overpowering. Before long the 'all clear' sounded – an equally eerie sound – and we thankfully got back into our beds. For the rest of the war I never put my gas mask on again.

The war became a way of life. A small square of butter, our ration for the week, was put on to separate dishes and marked off into seven strips, one for each day of the week but often finished in the first two days. The house grew colder. Baths, we were not sorry to find, became less frequent and the few inches of water were shared by one child after another. Frank Pakenham's pyjamas began to show beneath his sleeves and trouser legs. Nanny explained that he was absent-minded and adults were allowed to do this sort of thing but children were definitely not.

I looked on Elizabeth Pakenham with awe and admiration. She was dark and pretty and, unlike my mother, wore make-up. She believed in entertaining children by teaching them. She taught us Latin vocabulary by making us stand in a line and sending us to the end if we could not get the right translation. Her own children were given poetry to learn as a punishment, and she encouraged us to talk and ask her questions.

At that time she was standing as a Labour candidate in Birmingham, and her children were already well versed in politics and fought for the red mug at our elevenses each morning. Not knowing what it was all about, I asked her one day what Labour was. She talked to children in the same way that she talked to adults and told me very seriously that the Labour Party was the party that wanted to make *everyone* happy. I knew that was what *I* wanted and my political allegiance was set for the rest of my life.

Frank Pakenham was a charming, vague man, and many stories were recounted about his absent-minded habits and his generosity to the needy. It was said that he frequently took a taxi to Christ Church, telling the driver to wait at one gate and a short while later, forgetting all about it, would leave by a different gate and call another one. He was a soft touch for the Oxford tramps, and he himself told us that a tramp had called at his house one day asking for clothing. He had reluctantly given him a coat that he still occasionally used. Only a few weeks later, the man came begging again, wearing the coat. 'Is there nothing you can spare me?' he asked. 'All I have to keep me warm is this filthy garment.'

Frank had been asked to join the panel of a brains trust that was to take place in Oxford and as a treat we children were allowed to go and listen. I was squashed into the back of a car with Lady Beveridge and the Pakenhams, who spent the journey going through the questions, which they were not supposed to have seen, and deciding how they would answer them. I would have taken little interest had Elizabeth not suddenly turned to me and said conspiratorially, 'You won't tell anyone what we have been talking about, will you?'

One winter's day I was clutching the side of my younger brother's pram as Nanny took us for a walk up the drive. Far away, by a hedgerow, a man was lurking, occasionally bending down and finally disappearing altogether on the far side. Nanny said nothing, but the pram was quickly turned and we raced at full speed back towards the house. I heard her telling my mother that she was sure there was a German spy in the field. My mother rushed to the telephone and rang the police. For a while Nanny was the hero of the hour, but later that evening it was discovered that the so-called spy had been a botanist from Oxford University looking for some rare species. The whole episode was suddenly treated as a joke and the laugh seemed to be on Nanny. I suffered for her and held her hand tightly as we went upstairs back to the nursery. I knew she had been hurt and that they had all been just as mistaken as she had been.

By 1942 the Pakenhams and Taylors decided to return to their houses in Oxford. Antonia was still my only friend, and we stayed with each other regularly. Her mother, Elizabeth, had a new baby, and she told us quite naturally what it felt like to give birth and also how she used a breast pump if she had to go away. My own mother rarely discussed anything like this.

One day Antonia and her brother Thomas and I were sitting in the kitchen having lunch with their housekeeper, Mrs Pope. The doorbell rang and Mrs Pope returned from answering it looking worried. She said that a gentleman had arrived who said he had an appointment with Mr Pakenham. She had heard him come in earlier and go upstairs. She looked round the table at us and for some reason chose me. 'Just run up and tell Mr Pakenham that there is someone waiting to see him,' she said. I approached the bedroom door and knocked on it shyly. After a pause I was told to come in. Frank and Elizabeth were lying together in their double bed. Elizabeth half sat up and, trying to put me at my ease, said, 'What is it, Flora, you look as if you have seen a ghost?' I gabbled the message quickly and left the room as soon as I could. I felt acutely embarrassed. I imagined that this was how babies were made. I began to wonder how my parents had managed it when they slept in separate rooms.

One morning a smart young officer arrived at Water Eaton, driven by a glamorous young lady in uniform, who we were told was his 'FANY'. They were closeted with my mother for some time and she finally appeared for lunch looking distraught. She told us that the house was going to be requisitioned by the Army and we had been given two weeks to get out.

The officer and the FANY moved in to make sure that we were getting ready to go, and very shortly more soldiers appeared and began to move things out of the house. My father's cellar was raided and my grandfather's pistols were stolen. My mother was a hoarder, and boxes of her things were thrown down from the top floor of the outbuildings. I could not believe that this army was on our side. My parents were frantically trying to find somewhere for us to live.

To gain attention Edmund began to draw swastikas on the wall, which soon brought down my mother's wrath. She explained that the soldiers who were going to be trained at Water Eaton would be risking their lives when they were dropped by parachute behind enemy lines to stop the Germans coming. If the Germans did come, our father, as a professor, would be the first to be taken to a concentration camp. The house was changing before my eyes. Rows of lavatories appeared at the back of the house and before we left, the kitchen had become the soldiers' mess.

The outcome of the move was that Nanny was to leave us and go to work for one of the cousins whom she had brought up. Anne Phillimore's husband had been killed in France and she had been left with two young children. We were to rent a house, owned by Sir John Cockcroft of atom-splitting fame, in Cambridge while my father arranged for the LSE to be evacuated to Peterhouse. With us came Mrs Bray who was to stay on and work for us and her three sons. She was a down-to-earth Lancashire woman who accepted as her lot that she and her boys were crammed into a couple of rooms at the back of the house while we occupied the rest. The Bray boys went off to the local state school while we set off on our bicycles for private ones and there was little contact between us, but I spent many hours in the kitchen talking to Mrs Bray. She never grumbled but used to tell me, 'When the war is over and my old man comes back, you won't see me for a cloud of dust.'

At first I did not miss Nanny in the excitement of living in a suburban villa with neighbours on either side instead of our isolated existence in the country. Suddenly I felt that I was like everyone else as I walked up our street looking into the gardens and occasionally peering into their houses. When Nanny came up for an odd night to visit us, she took a pot of cold cream and some cotton wool out of her bag and told me to hold my face up to the light. My skin was ingrained with dirt, she said, as she polished my cheeks and ended up with a bit of grey cotton wool. Then she asked for my brush and comb and began to take all the tangles out of my long hair. I had become used to being unable to pull the comb though it. She told me I was old enough to look after myself and even if we did not have enough hot water, I was to wash my face with soap and cold water, night and morning.

At night, air-raid wardens patrolled the street – busybodies my mother called them – and knocked on the door of anyone whose windows were not properly blacked out. My mother refused to have proper blackout curtains as she had no intention of living in the suburbs for long and was determined that we would soon move back to the country. She rigged up a variety of old drapery with the result that, to the mortification of my father who preferred to be a good citizen, the air-raid warden would constantly be at our door telling us to turn out our lights.

All the animals had been dispersed. The cows were sent to graze on the LSE playing fields outside London, and my mother felt frustrated. During the First World War she had worked as a dispatch rider and ridden a motorbike round Hyde Park Corner. Now she had only the cooking to cope with. Mrs Bray did all the housework. It was not long before she was searching the outlying countryside for another house and soon found and bought an old mill house near Cambridge. It was dark and gloomy, with a history of suicide, a mill pond, a huge garden with no gardener, a couple of fields and a multitude of sheds. Mrs Bray and I wept at the thought of the move, but my mother was convinced that there she could do her war work, producing milk and food and keeping her family from starvation.

The cows were quickly brought back from the playing fields, hens took up residence in one shed, two pigs, doomed for bacon, filled another, and a few geese and ducks squatted in the mud around the pond. She soon arranged for a nearby American camp to deliver their swill, and we would bend over the bins of waste with interest as we identified yellow skins as grapefruit and the long skins, which were now only seen in pictures on greengrocers' walls, as bananas.

My father was to spend the week at Peterhouse in Cambridge where the LSE had been evacuated. Edmund was to be sent to Westminster, normally a London-based public school but now evacuated to Wales. My father considered that the education in Catholic public schools was inferior, so my mother had agreed to compromise, thinking that a Protestant day school would be less likely to lead him off the path to Rome. My younger brother Nicholas and I were to go to King Alfred's School, a 'modern' school that had been evacuated to an area a few miles away from our house.

On the first day of term, a teacher took me into her room. She went through a long list of subjects and asked me to choose the ones I wanted to do. When my list turned out to be short, she inveigled me into adding a few more, and I ended up with a timetable such as I might have followed in any normal school. The school was co-educational, and the children were mostly boarders and none too friendly to a newcomer.

At the end of the day I had to walk through some trees before I joined the road to pick up my lift home. One day I heard cries behind me and a group of small boys descended on me, threw me to the ground, pulled up my skirt and tried to remove my pants. By kicking violently I managed to beat them off. As I stumbled up I remember hearing one boy say triumphantly, 'I did see her crack!'

It must have been a result of this incident that prompted my mother to tell me at the end of the term that I would not be returning to St Alfred's but would become a boarder at a convent school in Ascot.

A huge list of uniform arrived, all to be purchased from Harrod's, and I was delighted with the idea that I might have some new clothes, an extravagance that my mother did not believe in. As she read through the list, however, my hopes fell. 'What are the nuns thinking of?' she exclaimed in horror. 'Have they forgotten they have taken a vow of holy poverty?' Where the list required six pairs of knickers she changed it to three, and so on, until I finally arrived at school with half the required clothing and a few unsatisfactory garments that she had made for me herself. Dressmaking was not one of her talents.

Nuns and Crocodiles

～

The nuns at the convent in Cambridge where I had been to school had talked in glowing terms about their other convent at Ascot. Whereas Cambridge was a large state-aided school with a few private boarders, Ascot was an entirely private boarding school and, as I soon discovered, a snobbish one at that.

I watched nervously as the nuns unpacked my trunk and silently listed all the items that were missing. These were promptly ordered from Harrod's and put on my bill. My pyjamas, made from two assorted bits of material, unheard of in those days, were held up for ridicule and one of the nuns compared me to Oliver Twist.

The nuns on the whole meant well and tried to be kind, but I found it difficult to see them as real human beings. They glided silently around the building in their soft shoes – beautiful creatures from another planet in long black habits with gently pleated skirts, flatteringly tight at the waist, and simple black and white wimples that completely covered their hair. Only the rattle of their rosary beads, hanging from their belts, ever gave them away. It seemed almost indecent if a couple of hairs escaped from under their wimples, and we would whisper to each other in awe, 'I saw Sister So-and-so's hair!'

They supervised all our meals but never ate with us – we wondered if they actually ate at all. They appeared and disappeared through a door into their side of the convent, where we were never allowed to venture. The nuns expected obedience without explanation and we were supervised during every minute of the day. When we moved from classroom to classroom or to the chapel or refectory, we had to form a line in height order with the smallest in the lead.

We slept in cubicles in a dormitory, each with a washstand and basin. Every morning we were woken up for Mass with the words 'Benedicamus domino' to which we replied sleepily 'Deo gratias'. Jugs of hot and cold water were brought to us then and again at night.

After the lights were put out, an elderly nun sat saying her rosary at the far end of the dormitory, and the most daring activity of the day was to get out of bed, dance around the room and then dash back without being caught. I soon found that the great advantage of a strict regime was the pleasure that could be obtained by breaking the rules. I felt a surge of strength when I challenged the nuns' authority, and it also made me popular with the other girls – and to be popular was what I wanted most of all.

Every morning, we were lined up outside the chapel for Mass and we put on our veils – black for every day and white on feast days. We filed into our benches where we each kept as many holy pictures as we could collect and a pile of Catholic Truth Society pamphlets that we never read. Swapping holy pictures helped to pass the time during Mass. Even so, the solemnity in the highly polished chapel lit for benediction by a mass of flickering candles, the beautiful singing of the choir, the emphasis on the importance of the occasion and the value of prayer formed a solid foundation for my religious beliefs that has never left me.

From the beginning of term until the end, we rarely left the school and then only in a long crocodile, walking in twos up to south Ascot and back again. On certain weekends, we were allowed to be taken out, and most parents managed this once a term. We stood outside the refectory waiting for them to arrive. Huge black cars would sweep in, one after the other, and drive off with their respective child. Finally, usually late, our battered Ford Popular would slowly crunch to a halt on the gravel. My parents saw no logic in spending money on expensive cars. The nuns would look pained at the sight of it, and I could not wait to get out and away.

Although I went back to school quite cheerfully looking forward to meeting my friends, as the term progressed I always began to suffer severe homesickness – a grinding physical pain in my stomach, a sensation that I was to feel again only in the months following my husband's death. The mind is unable to dominate the body, and however hard one tries, one cannot free oneself from it. My parents were understanding and promised me that as soon as the war was finally over we would have a house in London and I would be able to attend a day school there.

In spite of teaching Christianity, the nuns had an almost childish worship of money and titles. Their views on politics were equally simplistic. Before the general election, one of the nuns gave us a talk on politics. 'There are two main parties,' she told us, 'Labour and Conservative. However, there is only one party that the parents of everyone in this room will vote for and that is Conservative.' Her eyes swept around us confidently and I tried not to meet them. My father, who was too independently minded to ally himself to any political party, had told me that he thought that Britain would need a change of government after the war and he was going to vote Labour. Although I was happy to tell my friends that I was a Labour supporter, I did not have the courage to stand up and proclaim my views.

The nuns' attitude towards me changed abruptly after my father was given a knighthood. My mother's best friend, on hearing the news, telephoned her to commiserate. She thought it a terrible misfortune to become the wife of a 'common knight'. My mother explained to me apologetically that my father had been obliged to accept the honour for the sake of the porters at the LSE. 'It means a lot to people like that,' she explained. The nuns, on the other hand, were both surprised and excited. Even the fact that my father was a Protestant was suddenly overlooked. They kept asking me why he had received such an honour, the fact that, among other things, he had sat on a royal commission for education not having come to their notice. My mother insisted that my younger brother and I should accompany my father to the Investiture as we would enjoy it more than she would. The composition I wrote describing the scene was immediately chosen to go into the school magazine.

Compared to the nuns' comfortable life at school where unfortunate lay sisters did all the domestic work, my mother now found herself trying to look after the house, milking cows, making cream, butter and cheese, and curing hams, all at the same time. She found it hard to get help and if she did, no one stayed long when they discovered the chaos they had to work in. It left her permanently exhausted. The 'servant problem' was a popular topic of conversation among her friends, who had never lived without them and could not believe that they would not soon reappear.

As there was always hope that these mythical creatures might one day become a reality, we continued to live as if they were there, never eating in the kitchen and having all our meals passed through a hatch to the dining room. To our amusement, my father still walked around the room as he ate his porridge, often talking to himself at the same time, but as it was a smaller room than he was used to, he would often leave the dining room and do a turn in the drawing room as well.

In the chaotic back kitchen, hams hung from hooks in the ceiling, and below, large pans of milk lay set for cream that we later took turns to churn into cheesy-tasting butter. I once saw a maggot fall from a ham with a splash into the milk below. The airing cupboard more often than not contained a half-dead duckling in the course of being revived or, worse by far, a stiff little corpse that had not survived and had been forgotten altogether.

I was sorry for Nicholas, who was still at a day school. In the evening he had to sit beside my mother holding a paraffin lantern as she milked the cows. She was so busy with the animals that she had little time for us. All her activity was supposed to be for our benefit, but Nicholas and I would have preferred to have had more of her attention. This was reserved for Edmund, our elder brother, as it had been since his birth.

Nicholas was good at amusing himself. He liked experimenting and wanted to find out how everything worked. I was hugely disappointed when he explained to me that the money put into the coin box in a public telephone did not go through to the operator in some magic way but was counted by the number of pings it made.

Antonia Pakenham was still my closest friend, and we often stayed with each other, but she had grown up more quickly than I had. From having to learn poetry as a punishment, Antonia and her brother Thomas could quote a few lines appropriate to any occasion, which they frequently did, overwhelming me with their superiority.

Once, at their house in Oxford, a young master at the Dragon School, who had become a friend of the family, took us both out in a punt. After a while he stopped the punt, telling me to wait as Antonia and he had something to do. They scrambled on to the bank and retired behind some bushes. They soon returned and nothing was said, but an uncertain feeling of something being wrong took hold of me. I realised that a chasm had opened up between us. As it had been on the yew tree, Antonia had gone ahead and I was left behind.

In the village at home sex was heavily in the air. Every woman in the neighbourhood who was not kept under lock and key was being wooed by a desperate GI from the local US Army camp. Occasionally, at night, an American soldier and his girl would take refuge in what they thought was an empty space behind the pub but was actually in the driveway in front of our house. To the horror of my mother they would make love up against a wall and I would be told not to look out of the window. Naturally I did and was annoyed that it was too dark to see what was going on. The girls in the village all knew who was having sex with whom and where, but I was rarely allowed to come into contact with them.

I was once allowed to spend a day with the children of a

family who were considered to be sufficiently intellectual and respectable. As soon as they were out of reach of their parents, they took me into a deserted part of the garden and I was told that we would play a game where the boys (aged about twelve) would make love with the girls. A bossy girl decided who went with whom. One little boy who seemed over-keen was told 'not to take it out'. I was filled with horror and stood transfixed to the spot as I was paired off with another little boy who, to my relief, seemed nervous. At last I plucked up courage to say that I did not want to play the game and after a lot of discussion it was decided that as long as I swore that I 'would not tell', I would be allowed to opt out.

It was about this time that I became aware of a mild handicap that has dogged me all my life. A friend of my mother, whom I knew quite well, came to stay and we all went out for a picnic. When it was over, she sat in the car while we packed up. She had combed her hair and as I went towards the car I could not recognise her. I thought that someone else had taken her place. As soon as she spoke I knew it was her, but all my life I have been unable to recognise people – even those I know fairly well.

At Christmas, the soldiers at the local US Army camp invited all the children in the village to a Christmas lunch and present-giving. After much pleading, my brothers and I were allowed to go for a short time as long as we promised to stick together and not to stay for lunch. I, particularly, was warned never to leave my brothers' side. My mother seemed obsessed by the fear that I would be 'interfered with'.

On arrival, we were each given a large cardboard box and told to go down the lines of the soldiers' huts and call into each one. Far from the soldiers being licentious, they were mostly overwhelmed with homesickness. Photographs of their families were pinned up on the walls, and they patted us on the head, asked us our names and how old we were, and told us about their children they had left back at home. They each generously dropped an American candy or chocolate bar into our boxes, and we eventually arrived home for our Christmas lunch brimming over with more goodies than we had ever seen since the start of sweet rationing.

Our Christmas meal had become a fairly ad hoc affair, as the cows still had to be milked and my mother made few preparations in advance. She always wrote her Christmas cards while waiting to go to midnight Mass. Since she had given up rearing turkeys, we would have any old hen that was around, and the Christmas pudding was made just before lunch, 'much lighter and more digestible' she would assure us. She much preferred giving us a present during the year when she found something we would like and saw no point in keeping it. Wrapping them up also seemed to her to be an unnecessary extravagance. Having no Christmas present for me one year, she told me that she was giving me her mother's early Victorian desk, which stood in the drawing room. At the time I was disappointed and would have much preferred a parcel, but ten years later, when I got married, I reminded her and carried it off to my new house. My favourite part of Christmas was a card game called Commerce, which my father's family had played for many generations and must have dated from Georgian times. Each player had three lives, represented by counters. A chocolate was placed on each one and at the end of a round the loser had to give his or her chocolate to the winner.

Several days a week a squadron of bombers took off from the American Air Force base nearby and the number of planes could be counted leaving and checked again on return. Often there would be one or two missing. My mother often shed a tear as she counted them, but I was cocooned in the selfishness of childhood and took tragedies that did not concern me for granted.

When the war did finally come to an end we had to write a composition at school on what that meant to us. I received an A for writing about the relief I felt that no more lives would be lost, planes brought down and families left grieving. But as I wrote I knew that it was the fact that I would be able to leave St Mary's Convent and go to a day school that the end of the war really meant for me.

Youth Post-War

⁓

After a wartime childhood in the country, the thought of moving to London was a dream. My brief memories were of a visit to my parents' flat in Fetter Lane; an odd night in the bowels of the earth under the LSE where the caretaker and his wife had created a cosy space surrounded by the stored books; and a recollection of sitting in a taxi at night seeing lights instead of country darkness – all of which contributed to my expectations of an enchanted city.

I was not put off by the scars left by the war. Bomb damage could be seen everywhere. There were empty spaces where a house had been completely wiped out and willowherb grew rampant on the bomb sites.

We were to live in a flat that had been made in the top two floors of a tall bomb-damaged house in Kensington still propped up by a wooden buttress. It was one of the three London houses that my mother and her sisters had inherited from their grandfather. Their house next door had been bombed out of existence and only the rubble remained. There were strict laws governing the amount of money that could be spent on repairs and the rest of the house was left untouched. We climbed up the damaged main stairs and passed the derelict rooms where remnants of wallpaper hung off the walls. Everything was covered in the thick dust that bombs leave in their wake.

We were to return to Mill House at weekends, but my mother insisted on bringing up some hens to keep on the bombed site next door and devised the practical method of feeding them by throwing all our waste scraps out of the kitchen window. A block of luxury flats had been built on the other side, and the residents soon began to complain as the amount of refuse left by the hens accumulated. My mother was indignant. This would turn into compost, she explained, and she did not like good scraps being wasted. Her intention was to make a heap at one end of the site, but she could not persuade my brothers or myself to do this, with the result that the waste increased and so did the complaints.

Undeterred, she decided to bring some ducks up to join the hens. As petrol was still rationed, we often had to travel backwards and forwards to Mill House by train and bus. As we stepped down one day from a double-decker bus, my mother and I each clutching a basket with ducks' heads sticking out of it, the conductor turned to us and said in a sarcastic voice, 'Madam, next time you travel, I advise you to take the ark.'

By this time I had reached an age when I longed to be like everyone else. I wished I lived in the elegant block of flats opposite and that animals would get out of my life. But we had other compensations. There was a trap-door on to the very sooty roof of the house, and on hot days we took up old punt seats and sat having a picnic as we looked for miles across the roof tops. At that time, with rationing still in progress, cakes were a great rarity and could be bought only if they were eaten in the café or tea shop where they were sold. We often gazed at them through the window of a small tea shop in Notting Hill Gate, then a sleazy, unattractive area. My mother considered it unhygienic, as well as extravagant, to take us all out for tea. She would go in on her own and order tea and then whisk the cakes into her bag and bring them home. We would sit on the roof, eating them in sheer ecstasy.

There were two brands of ice cream on the market, Walls and Eldorado. My mother said we were never to eat Eldorado ice cream as a friend of hers had visited the factory and found it dirty. One day, for a treat when we were waiting to meet my father off a train, Nicholas was allowed to go and buy us ices. He could find only Eldorado. My mother had a fit when he brought them back and said that we could not possibly eat them. 'Give them to those two children over there,' she ordered, pointing to two shabbily dressed boys standing alone. 'But why won't they get ill?' I asked indignantly. To this I received no answer.

Clothes were still rationed. I longed for new clothes, but my mother insisted that she had either lost the clothing coupons or that they must be kept for sheets. She thrived on the fact that new clothes were out of reach and triumphantly bought a parachute that was being sold off by the Ministry of War. Parachutes were made of natural silk, a luxury that had not been available for a long time, but they had to be unpicked and the odd-shaped segments sewn together again. My mother found this a great test of her ingenuity, and I was soon the ungrateful possessor of a wardrobe of silk clothes in bizarre designs.

Even though she did not believe in many or expensive clothes, she was very particular about the kind of clothes, and she was adamant that in the country only flat-heeled shoes and tweeds – and no black clothes – could be worn. It was an extension of her views on the use of language, which was supposed to show the world what kind of background you came from – like being a member of an exclusive club. You must never talk about a 'suit', only a 'coat and skirt' and 'blouse' had to rhyme with 'shoes'. It was anathema to her to hear anyone say 'pardon' or use the word 'toilet'. Brompton Road had to be pronounced 'Brumpton' and Ovington Gardens to rhyme with 'hot' and not 'goat', and of course Catholic and Mass had to have a long 'a'. As her mother had been born in early Victorian days, many of her pronunciations went back to that era.

I was deliriously happy at being out of boarding school. The freedom of travelling to a day school on the Underground and moving around London on my own instead of being taken everywhere was exhilarating. A great friend from school,

Serena Dunn, had left the convent at the same time as I had. We were now both at different day schools. I went to the Holy Child Convent in Cavendish Square, but we met constantly at weekends, and her father often took us out to the cinema in the evenings. Serena lived for a time in a flat in Arlington House. We roller-skated all over the ground floor and then up Arlington Street where there was a side door into the Ritz Hotel. Our ambition was to make a dash through one door on our roller skates and come out through the main door into Piccadilly. We would linger casually by the side entrance waiting for the doorman to be out of sight, but just as we were ready to go, his huge top-hatted figure would reappear in front of us and just as casually block our path.

I loved going away from home and was often invited to stay with Serena at her father's house in Wiltshire. It was the first time that I came into contact with comics, which we read avidly, lying in bed with the dogs beside us. There was a stable with horses and show ponies, and her father took us out riding. Serena's parents were divorced, and the house was looked after by housekeepers. I didn't realised at the time how much she missed her mother but envied her having such a charming father who spent so much time amusing her.

As I grew older, my mother stayed in the country more often or disappeared up north to Huyton, taking only Edmund with her. Her land was to be bought by compulsory purchase and used as a site for factories. She was put out when she heard that the road running slap-bang through her old farm was to be called Harold Wilson Avenue, after the local MP, but, hoping that it would bring much needed employment to the area, she did not put up resistance and donated an extra piece of land for a playground. Later, after a Huntley and Palmer's biscuit factory was built on the site, she would pass round their biscuits, saying with a caustic smile, 'Made on the farm'.

Nanny was now in London where she was a companion to a woman who had had a stroke and had lost her power of speech. Although it was never mentioned to me, it transpired that when Anne Phillimore's children grew older she had employed a governess for them and this woman had ousted Nanny. My mother castigated Anne, whom she had never liked, but was also determined that Nanny was not her responsibility. She said that Anne lived in a big house and should have looked after her for good, but Nanny was still fond of Anne and would say nothing against her.

Nanny never changed. She always looked exactly the same. As a child I had thought she looked old, but she never appeared to get any older. When she visited us I began to realise that my mother was jealous of my affection for her and I felt uncomfortable at the way that she was treated. She always kept a distance between them and never invited her to a proper meal but only for tea. When I visited my Aunt Freda, a sister with whom my mother was not on speaking terms, and found Nanny sitting in her drawing room drinking a glass of sherry I could see the difference. When I heard that Nanny thought she might be alone one Christmas I suggested to my mother that she came to us. This was firmly vetoed. My mother insisted that she liked to have only her family with her at that time.

Nanny still made her annual visit to Ireland and told me that her niece had bought a car and took her out for drives. 'She hasn't learnt to go into reverse yet,' she told me, 'so she always tries to make sure she doesn't have to turn round.' 'What happens if she makes a mistake?' 'Oh, it doesn't really matter. She gets out and stops the first car coming the other way and asks the driver to do it for her.'

One of her American relatives who worked for an airline came over to London regularly and occasionally took her out to meals in expensive restaurants. I was very excited when she described sitting near Elizabeth Taylor. 'What was she like?' I asked. 'Oh, just a pale little thing, you would hardly have noticed her.'

Nicholas had now been sent to Ampleforth, a Benedictine boarding school. He only told me later how unhappy he had been. He was put into a house where not only the boys but the housemaster himself were all interested in shooting or fishing. Even if he had wanted to he would have been unable to do either as he had been born with no sight in one eye. This had not come to my mother's attention until he was six.

I would often be left at home with my father. He took me regularly to concerts, the ballet and art galleries and to Wagner operas at Covent Garden. Nearly every time we went out we would be approached by someone who knew him. All the students who had passed through the LSE recognised him and many had ended up in prominent positions.

He loved music, Beethoven especially, and would listen to the radio or to records at home, concentrating on every note, while I had to be careful not to move or make a sound and often breathed a sigh of relief when, after a few anticlimaxes, the symphony finally came to an end. His knowledge of paintings was huge, and he enjoyed buying pictures and identifying the artists. He had no interest in their value. If he started talking to me about a painting in a public gallery, a small crowd would often collect around us to listen.

Although I missed the laughter and chatter with my mother when she was away, I enjoyed being alone with my father. He brought a peaceful presence to the house when he sat in the drawing room reading and smoking his pipe or playing a game of piquet or chess. I admired him enormously – my mother encouraged this – but I could never get close to him. He had allowed my mother to send me to convent schools where education was not a priority and I had become a fun-loving sociable girl whom he found hard to understand.

He had a standard of excellence to which he thought everyone should aspire. When I went through a phase of writing poetry and nervously showed him a poem that I was pleased with, he merely went through it, showing me how to make it scan properly. When my mother and I painted he hardly felt it worthwhile looking at our work. It was not in his nature to give a dishonest opinion. The knowledge that we could never impress him made us three children grow up with little confidence in our abilities.

The LSE had become a lively place after the war. When the then prime minister, Clement Attlee, a former member of the staff, returned to give a lecture, my father, knowing of my allegiance to the Labour Party, arranged for me to leave school early and come and listen to him. Before the lecture I was introduced to him. He was a small man with a moustache, and I was surprised to see him standing in an empty space in the crowded room. After we shook hands, he said a few polite words and then fell silent. This, I was told afterwards, was his hallmark. A conversation with Attlee soon came to a halt and, unlike other prime ministers, his crowd of followers were inclined to keep their distance.

Professor Harold Laski, a Socialist professor with a flamboyant style and extreme ideas, was one of the most popular lecturers in the LSE. My father introduced me to him and, perhaps to make up for his own lack of support, had described my political views. From that time onwards Professor Laski regularly sent me books inscribed in his minuscule handwriting 'To Flora from her humble admirer'. He had been chairman of the Labour Party during its recent victory in 1945. At the start of the campaign, he wrote to Attlee in his ebullient but tactless manner advising him to resign as he was 'the wrong man for the job'. Attlee replied characteristically: 'Dear Laski, thank you for your letter, contents of which have been noted.'

This exchange later resulted in Laski not being given the American ambassadorship, which he had been hoping for. His views became even more extreme, and he went on lecture tours attacking the Americans and praising Stalin. This naturally embarrassed the new government and elicited the famous Attlee remark: 'A period of silence on your part would be welcome'.

The Beaverbook press set out to get him. They misquoted in banner headlines 'New Laski sensation: "Socialism even if it means violence"'. Laski immediately issued writs, certain that he would win, but the 'special jury' selected from a panel of property-owning jurors turned against him, he lost the trial, was ordered to pay costs and was deeply humiliated. I was close to tears as I followed his degradation in the evening paper each night. Laski was devastated and offered to resign. Five thousand admirers contributed to his costs but his spirit had been broken.

Professor Tawney, the economic historian, was a good friend of my parents. He was a 'scholar, a saint and a social reformer' as well as a warm cuddly man with a white moustache and kind eyes, always dressed in clothes that had seen better days. His main luxury was his pipe. On one occasion, before giving a lecture, he absent-mindedly put his pipe into his pocket while it was still alight. First there was a whiff of scorching and finally smoke began to appear around him as he still continued to lecture. Before flames actually broke out, a porter rushed in and, in the nick of time, managed to rip off his jacket. When the porters were asked why they had not done anything sooner, they replied, 'We just smelt old rags burning and had no idea it was coming from the Professor.'

My father was often awarded honorary degrees. When he was granted one by Dublin University I was only twelve, but my mother insisted that I go instead of her, the excuse being that we could stay with my godfather, Tom Gaisford St Lawrence, whom I had never met but from whom I received an identical Christmas card every year with a photograph of his castle, Howth, outside Dublin. His spinster sister Dorothy, a fierce hunting woman, lived with him and bred Dalmatians. On our arrival, one bounded down the stairs to greet us. I put out my hand to stroke it and was immediately given a painful bite. Dorothy looked at my hand and said it was nothing much but whatever I did I was not to tell Tom. I do not remember seeing her again all the time we were there.

Tom was a quiet, middle-aged bachelor. My father never made small talk and I was struck dumb with shyness so I remember dinner being conducted in near silence. Added to this, on the first evening I was very taken aback when I noticed that a fourth place had been laid, which I presumed was for

Dorothy, but she did not arrive. Then I remembered being told about the curse that a Queen of Ireland had made when she had been refused hospitality at the castle. It was lifted only on condition that in future an extra place was always kept ready at the table and the front door should always be open. These conditions had been observed ever since, and an inside porch had been built around the front door to make it practical in winter.

I was mortified by another incident on that visit. As the only female I was served first, and when it came to the dessert, the butler laid an empty finger bowl down in front of me. Instead of removing it, I put my strawberries into it. I soon realised that I had made a mistake and, being at a highly sensitive age, I was sure that the impassive butler was laughing at me behind his mask of indifference and imagined him relaying such a terrible *faux pas* to the rest of the staff. I remember these incidents far more clearly than the degree ceremony itself, but I do recollect being shown the Book of Kells and feeling excited by its beauty and antiquity.

After a few years, my father wanted to get his books and furniture out of store, and we moved into a large inconvenient house in Palace Gardens Terrace. These houses have now each been converted into several flats. The kitchen was in the basement and the food had to be wound up in a lift to the dining room on the ground floor. Above it were three storeys with a wide staircase; at the back there was a delightful garden looking on to an even larger one that turned out to belong to the Russian Embassy.

In the spring the whole street was awash with blossom from the flowering cherry trees that lined the road, and in the summer we sat outside under a vine-covered trellis. It was a house that required a lot of domestic help, but as it had accommodation in the basement it was easier to attract staff. My mother still cooked. She had taken cookery lessons and was sure that, except for one Austrian cook, she did it better than anyone else. We were not so convinced. She was, however, quite unable to clean up the kitchen afterwards or do any form of housework, and I do not think I ever saw her hoover or dust in her life. She had decided that immaculately kept houses were 'middle class' and showed that their owners had nothing better to do.

There was a tutorial establishment a few doors down our street, and it was decided instead of my going over to join their class, the two other girls and the tutor would be sent over to us. One of the girls, Helen, was the youngest of three pretty sisters whose mother had stage and screen ambitions for them and made them exercise in front of her every morning. She was a small, eternally young-looking woman who went shopping in Harrod's every Saturday accompanied by both her husband, who looked like Churchill, and George, a gentleman who adored her till the end of her life in spite of the way she continually castigated him. They were different from the families I already knew. They lived in a mansion flat in Bayswater and I loved visiting them. I envied the close companionship between the sisters and even the strict regime that their mother put them through. One of the sisters, Ann, was recorded singing the Christopher Robin poems and got small parts in films and on the stage. My mother thought that anyone who was in the theatre might be 'fast' and was agreeably surprised when we met Ann on a bus coming back from the theatre one evening dressed in a brown raincoat and looking as respectable as anyone else. Helen has remained a lifelong friend, and many years later I went to visit her when she was trying her luck in Hollywood.

A Girl about Town

~

In the summer of 1947, as soon as it was possible to travel abroad again, my father decided to take us all for a holiday in Switzerland. We were to stay in Zermatt. I was thrilled at the thought of going to a foreign country and could not imagine one where the inhabitants would speak a different language and even the advertisements and road signs would be incomprehensible. We went by night train to Basle where we had to change. In the station buffet we were given pure white bread rolls and unlimited fresh butter for breakfast, a treat after the beige-coloured bread we had become used to in Britain. A smaller mountain train took us to Zermatt where we walked up the main street to our hotel. I was dying to look at the souvenir stalls lining the road, but my excitement was marred by overhearing my mother grumble to Edmund about what a terrible touristy place it was and she could not imagine why our father had brought us there. My mother never liked to think that she was a tourist when she went abroad.

The Monte Rosa Hotel, where my father had stayed in his climbing days, was now the best hotel in the town. While Nicholas and I enjoyed the luxury, my mother could not wait until she had moved us all out to a stuffy pension outside Zermatt. She revelled in the fact that foreign currency was limited and we must spend as little as possible to make it go further. My father seemed not to mind the change of plan and took us children on long walks through the pine trees and up above the snow line. We finished with a day on the vast

Gorgengrat glacier. He roped us together as we walked across the white icy expanse, feeling that we had left behind the world we knew and had reached an enchanted place that must lead to eternity. The glare and the lack of a focusing point added to the unreality. Occasionally we came to a crevasse where we stared down into a deep gorge of faintly blue-tinged ice.

As the wartime restrictions eased at home, we began to make contact with families and relatives with whom we had been out of touch. They visited us in London, and I went to stay with my mother's cousins in Lancashire at Ince Blundell Hall where my grandmother had been brought up.

The house had an outstanding art collection and a pantheon that had been built to contain the antique marble statues and busts collected by a Blundell ancestor in the eighteenth century. A legend had it that the house had passed to the Welds in a romantic fashion. Joseph Weld had been in Paris at the time of the French Revolution and had met his cousin Charles Blundell, who was in debt and unable to leave France and return to England. Joseph lent him enough money to escape and in gratitude Charles Blundell, who had no male heirs, left him the house. Blundell relatives were far from pleased and tried to prove his insanity in court. To support their point of view they testified that when Charles had been caught in a rainstorm he had taken off his clothes and sat on them to keep them dry.

My great-uncle Charles Weld Blundell's will had been made before the First World War and as he had two sons he had expected that one would inherit. Sadly, the war had taken both their lives. His daughters had been given a life rent, but after their deaths it would go to a distant male cousin. The eldest daughter, May, lived in the house with her husband and daughter, Pookie, and her sister's widower, John, and his four children. The two youngest, Mary and Anne, were nearer my age and became great friends. I revelled in the luxury of the house, which was kept up to pre-war standards, and only learnt afterwards how my cousins had disliked living there and had wished they had been brought up in a small house of their own.

At breakfast a hot plate sat on a sideboard laden with bacon, eggs and kippers, and each morning freshly baked scones, which no one ever ate, were set out on the huge dining-room table. Both families had their meals together. My one dread was to be seated next to Pookie, May's daughter, an only child who had been brought up quite differently from her cousins and spoilt beyond measure. She was in her twenties, a sophisticated young woman, slim and beautiful, who went to Paris to buy her clothes and have her hair done. She lived most of the time in a flat in Park Lane in London. She never ate more than a few mouthfuls and talked continuously in a low affected voice that I had great difficulty in understanding. I felt I had to give her my full attention while listening to the non-stop prattle when I would far rather have concentrated on what I was eating. She horrified her mother by the way she addressed the servants and continually criticised them. When she imagined that a new butler was bending too low as he served her she pointedly put her hand over her low-cut dress and explained to me in his hearing that he had worked as a waiter and wanted people to remember his face and give him a tip.

Ince was one of the earliest houses to open its doors to the public, and it was done in such a discreet manner that it is surprising that anyone came to see it. May did not even like to mention the subject, and on the days that it was open she merely announced that lunch would be served 'a little earlier' that day. This meant that the butler had time to be ready to show the handful of visitors through the back entrance into the pantheon and gallery and the few rooms they were allowed to see. Her brother-in-law, John Weld, would point at the visitors from the library window and ask with a smile, 'Have you ever seen half a crown on two legs?' He was a courageous man who had lost a leg in the First World War in which he had fought all the way through as a private, refusing to take a commission. Lack of a leg did not prevent him from keeping bees and chasing after them when they swarmed.

When we were in London my father was occupied most evenings with meetings and official dinners. He also tried to invite the leading students of the various societies to small dinners so that he could get to know them. He entertained both in his private dining room at the LSE or in his club, the Athenaeum. He insisted on travelling by Underground and I often saw him return home exhausted. It would never have entered his head to take a taxi. My mother took little part in the life of the School. She preferred the company of close friends and relatives, most of whom were Catholics.

She did not enjoy social life and joined my father for formal dinners only when it was absolutely necessary but delayed her departure by cooking our supper before she left. She then had an agonising search through her belongings to find stockings without holes and tried to tidy her long hair, which she always wore up. She rarely went to a hairdresser. My father trained his secretary to ring up three-quarters of an hour before to ask if she had left. I was equally well trained to answer that she was 'just leaving', however untruthful that was, and nine times out of ten she would not get there on time. Whenever she could get out of accompanying him, she did. As soon as I was old enough, and well before, she would persuade me to take her place. When it was a question of meeting students I enjoyed it, but there were other occasions when I felt miserably shy and out of place.

My parents gave few formal dinner parties at home, but there were often extra people at meals. My father enjoyed receiving information and plumbing a subject to its depths. He had an excellent memory. He could give us an answer on any subject we cared to ask him. If he felt unsure, he would immediately go and look it up in his vast library. He was ascetic in his tastes, and food, like clothes, held no importance for him, although he dressed in a conventional manner. He scarcely noticed what he ate and, to my mother's annoyance, was inclined to mash up all his food as soon as it was put in front of him. He lost interest in wine after his wine cellar at Water Eaton was plundered. Our visitors were never offered more than a glass of sherry before dinner and a moderate amount of wine with the meal.

He hated small talk or inaccurate statements, and I soon found that the quickest way to gain his attention was to make a stupid, but what I hoped was a witty, remark. He would immediately focus all his attention upon me and say despairingly 'My dear Flora'.

My mother maintained that his inability to suffer fools gladly terrified her friends and relatives, and she grumbled that she felt nervous about asking them to the house. He was quite unconscious of this. When Claude, a fourteen-year-old French girl came to stay, he tried to put her at her ease on her first evening by asking her what were the differences between the French and English armies.

One of my mother's relatives was flattered to gain his attention when she told him she had climbed in the Alps when she was young. He quickly began to cross-question her as to the names and heights of mountains that she could not remember, and she answered with wild guesses. My father became more and more impressed, brought out an atlas and, as her finger wavered over the Alps, he began to wonder whether she had been one of the first women to climb Mont Blanc. Aware that her climbing had actually been walking on the lower slopes, she was at last forced to disillusion him, whereupon their conversation came to an abrupt close.

My mother had a great sense of humour. She loved conversation and sitting over meals for hours. If anyone suggested clearing the table, she would say 'they will do it', forgetting that there was either no 'they' at all or that 'they' consisted of one unfortunate woman longing to go home. Religion was one of her favourite topics but was discussed when my father was not there. She was an intellectual Catholic and dismissed all forms of worship other than the Mass as 'non-liturgical'. She took no notice of a sermon she disagreed with and had the recusant Catholic opinion about priests. They were there to serve and not to dictate. One of her relatives, who had a chapel in his house, told the priest that

Mass must never last longer than half an hour and if it ran one minute over he would burst into a loud warning cough.

Her political views varied depending on who she was talking to. With her ultra-conservative relatives she was a socialist as she had been horrified by the poverty she saw in Lancashire when she farmed there between the wars. However, she was scathing about many of the Oxford socialists she knew who she thought promoted one style of life to the electorate and lived a completely different one themselves.

Our different religions separated the family, and as we children were all brought up Catholics like my mother, it tended to isolate my father. At that time, Catholics were not allowed to attend any Protestant services, and if we did attend a wedding or a funeral, we were supposed not to take part in the service, which meant sitting down firmly in your seat and not kneeling or standing with the rest of the congregation. My father was interested in architecture, and we often drove around the Cambridgeshire villages looking at churches. When we went into a Protestant church I was terrified that I might say a prayer by mistake.

The Mill House was sold and a house in Cumberland was bought for holidays. It was in a remote part of the Lake District and ideal for walking. Many friends and relatives came to stay with their families. My father led us on long walks over the hills, but my mother never accompanied us, claiming that she had a bad heart, a myth that she maintained until she was 96.

After a few years we moved house again in London, this time to a gem of a Regency house in Brompton Square. My grandmother maintained that it had once been a plague pit. The first-floor drawing room had two pairs of French windows looking on to the pretty garden in the square. We were five minutes' walk from the Oratory, one of the grandest Catholic churches in London, while from my bedroom window at the back of the house I could see the lit-up dome of Harrod's. This time the house was made more convenient, with a new kitchen on a half-landing near the dining room.

I left school with no idea of what I wanted to do. In spite of gaining good marks in other subjects I had never been able to pass a maths or Latin exam so my parents' hope that I would follow Edmund to Oxford was thwarted. I had become sick of education and preferred the idea of spending a year in Paris with my cousin, Anne Weld Blundell, at a domestic science school. We were taught how to cook, to make dresses and hats and to iron. The French girls were already adept at these skills, but I was so incompetent that the teachers often ended up demonstrating on my materials. I did at least learn some French. The grand finale was ironing a *chemise d'homme*. By that time I was staying with my French friend Claude, so her father, a barrister, nervously lent me one of his shirts.

When I returned home I decided, like many of my friends, to go to a secretarial college. At the time of the 1950 general election I found myself sitting alone and depressed in the cloakroom as the other girls rejoiced in the fact that the Labour Government's majority had been reduced to seventeen.

I was invited to watch the funeral of George VI from a house near Paddington where all the down-at-heel boarding houses had let out their windows for the occasion. A sadness hung over the city while, to the sound of muffled drums, the procession moved slowly forward. On the way home, walking down Kensington Church Street, I noticed that the shop windows had all gone into mourning. Even a lingerie boutique had been dressed with black and white brassières and corsets.

While learning shorthand and typing I led the same life as most of my friends who were 'coming out' as debutantes. My mother would not have dreamt of giving a dance for me, but she made up a party for Queen Charlotte's ball where we wore white and curtsied to a huge birthday cake. She also presented me at court where the new Queen Elizabeth and Prince Philip must have suffered many hours of boredom sitting on their thrones while teenage girls in hats and frilly dresses, who had been taught how to curtsy, passed in turn in front of them. The mothers sat in rows on gilt chairs watching while a military band played cheering music in the background. I went to parties in London and in country houses, and was invited to Commem balls at Oxford and May balls at Cambridge where we wore strapless dresses with huge skirts supported by crinolines or stiff petticoats. On one occasion I was able to smuggle a small boyfriend into a ball underneath my skirt. Young men invited me out to dinner in restaurants or occasionally to their flats (thought to be dangerous) and we occasionally ended up in a night club. Like most of my friends, I did not have a steady boyfriend but had more fun wondering who would ring up next. A certain amount of kissing and cuddling went on, but we were discouraged from anything further by the pre-Pill fear of getting pregnant.

I took a few temporary secretarial jobs, including one in the House of Commons Library. It was a sought-after job and was passed from one friend to another. In contrast to MPs' secretaries we were employed by the House. We entered through Westminster Hall and worked in rooms looking on to the Thames under the actual Library and had our lunch in the Lords' Bar. I worked for the Statistician. If a member wanted to know any statistics for a speech, he had only to ring down and ask for them. Every morning I typed out statistics mentioned in the previous day's *Hansard* on to reference cards.

I soon realised that I had also been taken on to sort out some huge tomes that had been stored in a basement nearby. The aesthetic young men who worked in the Library maintained that they had bad backs and were unable to lift them. I resented being given this task. My mother had always told me not to lift weights as she believed that it prevented a woman having babies. If I had been out late the night before, I would ask to be rung on the extension when it was time to go home and then fall asleep on a pile of books.

The coronation of Queen Elizabeth II took place while I was still employed at the House of Commons, and I was issued with a ticket for a place on the pavement opposite Westminster Abbey. I was also given a ticket for a special Underground train that was to run to Westminster on the morning of the Coronation. At Kensington High Street, I stepped into the sparkling clean train and found myself completely surrounded by peers and peeresses sitting in silence looking a little awkward dressed in their coronation robes and holding their coronets and tiaras. A faint smell of mothballs filled the carriage. An elderly peeress opposite me looked down sadly at her feet. She was wearing brogues and had realised that she had forgotten to change her shoes.

In the autumn of that year, 1953, I accompanied my father to South Africa where he was to be awarded an honorary degree by the University of Natal. We stayed first in Cape Town with an old friend, Professor Alan Davie. Mrs Davie was a member of the Black Sash movement, a group of women who appeared when racist politicians were speaking and sat in front of them wearing black sashes, which were known to be a sign of disapproval and which succeeded in unnerving many a speaker. The colour problem was blatantly visible, and I was horrified to see signs outside post offices with separate entrances for Europeans and non-Europeans. We were taken to see clinics and small projects that had been set up by the university in the black townships but were aware that they were but a drop in the ocean. I loved Cape Town with its huge uncultivated mountain towering over the urban development below in the same way that I later felt Castle Rock does in Edinburgh.

We proceeded to Durban, where our host, Professor Malherbe, the Vice Chancellor of the University of Natal, and his wife put us up in their house, entertained us lavishly and could not do enough for us. At a picnic we met the poet Roy Campbell who presented me with a python skin. The Malherbes were Afrikaners and talked of the Zulus, the black tribe in that area, with great affection and took an interest in their welfare, but it was evident that they thought of them as being a different kind of being and one that was inferior. I was reminded of the way that the 'upper classes' treated the 'working classes' in Britain.

As I had been dreading, we stayed with the Malherbes over a Sunday when I felt obliged to go to Mass. As I grew up

Catholic, obligations such as Mass on Sunday and no meat on Fridays were beginning to infringe on everyday life. I did not want to be a nuisance so my father suggested that I borrow a bicycle. The house stood on a steep hill above the town with a splendid view of the bay. I got up and set off before the rest of the household was awake. I gained speed rapidly as I went down the hill but when I felt for the brakes on the handlebars there were none there. Convinced that my life was about to come to an end as I careered forwards, I said a desperate prayer and something made me back-pedal. To my infinite relief this happened to work the brakes and I was saved.

When black Africans found that they were to be banned from a celebration following the degree ceremony, my father took their part. It was taken up by the press, who waited for him on our return to Cape Town. He reiterated his opinion that in his mind blacks and whites were equal. This was not an emotional opinion on his part but a conclusion based on his findings when he had studied the relationship between pigmentation and mental potential. On our way back to Cape Town we were advised by white South Africans to visit the all-black university of Fort Hare which Nelson Mandela had attended. We were not at all impressed by its inferior facilities. After he retired from the LSE, my father devoted himself to setting up universities overseas, one of the first being the University of Rhodesia. Although separate colleges had been projected, he insisted on one multiracial university.

I stayed on in Cape Town where I was given a job in the Social Science department of the university, helping to carry out a survey of Cape-Coloured education. It was a job that white South African girls would not do, and it gave me an insight into the segregation of this race – people of mixed parentage or descent – who were accepted by neither the Blacks nor the Whites. One of the embittered headmasters I interviewed put the position clearly: 'If you went back and said that I had raped you,' he told me, 'you would be believed and however much I denied it I would be considered guilty.'

After spending a month with a friend on the island of St

Helena, I returned to Britain. I had begun to paint water-colours in Cumberland and made up my mind that I wanted to go to art school. Getting accepted in those days was a little easier than it is today. I presented myself at Camberwell School of Art with a few of my paintings. Gilbert Spencer, brother of the painter Stanley Spencer, was on duty and gave them a cursory glance. After murmuring 'good sense of composition', he enrolled me on the spot. As I was now twenty and older than most of the first-year students, I was put into the second year of a foundation course.

Falling in Love

~

I first met Peter Maxwell Stuart in 1954 in the house of a Spanish journalist who rejoiced in the name of Jesus. He was the London correspondent for a Spanish newspaper and held open house on Sunday evenings. We drank red wine, and the more Jesus drank the more difficult his English became to understand.

His girlfriend introduced me to Peter, who was tall and thin with huge blue eyes and wearing a dashing fancy waistcoat – the fashion of the time. He was older than my other boyfriends, which immediately made him more interesting. We were attracted to each other at once, and we arranged to meet again. I soon learnt that Peter's passion was the cinema, and our first date was at the Classic in King's Road to see *The Seven Samurai*, a Japanese Samurai film that I pretended to enjoy.

Peter was brought up in England, first in Ascot and Sunningdale and then in London. His father, Frank Maxwell Stuart, was the eldest son of a large Catholic family of six boys and five girls. Frank, as the eldest, was fortunate in being sent to the School of Mining Engineering, but between the two World Wars it was not easy for him to find employment. He was taken on by Rio Tinto but only under short contracts when he would disappear for months at a time to explore the Amazon or into the jungle, searching for gold and precious minerals. His returns home with exotic gifts and stories of his adventures were not welcomed by his wife, Dolly, who had been left at home with three children under five and little to support them. She was frequently obliged to call on her own family for help.

Meanwhile, Frank's bachelor uncles, who had made him their heir, lived a comfortable life in Yorkshire unhampered by any necessity to earn a living. They went to Scotland each summer for the shooting and stayed at Traquair, their estate in the Scottish Borders. Unaccustomed to children, they did not welcome them at Traquair, thinking that they were a danger to the house. So when Peter's family spent a holiday there they were obliged to take the schoolmistress's house in the village. Peter vaguely remembered a young cousin telling him that one day he would inherit the place but he had far more vivid memories of the old housekeeper taking him into a small panelled room and cutting him a piece of her home-made fruit cake.

Peter was sent to a boarding prep school and then to the Benedictine College of Downside, which he hated and left when he was sixteen. There was nothing to finance his further education, so his father took him to see a Catholic friend, the whisky merchant John Calder, and asked for his advice. Calder arranged for Peter to join the firm of John Haig and Company in Fife, telling him that he himself had started at the bottom and he advised Peter to do likewise.

Peter got digs with a friendly landlady in Markinch and set to work as an office boy. He made tea for the typists and learnt, among other things, the useful skills of wrapping up neat parcels and arranging envelopes in lines so that they could all be dampened with one sweep of a sponge.

When the Second World War broke out, Arthur, the last surviving great-uncle, after giving everyone a few anxious moments when he announced his intention of marrying his nurse, decided to make Traquair over to Frank. Peter's sisters, now grown up, stayed in London to do war work while his parents and younger brother, Michael, went to live at Traquair. His father soon volunteered for bomb disposal. Peter would manage an occasional weekend visit, bicycling from Markinch, taking the ferry across the Firth of Forth and bicycling the next forty miles to Traquair. When he was old enough, he volunteered for the Army, first in the Royal Scots and then transferring to the Indian Army – 'as the food was better', he would say with a laugh. He ended up in the Burma Campaign and came back at the end of the war in a hospital ship, suffering from dysentery and malaria. He did not like talking about his war experiences and always played down the danger and illnesses he had suffered.

After a few more years in Markinch he was transferred to the Distillers Company offices in London where he was made assistant advertising manager. He was also given the task of researching the history of the Haig family for a book celebrating the company's centenary. At the time we met, Peter was living in a large flat in Eaton Square that he shared with three or four friends at a nominal rent as the owners preferred to live in the country and only occasionally made visits to London. His social life had taken off, and in his late twenties and early thirties he had become a 'debs' delight'. We met about a year after the Coronation, at which he had been given a position as Gold Staff Officer – the perfect position for him as he loved pageantry. Owing to his permanently impecunious position, he was obliged to sell his coronation stool immediately after the ceremony.

London became a different place after I met Peter. He loved the city and, as a boy, had been allowed to explore it on his own when he started to write a guidebook. He knew many small back streets, old buildings and narrow passages that I hadn't come across before, and I often went to meet him in his huge office in the impressive Adam house in St James's Square owned by the Distillers Company before he took me off to see some new haunt.

His salary was not as impressive as his office, and he had once tried to supplement it by taking an evening job as a barman in a pub behind St James's Square. When this was reported to his directors, they were horrified and he was asked to give it up. Since then, he had started to write articles for

American magazines, his speciality being London social life. He liked a dare, and for a newspaper he had once gate-crashed the Royal Command Film Performance, arriving in top hat and tails on his bicycle which he grandly handed to the commissionaire.

He had a great sense of humour and had no interest in promotion, knowing at the back of his mind that one day he would have to look after Traquair. He got on far better with the commissionaires, the chauffeurs and the women in the canteen, who called him 'Maxy', than he did with his directors.

It was not long before Peter and I knew we were in love and decided to get married. I had met his father, Frank, who would make an annual trip south in the autumn. During the summer he opened Traquair to the public two days a week, and he was as excited as a schoolboy home for the holidays when he put some of the takings in his pocket and headed for London. He had the same cheerful, easy-going nature as the rest of his family. My mother and he soon found that, like all recusant Catholic families, they had many relatives and friends in common. He was enthusiastic about our marriage, but how Peter's mother, Dolly, would react was a matter for conjecture. She was known to be unpredictable and often objected to people on sight. 'Don't worry about Dolly, she's as mad as a hatter,' Peter's Aunt Emily reassured me, but I was not looking forward to the meeting at Traquair, which it was decided would take place next time that we were staying in our house in Cumberland.

Traquair

~

I sat in the back of my parents' aged car as it veered erratically
down the avenue that leads to Traquair House. My mother's
driving seemed even more unpredictable than usual. My father
sat next to her with a pained expression and muttered, 'Teresa,
take care,' as we bounced into a pot hole. I felt apprehensive as
I was about to meet my future mother-in-law for the first time.

The ancient building that I had heard so much about
came into view. It was tall and severe and peppered with a mass
of small windows, but two low wings came forward at either
side in a welcoming gesture. There was no formal design, and
it was very different from the country houses I knew in
England. A mass of daffodils grew in the rough grass in front
of the house but, unlike the sweeps of yellow we had left
behind in the kinder Cumbrian climate, they were still in bud.
We drove through beautiful wrought-iron gates into the courtyard and parked outside the front door, which was enclosed in
a small porch slightly to one side of the main façade. I pulled
the doorbell and heard it clanging inside.

I was relieved when Peter appeared, smiling broadly, and
everything seemed normal again. He welcomed us into the
dark, stone-flagged entrance. In the background I caught sight
of a small bird-like woman who I knew must be his mother
and who was obviously intending to take a peek at us and then
disappear until later. She was taken off her guard however,
when my mother rushed forward saying, 'Dolly! How nice to
see you again.' They had apparently met years ago in their

distant youth. Dolly was a small fine-featured woman with large blue eyes and wild grey hair. She talked to us pleasantly while eyeing us up and down and decided that Peter should take us round the house before it got too dark and we would then join her for tea in the kitchen.

Peter warned us to keep our coats on. There was no electricity or heating in the house, and the passages and winding stairs were cold and dimly lit by the small astragal windows. He led us up to the high drawing room on the first floor, a surprisingly light room as it spanned the width of the house with windows on both sides. Peter explained that with the help of a government grant a certain amount of restoration had recently been carried out and some interesting discoveries had been made. A blocked-up window had been opened up and when the ceiling was repaired, sixteenth-century beams decorated with bright patterns and quotations from the Bible were found underneath.

He glanced at me occasionally as he recounted the history of the house, and I knew that he was nervous in front of my father, who listened intently to every word and occasionally asked a searching question.

Peter then led us into the oldest part of the house – the original peel tower – where there was a small panelled dressing room and the King's room, which he told us had been used by the Kings of Scotland and by Mary Queen of Scots when she came as a guest to hunt.

My father looked out of the window. 'What's the height of those hills?' he asked. Peter mumbled a bit and said he was not quite sure but the trees on the top were known as the 'Bush aboon Traquair' and many poems and songs had been written about them. He then warned us to hold on to a rope and to take care climbing down an uneven narrow stair, hidden in the width of the wall, that led us back to the ground floor.

At this level there was a series of dark cellars with vaulted ceilings that were once used for hiding cattle when the English came raiding across the Border. From there we passed through into the west wing and into a light, airy chapel. Fifteenth-century oak carvings of the life of Christ hung on the walls, and a striking white marble altar carved with the symbols of the Passion stood at the far end. Peter explained that it had once been a billiard room but when Catholics were allowed to worship openly in the nineteenth century, it was made into a chapel. Before that time Mass had to be said secretly in a small room on the top floor where the entrance to a hidden stair was concealed in a cupboard.

Peter led us across the courtyard to the opposite wing to see the dining room, hung with family portraits. In the small lower drawing room leading off it, Frank had displayed some of the house's treasures – a Jacobite Amen glass, miniatures and seventeenth-century embroideries. As the whole place was freezing cold, I was relieved then to be led into the kitchen for tea. The room had a high ceiling and one small window. It had been modernised, with a composition floor and a Formica-topped table. The kettle was simmering on an old Esse stove. Next to it was a Calor Gas cooker and next to that a small solid-fuel hot-water boiler. Dolly was standing by the Esse, ready to pour water into a large china teapot, and told us to sit down at the kitchen table, which was laid out with scones and a fruit cake. Peter told me later that shortly before our arrival he had been asked to rush down to Innerleithen to buy them at the local bakery.

Once we were all settled, Dolly began to tell us what a nightmare the house was to live in and how badly the restoration work had been done, ruining the old atmosphere. She went on to say that she had lived there on her own, right through the war, with no electricity. Now and then she flashed a glance at my father to see what impression she was making on him, but he was oblivious to female wiles and she got no response.

While she was talking, the kitchen door opened and Peter's father, Frank, came in. 'I had no idea you were here,' he apologised, 'no one told me.' Dolly shrugged her shoulders dismissively and Peter rose to get him a cup. He looked delighted to see us. He told us that he had been cleaning a picture with a raw potato – a new method that someone had told him about. My father frowned doubtfully, but I was thankful that he made no comment. I was later to learn that Frank was an inveterate handyman and was busy restoring as much as he could, often skilfully. He had even taken lessons in petit point so that he could work on old bed hangings. Those were the happy days before museum experts insisted that no restoration could be done without it costing hundreds of pounds.

My mother and Frank immediately got into conversation, but my father soon began to look bored. He took his watch from his waistcoat pocket and said it was time for us to go. Peter gave me a wink as we left, which signalled that he thought the visit had gone well.

As soon as we were in the car my mother started to go into ecstasies about the house. She had always heard about Traquair from her mother who had had her eye on one of Frank's uncles. Being a Catholic stronghold, it had all the qualities and charm that she admired. After a while my father could bear it no longer. 'I don't know what you are talking about my dear,' he said patiently, 'there is absolutely nothing of any importance in that house whatsoever.' Fortunately, he had a higher opinion of Peter himself and both our families approved of our forthcoming marriage.

When we were back in London, Peter was a regular visitor. He had a voracious appetite while never putting on weight. He put it down to nervous energy. My mother enjoyed feeding him and gossiping about mutual friends and relatives. He was the first boyfriend that she did not criticise. My father, who always followed my mother's judgement in these matters, was equally content. Although Peter and he had little in common, he obviously respected him and knew I would be in safe hands.

Peter introduced me to his maiden Aunt Emily, the sister who spent her life looking after her mother and was now constantly at the disposal of the rest of her family. She lived in a homely house in Pimlico which was open to all her relatives.

The key to the front door hung on a string inside the letter-box. She had all the Maxwell Stuart kindness and good humour and welcomed me with open arms.

Four of the brothers had been killed in the First World War. Their letters, which I later read at Traquair, were heart-breaking. One of the boys, Edmund, wrote home in 1916: 'I am in the death trap known as the Salient, burrowing tunnels under the Hun ridden trenches, in fact looking for trouble. For five long shell ridden months I have been here and feel ten years older than when I landed.' He volunteered to stay on to instruct a relieving company and was killed by a shell. He was twenty-four. Their father had accepted his sons' deaths with a quiet resignation. 'I must say that the patriotism of my family stands out somewhat conspicuously,' he wrote, 'seeing that out of my eleven children four sons have been killed, two are at present serving, the seventh still being at school and of my four daughters three have served as nurses and one is in religion.'

The youngest brother, Philip, who had suffered severely as a Japanese prisoner of war, lived with Emily. He was a large, heavily-built man with a scar across his ruddy face. He appeared relaxed during the day but at night, Aunt Emily told us, was tortured by nightmares. Although he liked women he was shy with them and did not have a girlfriend. Uncle Phil, as he was known, supported himself by getting intermittent work as a film extra. Every afternoon he rang his agent and learnt whether there would be any work for him the next day. He soon learned that the more different styles of dress he owned, the more work he was given and cleverly hit upon the idea of keeping them all in the local pawnbroker's where they were well looked after.

Another brother, Willy, had also suffered in the Second World War. In his younger days he was a champion ballroom dancer and won cups and gave demonstrations all over the world. Emily would take the cups round to the pawnbroker who would greet her by saying, 'I read in the paper that Mr William had won another cup so I knew you would be in soon.'

Peter's Aunt May was married to a retired surgeon and was the most formidable of the family but, like the others, she loved being among people. As she also disliked keeping house, they spent most of their married life living in hotels. In her seventies, when she wanted extra money for Christmas presents, she took her first job sorting mail for the Post Office and enjoyed every minute of it.

Effie, Frank's twin and the eldest surviving sister, had entered a convent when she was only eighteen. She adored her family and was a compulsive letter-writer in spite of belonging to an order that discouraged its nuns from writing letters. Everyone wrote to her with their news and secretly sent her stamps and writing paper so that she remained the fount of family gossip. She also managed to get up to London at intervals when she was being transferred from one convent to another. A great family reunion would take place in Aunt Emily's house where the three sisters never stopped talking, all at the same time. I asked Aunt Emily once when Effie had first got her vocation. 'Effie, a vocation,' she laughed, 'she's just trying to be a good woman.'

Years later, when Peter and I were living at Traquair and Vatican II had introduced many changes in the Catholic Church, nuns were permitted to go home for a short visit. We invited Aunt Effie to Traquair. She was allowed to come for one night. It was more than fifty years since she had stayed there and she was bubbling over with excitement as she tried to remember everything. She asked if she could go through the door that she had seen her grandmother disappear through and had always wondered what was on the other side. In the evening we sat in the high drawing room. She drank a glass of sherry and smoked a cigarette, holding it in twenties' fashion between her thumb and forefinger. 'Just one, to see if I can remember how to do it,' she explained. When her young reverend mother came to fetch her the next day, we said we hoped Effie could come again. She shook her head. It was like putting a wild bird back into a cage.

The deaths of their four brothers had brought the rest of

the Maxwell Stuart family closer together, and they all gossiped and corresponded with each other regularly. Peter's mother, Dolly, found this hard to deal with. She felt they wrote and told each other 'every time I blow my nose'. As she loved to shock people and had constant rows with neighbours, they had plenty to write about. The result was that, after several family rows, she had put the fear of God into her in-laws and they were no longer welcome at Traquair.

Honeymoon Years

~

Our wedding took place the following September in 1956, in St Etheldreda's, Ely Place, one of the oldest Catholic churches in London. The reception was held at the London School of Economics in the Founders Room, a beautiful room at the top of the building that was dedicated to the School's founders, Sydney and Beatrice Webb, and to which my father had donated some of his pictures and furniture. Our Catholic relatives entered in trepidation, convinced that they were entering a hotbed of socialism. I could never understand why Christians, who are presumably trying to emulate Christ, were so frightened of a political party that believed in sharing wealth.

Our married life in London was spent in a terraced house in Chelsea. Each morning Peter rode off to work on his bicycle, an elegant figure in a dark suit and bowler hat, his briefcase on end in the bicycle basket. I had left art school having completed only one year. I had enjoyed it but was convinced I would never become a professional painter. I had learnt enough to enjoy sketching and painting in my spare time and had specialised in calligraphy.

My father had presented me with a substantial sum of money that gave me an income. I knew how he would like it to be spent – a house, furniture, pictures and foreign travel were in his eyes worthwhile – but I wanted to be independent and to earn money that I could spend exactly how I pleased. I took a part-time job as secretary to Peter Haigh, television's most eligible bachelor at that time. He had been one of the BBC's first news readers, presenting the news in a black tie. He was a charming man and easy to work for. He took Peter and me to watch a rehearsal of the hugely popular *Goon Show*, which Peter loved but which I never managed to find funny. Peter Haigh had recently been given his own film review programme and was sent tickets for all the press screenings, which he urged me to go to on his behalf. As they were shown in the morning, not far from Peter's office in St James's Square, he could not resist occasionally nipping out of his office to join me.

Peter Haigh received a huge amount of fan mail that I had to deal with. Early television presenters had a striking effect on their viewers, who looked on them as close friends and wrote them intimate letters, often asking them to solve their personal problems – anything from how could you learn to make ships in bottles to a schoolgirl asking how she should cope with her headmaster's sexual advances. Peter Haigh's popularity began to wane when he married Jill Adams. She had been a Rank starlet but was finding that work was drying up. Peter, too, was worried that his own career was on the line. They decided to leave Britain and run a bar in the Algarve in Portugal.

I decided to return to calligraphy and after further training began to work freelance. Among other commissions was the lettering on the Queen's private Christmas card (designed by her doctor) and a daily job writing out menus for an expensive restaurant in Beauchamp Place. The payment included a free meal for us both once a month. Parkes, as it was called, was run by a chef, Ray Parkes, and his partner, Jack. It was one of the first restaurants where customers could see into the kitchen and Ray was the main attraction. As well as producing mouth-watering food, he could sing every part of a complete opera as he worked. The restaurant became one of the most fashionable in London. Ray told me how two-faced his clientele could be. They would treat him as their best friend when they were trying to get a table but scarcely acknowledged him if they met in the street. He composed the menu only after he had been out shopping each day so I could never write them in advance but had to wait for a telephone call and deliver them that evening.

Years later, when I returned for a visit, I found some of my old menus had been framed and were decorating the stairs. Not entirely for the beauty of the calligraphy, I gathered, but to remind customers of the happy days when the cover charge was two shillings and sixpence and the most expensive main course was under a pound.

I also joined a Care Committee. At that time, the London County Council arranged for every primary school to have a committee of part-time voluntary members who were sent out to visit the homes of any child who the teachers thought might be in need of help. If the family income was low enough, they were eligible for free dinners and clothing grants. We also attended school medicals. If the parents could not be there and the doctor wanted information on the family, we were used as a liaison. I felt sorry for the skinny little boys standing shivering in front of us while the doctor roughly groped for their testicles.

We had virtually no training, and although some of the mothers were lonely at home and enjoyed a chat, I felt uncomfortable as a privileged woman in my early twenties asking them to fill in a form with all their personal details. The visits did more for me than I did for them.

Peter was given four weeks' holiday a year and we travelled as much as we could. During the first year of our marriage we set off on a four-week trip to the United States. We made as much use as possible of the Greyhound bus bargain ticket of ninety-nine dollars for ninety-nine days. We travelled down to New Orleans and back up to New York. We visited various contacts en route, and my old Nanny had arranged for us to visit her elder brother who had emigrated to America and lived in Kansas City. They were a devout Catholic family. Their only son, Jack, was a priest, and his mother had a picture of Our Lady above the kitchen sink and told us that she chatted to her while she was doing the washing-up. Nanny was known as Aunt B and spoken of with awe. What she had written about us I do not know, but we were treated like royalty and intro-duced to ex-President Truman, a mild, relaxed man who received people in his Library in the city. He shook our hands and asked us about Scotland. Our friends made us believe that it was more his pleasure than ours. 'Be sure and let him know how you're getting on,' they urged.

The following September we visited the Holy Land. The Palestinians would not allow into their territory anyone who had an Israeli stamp in his or her passport so we travelled via Lebanon and Syria, first flying to Beirut where we stayed a few days and were entertained by Lebanese business colleagues of Peter's. We then took a seat in a shared taxi driven by a manic Arab who took us at breakneck speed to Damascus. At one point I gasped to Peter, 'We will soon be passing cars on the wrong side,' and a few minutes later that was exactly what we did. We had only a short time in Damascus where we were longing to see the Blue Mosque but had to visit the Syrian Haig whisky representative first. He was delighted to meet Peter and proudly showed us the dusty showcase in his office where the products he represented were displayed. The bottle of Haig whisky was arranged next to a packet of Tampax. He promised that his driver would take us to the Mosque but time was running out as he insisted that we drink endless cups of sweet black coffee. Finally we were driven through the narrow streets, scattering the inhabitants as we went. I was further embarrassed when the Syrian driver led us into the prayerful atmosphere of the Mosque at a time when it was obviously closed to outsiders, and angry bearded men rose up and signalled to him to take us out.

We stayed several days in Jerusalem and took a local bus up to Bethlehem. A small Arab boy of no more than eight or nine nonchalantly brought out a packet of cigarettes, offered us one and took one himself. I made it the opening of my first radio talk, which I gave on *Woman's Hour* when we returned. We spent an afternoon in Gesthemane talking to a charming elderly Arab who seemed to have all the time in the world and was far better versed in the New Testament than we were.

The only way into Israel from Jerusalem at that time was through the Mandelbaum Gate. An Arab porter carried our cases to the exact middle of No Man's Land and an Israeli porter on the other side ran out and picked them up. When we emerged into the open we saw a changed landscape. Instead of arid hillsides, crops were growing on them. In the heat of the day women dressed in khaki were working with pickaxes making a new road. The Israelis were in a hurry to make a new country. We were ridiculed for wanting to see places mentioned in the New Testament. 'They are not interesting. Come and see our new hospital instead,' the taxi driver in Nazareth said to us.

We spent several Christmases at Traquair, which were celebrated in as low-key a fashion as ours at home. It was a standing joke that Dolly's first words were always 'When are you leaving?' It was a supreme effort for her to have us to stay. Before our arrival, she would fill an ancient oblong copper warming pan with hot water and carry it up two flights of stone stairs to air our half-tester bed, often leaving it in without any warning so that we hit our toes when we got into bed.

It was a struggle in the morning to leave the warmth of the bed, piled high with heavy hand-woven blankets, many of them bearing a coronet and a dating from the nineteenth century. I had been brought up without heating but the cold at Traquair was unbelievable. In the evening I dreaded leaving the warmth of a wood fire and setting off up the icy stairs to the equally icy bedroom. Even after electricity was installed, the house was not much warmer. Dolly suffered from permanent Catholic guilt if she indulged in any pleasure and insisted on turning off electric fires after a short time, convinced that they were a luxury and clocking up like taxis. She spurned an electric iron and was much happier with an old flat one, though she had little idea how to use either.

Dolly had grown heartily sick of living at Traquair. She had, after all, been brought up in Edwardian days in a well-staffed country house and it upset her not to be able to keep to those standards. With occasional help she valiantly attempted to cook, but cooking remained a mystery to her. 'When I put cutlets in the oven why do they sometimes come out raw and other times come out quite black?' she would ask me plaintively. It irked her that Frank could live so contentedly when money worries still haunted them. Death duties had forced him to sell a large part of the estate and he had found the house in bad repair and full of woodworm. As he had written to Peter at the time, 'inheriting property these days is not all pleasure'.

In June 1962 my mother-in-law and brother-in-law were on their way down to London to stay with us when we received a telephone call to say that Frank been found dead at the top of the house. It was thought that he had rushed up there to answer the telephone and had had a heart attack. He was in his late seventies and had never been ill, so it was a shock to us all.

We went up to Traquair where his coffin lay in the chapel, and Dolly and I picked early summer flowers from the garden to lay on it. The Bishop came down from Edinburgh to say his funeral Mass in the Catholic church in Innerleithen, and he was buried in the Maxwell family crypt at Terregles.

Except for a farm that his brother Michael inherited from his father, most of the estate had already been made over to Peter and he now owned the house. He decided to close it to the public for the rest of the season while we went back to London to make our arrangements.

Peter had two elder sisters and a younger brother, but male primogeniture has always been the British way of handing on estates. It does not make for good relations within families. Dolly adored her younger son, Michael. He was the baby of the family and she had brought him up herself. He had always lived at home while farming some of the land. She kept telling us that it was he who should have inherited the estate.

The income from the estate barely covered the costs of running it, while opening the house to the public brought in only pocket money. But at least we would have somewhere to live, and my father, in his usual quiet way, made some further capital over to me.

It was certainly a challenge. We hoped optimistically that if we increased the visitor numbers we could make the place viable.

Inheritance

~

Peter and I settled into a two-roomed cottage built into the wall of the old garden. A lean-to kitchen and bathroom had been added at one end. The historic date 1745 was carved over the front door. The cottage stood on the 'temporary avenue', which had been made, so it was said, after the fifth Earl of Traquair had bid Prince Charles Edward Stuart farewell on his march south. The Bear Gates at the top of the original avenue, now grassed over, had been locked and a vow made that they would not be opened until a Stuart king was crowned in London.

The first year was difficult for all of us. Dolly and Michael were in the big house trying to decide where they would go. Having told us how impossible it was to live at Traquair, Dolly had begun to see the good points. She had lived there for over twenty years and her good taste was responsible for many improvements. When the architect and Frank wanted to replace the Victorian crimson flock wallpaper in the panelled drawing room, she insisted that it should be painted in two shades of light grey. She rehung many of the portraits and had the passages painted white. They had previously not only been painted in 'drab', a colour often mentioned in old accounts, but had been further darkened by candle and lamp smoke. She was responsible for planting the mass of daffodils followed by the sweet-smelling white narcissi that come up each year in front of the house, and where there had once been dreary laurels, she made herbaceous borders.

The walled garden was run by a Highland family who lived opposite us and provided fruit and vegetables instead of rent. Mr Milne had a faraway look in his eyes and a gentle soft voice. He later confided to me that he often saw little green men in the grounds but did not talk about them in case he was laughed at.

On the far side of the garden were the kennels and the gamekeeper's house. The keeper was a swarthy, silent young man dedicated to his work. He looked after what remained of a grouse moor and reared pheasants for the syndicate of six guns who rented the shooting, with one gun kept for the house.

There was a shoot most Saturdays during the season, and we would be presented with a brace of pheasants that Mrs Storrie, the keeper's wife, plucked and prepared. She was a plump, chatty woman who could recount dubious gossip while smiling sweetly at the same time. I roasted the birds for lunch on Sunday, and we proceeded to eat them in different guises for the rest of the week. We had just finished the soup by the following Saturday when it was time to receive the next brace. Game soon ceased to be a delicacy.

My mother-in-law enjoyed men's company and looked forward to the shooting days. Sometimes she would walk with the guns and would always ask them back to tea in the dining room. If Peter had been out, I would occasionally join him and the others in the old mill, where the Miller brothers lit a fire and everyone brought out their 'piece'. The lorry-load of beaters recruited from round about ate their sandwiches in a shed next door. At first I disliked the pretentiousness of the sport more than the cruelty. The act of dressing up in combat gear and using a gun to shoot a few harmless semi-tame birds seemed to bring out a whole new persona in men, particularly when they were trying to pose as country gentlemen.

As I gradually learnt how the pheasant chicks were reared with tiny sticks of wood pushed through their beaks to prevent crowding and thought of the maimed birds who were not retrieved and left to die after each shoot, I began to hate the sport. Gamekeepers were under such pressure to produce enough game that if a cat were seen near the pheasant coups it was shot on sight. I was horrified one day to meet the Traquair schoolmistress in the vet's waiting room, holding her cat whose ear had been shot off by our keeper. I was shocked that she seemed to take the incident as a matter of course. Many years later, when we were away, a young keeper was persuaded by the syndicate to let them shoot the wild duck on the well pool. Peter began to see my point of view and when the keeper left he was not replaced. No more pheasants were reared and shooting on most of the land was given up.

The Traquair estate consisted of about five thousand acres. There were five let farms, forestry and a stretch of the River Tweed. It had been held together for several generations by the Miller family who, besides acting as stewards, were skilled joiners by trade and had passed their talent down from one generation to the next. The present generation consisted of two brothers, Tommy and Ian. Tommy had no children and Ian was unmarried so they were the last of the family. They lived in the same untouched cold cottage in the village where they had been brought up. Tommy had an office in his house and reported to the factor who came down from a firm in Glasgow once a month. Tommy welcomed us on our arrival with a subservient courtesy that I did not know still existed. He was a quiet, beautifully mannered man and it took a while before we could talk naturally to each other. Although he always showed the greatest respect for my mother-in-law, whom he referred to as 'Madam', he found her capricious nature hard to understand. One morning, he told me, Dolly had asked Tommy and Ian to mend a leaking pipe in the kitchen. She said that she was going out for the day and left them to it. While they were working with a blowtorch the flame caught the woodwork and before they could do anything the woodwork burst into flames. After throwing on water they managed to put the blaze out and then tried frantically to get rid of the smell and clear up the mess before Dolly returned. As soon as she came into the room she gave a sniff and asked what had happened. They had to confess. 'Why did you try to put it out?' she demanded indignantly. 'You should have let the whole place burn down.'

The two brothers were devoted to each other. Tommy's wife, Irene, was a talented pianist with a mind of her own. She was in demand as an accompanist and in the days of silent movies had played in the local cinema. She told me that if she became too involved in the film she would start to slow down and her mother would make a sign to tell her to speed up. She was unable to get on with her mother-in-law, so she installed herself in Innerleithen where she gave music lessons until she was ninety. Each evening Tommy would drive down to have his evening meal with her and later Ian would walk down with his cherished dog and the two brothers would drive back to Traquair.

Before electricity was installed, one of Tommy's jobs was to creep around the big house in the early morning to collect all the lamps and candles which he filled or trimmed before putting them away in the small lamp room. He laid the fires, brought in the logs and disappeared silently before anyone was up.

Lady Louisa Stuart, the last of the direct line of Stuarts, had left money for a substantial Catholic church and priest's house to be built in Innerleithen. Its spire dominated the skyline. Dolly made a point of bicycling down to the eight o'clock daily Mass, but Peter took pity on her and went with her in the car. Catholics were very much in the minority in the south of Scotland, and Dolly told me that, particularly in the early days, she had felt herself regarded with suspicion when she was seen going into the Catholic church. She suffered from an exaggerated Catholic conscience and believed herself to be in need of mortification. This did not prevent her from sharing my mother's attitude towards priests. One Sunday morning I was sitting next to Dolly in her usual pew in the front of the church when an Irish priest of the old mode started to harangue the congregation on the poor collections and declared that he did not wish 'to see another copper in the plate'. When it came round, to show her disapproval, she picked every penny and halfpenny out of her purse and threw them in with a loud clatter.

I attended daily Mass with them only occasionally. We had to fast before we received communion and afterwards I would be dying to get back for a cup of coffee but Dolly, refusing to give in to human frailty, insisted on doing her shopping. It was tantalising visiting the grocer's, which was run by a mother and son. They cooked up their breakfast in the back of the shop and the smell of frying bacon would waft out to meet us.

Dolly was usually insistent that she buy a fillet or a cutlet for Michael, but the sight of raw meat disgusted her. The accommodating butcher would come out on to the pavement while she pointed to what she wanted in the window. He then went inside, wrapped it up and delivered the parcel into her hands.

Innerleithen is about a mile away from Traquair, and the land was once part of the estate. The town grew up around a woollen mill, and the last earl nurtured the small town and took an active interest in building new houses. As a young man he enjoyed his jaunts to London, which is apparent in his choice of names for the streets. There is a Bond Street and an Oxford Street. Innerleithen became famous for the quality of its cashmere garments, which were exported all over the world. During the Second World War it was found that women could take over skilled men's jobs and now both men and women were employed. At its peak, the mill was the heartbeat of the town. It determined whether people were on short time, overtime or shift work, covering twenty-four hours, with the machinery kept going all night. The trade in the shops and everyone's livelihood depended on the mill's order books.

The narrow main street runs slap through the town and gives a dour first impression with its grey stone houses and small shops on either side, but its inhabitants, I soon discovered, were anything but dour. Everyone seemed to know everyone else as many families had lived there for generations and had intermarried and all the children started at the same school. The women were so much at home in the town that they came out to do their shopping with their hair in curlers. They might be wearing down-at-heel shoes and an old skirt and pinafore but it was often topped by a luxury cashmere sweater – the workers were allowed to buy the rejects at low prices.

The shops were friendly places and shopkeepers could keep a whole queue of people waiting while they cracked jokes or inquired sympathetically after a mutual acquaintance's health. No one was in a hurry. Only at twelve o'clock when the hooter sounded and the workers poured out of the mill and into the shops was there any sign of urgency.

The Scots, I discovered, were very fond of their 'butcher meat'. When the mill went on short time the butcher was the first to know. As the best beef and lamb were produced on local farms, they were connoisseurs. Soup was the mainstay of the diet and good pieces of meat were used to make it.

There was a mouth-watering choice in the baker's. As many women worked full time, they had little time for baking at home. The only thing I missed were fruit and vegetables. The one small greengrocer's shop was run by a Pole. The first time I went into the shop it was early spring. He had nothing but onions and potatoes and huge imported carrots. I asked if he ever had green vegetables and he shook his head sadly. 'Not often – the Scots are like sheep, they like their root vegetables.'

There was a small community of Poles in the town as the Polish army was based in the district during the Second World War. Many of the girls were swept off their feet by the charming Polish soldiers who kissed their hands and paid them compliments, rather different from the macho Scots approach. Several marriages took place and there were still Poles left in the town who spoke with an incomprehensible accent while their children spoke fluent Scots.

Above the town was the Doo Well whose water was said to have healing properties. It was purported to improve eyesight and encourage fertility. When spas came into vogue, the earl started to develop the well and built an attractive pavilion beside it. For a while Innerleithen became a fashionable place to spend a few days. Invalids were wheeled up the hill in a bath chair to take the waters. The local paper printed a list of 'Who is staying in Innerleithen this week'. Sir Walter Scott, who had built his house, Abbotsford, nearby, observed the Earl's attempt to promote the spa with amusement and wrote his only satirical novel, *St Ronan's Well*, about it. After the book came out in 1823, the name of the Doo Well was changed to St Ronan's.

There were still a few old tradesmen in the town who could remember the great-uncles and enjoyed telling us some good tales. The plumber, who was just about to retire, could still remember accompanying his father when he had been called up to the 'big hoose' for an emergency. Uncle Arthur had dropped his false teeth down the lavatory and had inadvertently flushed them away. He was desperate to have them back and Mr Euman was asked to trace them. The plumbing at Traquair had been a mystery even to him. He decided to flush different bits of coloured paper down while his son searched among the trees at the back of the house. It was thought the effluent might soak away before it eventually ran into the Tweed. Fortunately, the teeth were never traced.

We wanted to reopen the house to the public the following July but were able to make only a few changes while Dolly and Michael were living there. Peter worked in his father's office in the house, formerly the old smoking room, where some of his great-uncles' pipes still hung in a rack on the wall, but otherwise we tried to keep out of their way as much as we could.

I was determined to make some kind of temporary tearoom as I knew this was an important part of a visit to an historic house. Dolly had tried to serve teas when they first opened the house to the public and there was no electricity. She had to boil up an immense kettle in her kitchen and then run across the courtyard with it to make the tea. I asked the visitors when they arrived if they would want tea afterwards, and they always said "no", she complained. 'Then when Frank had spent hours taking them round the house they would come out freezing to death and say they would like some after all. It took ages for the kettle to boil and they grumbled that they had to wait so long.' Now electricity had been installed and the Miller brothers, as resourceful as ever, cleared out a room in one of the wings and made six new tables.

Frank had not made a gift shop, fearing that he would take trade from local shopkeepers, so he had sold only postcards and paperweights that he made himself – he had acquired a load of cat's-eyes and carefully stuck a sepia photograph of the house underneath and covered it with green felt, creating very classy paperweights. Not many years later, I was proudly offered one by an antique dealer.

I decided that if we brought more visitors to the area by widening the attractions in the house, local shops would in the end benefit as well. Although we had missed the main Gift Fair, I visited a few wholesalers in London and bought an assortment of goods. We put a large table from the laundry into the lower drawing room and made this into a temporary counter.

Although we had little time or opportunity to make many changes in the house, we did move the showcases and their contents from the lower drawing room up into the old lumber room on the second floor and made this into a Museum Room. It had once been the top floor of the old peel tower and had the remains of a lively sixteenth-century mural on one wall. The walls had been replastered in the recent restoration, the corners had been rounded off and it had been made to look, according to Dolly, like a 'palais de danse'. Peter also arranged to have the splendid yellow bed, which Mary Queen of Scots was supposed to have slept in and which his father had just finished renovating, moved into the King's Room.

On the first of July 1963 we reopened the house. We had distributed hastily printed leaflets and posters and Peter, who was well versed in advertising, invited the press to a buffet lunch that I cooked in our cottage and brought down to the tearoom. He took them on a tour of the house and explained that we hoped to open up more rooms later. About twenty journalists turned up and we got good publicity in all the Scottish newspapers as well as a few nationals.

For the next three months we opened every afternoon except Fridays, with Jack, a student guide, helping Peter to take round continuous tours while I sold the tickets and looked after the shop. I felt uncomfortable selling a ticket to see round our house to someone we knew. Peter did not make it easier by saying, 'No, you mustn't pay: just buy something in the shop instead.' I could see their eyes searching desperately for an inexpensive object that they could possibly use. My inability to recognise people was a huge handicap – after selling people a ticket on arrival and chatting with them I would greet them as newcomers when they came out again and ask them if they wanted to buy a ticket.

Mrs Storrie, the keeper's wife, or schoolgirls, looked after the tearoom, but one particularly wet afternoon when few visitors were expected, I manned both shop and tearoom, dashing across the courtyard from one to the other. 'Dinna be in such a hurry, hen,' said a kindly woman as I arrived panting to ask what she would like. In the evenings I baked scones and cakes and Peter and Jack worked in the grounds.

Our main objective was to attract coach tours, and the sight of a bus coming down the avenue cheered us no end. We were disappointed when only a handful of passengers would decide to come into the house while the rest got out and went straight to the 'Ladies' which we had made in the old Lamp Room. They often did not even go into the tearoom as they had booked a tea stop farther on.

Meanwhile, Dolly kept a wary eye on the proceedings from her little sitting room on the first floor. Whenever a bus drove up alongside the Wine-Glass Lawn and damaged the edging, as they frequently did, she would fly down with great speed and give the driver a severe ticking off, telling one man that he was not fit to be in charge of a bus and should never return. Peter would then have to catch the driver before he left and beg him to take no notice but to come again as often as he could.

During the season, a group of architects and historians working for the Royal Commission on Ancient Monuments spent six weeks at the house. They were gradually producing a volume on each county in Scotland, recording all the buildings of age and interest. They patiently measured and photographed every room and outbuilding and tried to assess the age of each wall to find out how the house had evolved. When the time came for them to go into Dolly's bedroom, which was thought to have been an earlier dining room and had a decoration of vines and grapes above the fireplace, everyone was terrified to ask her permission. Peter suggested waiting till she went out on her afternoon bicycle ride. As she disappeared up the avenue he signalled the 'all clear' and they quickly finished before her return.

Our first season ended with a fling. A phone call from the British Travel Association in London told us that they were organising one of their 'British Weeks' in New Orleans. One of the major stores had asked if they could exhibit Mary Queen of Scots' relics and would we be prepared to lend the quilted silk cover from the King's bed and the carved oak cradle in which Mary Queen of Scots had rocked her baby, who was later to be James VI. We were invited to the opening and Peter was asked to give a lecture on the house. After checking that the items would be properly packed and insured, we agreed without hesitation. Being new to tourism, the fact that we would have to shut up the house a few days before the end of September, our official closing time, did not worry us. We felt that the publicity we would get in the United States would justify inconveniencing a few visitors. We merely hung a notice at the entrance saying that we had been forced to close a few days early and off we went.

We flew from Glasgow to New York and were joined on the plane to New Orleans by the strange combination of Norman Hartnell, the Queen's dressmaker, and a Town Crier complete with his bell. We arrived at New Orleans in the early hours of the morning by our time, but about 6 o'clock in the evening by theirs. We were floodlit and photographed coming off the plane and then given a police escort through all the red lights to our hotel before being whisked off to dinner at 'Antoine's'.

Our hosts were the town dignitaries and the stores' executives and their wives, all dressed up to the nines. I was taken aback when one of the wives whispered to me after the first course, 'Shall we go to the little girls' room?' Feeling jet-lagged, I asked curiously 'What little girl?' before realising that it meant that all the women left the table and retreated to the ladies' room to readjust their hair and faces before returning to the table and continuing with the rest of the meal.

We were put up in a luxurious old-fashioned hotel and I had breakfast in bed brought in on a large trolley. While I ate pancakes and syrup, I watched Peter being interviewed on breakfast television. We had trips to the French Market and listened to jazz in Bourbon Street, as well as attending dinners for the opening of the British Week. Norman Hartnell seemed put out that he had to share the limelight with us and scarcely exchanged a word. There was a nasty moment when he could not be found, just before the big opening, but he reappeared looking jaded in the nick of time. Peter's talk on Traquair was packed out and a great success. He was introduced as the 'Twentieth Laird of Traquair', and at the end of the talk a young woman came up and shook his hand saying, 'I am Mrs Laird, we must be related.'

We ended our visit to the South by hiring a car and driving into Mississippi to stay on a cotton plantation with Mrs Polk, a descendant of the fifteenth American President. At Traquair I had chatted to a visitor in the tearoom who turned out to be her cousin and when she heard that we were going to New Orleans she had arranged the visit.

We stayed in her nostalgic plantation house and ate the best southern fried chicken I have ever had. Mrs Polk told us later that she had asked the maid who served us not to give her any wings or legs as she would not be able to resist picking them up in her fingers and thought we might be shocked. She had been brought up on a plantation and saw the liberation of the slaves as liberation also for the plantation wives who, she maintained, had spent so much time looking after them. The cotton grew like large cotton-wool balls on stalks and was being picked mechanically while we were there.

Before we left, Mrs Polk gave me a small cookery book that had been compiled in aid of her church in their local small town of Inverness. It included, among other delicious recipes, a whisky mousse which I guessed must have originated in Scotland. I have used it for special occasions ever since and have given it to American visitors as an old Scots recipe. We kept in touch with Mrs Polk until her death. The friendship was a great reward for working in the tearoom.

Taking Over

~

In the spring of 1964 I was surprised and delighted to discover that I was pregnant. We had been married for seven years and had never used any form of birth control but I had not had a hint of a pregnancy. When we first got married, we imagined that, like many of our Catholic relatives, we might find ourselves inundated with children. I felt there was plenty of time, so for a few years I was happy to be childless. Later on we took medical advice but no problem was diagnosed. We were just told to wait.

I had begun to long for a child and prayed for one every day, but I managed to resign myself to the fact that it seemed I might never have one. I consoled myself with the thought that Peter and I were blissfully happy together and maybe, even more so, than if we had children. I was, however, annoyed by friends and relatives making sly comments. Only Nanny, who was at last happily settled living with Jocelyn, Anne Phillimore's brother in London, understood how I felt and advised me to drink olive oil. I could not bring myself to do this.

So the fact that I was now actually about to have a child was a huge excitement. It was due in November, after our season was over, and after we had moved into the big house. Dolly had decided to move into the old factor's house which had become vacant nearby. She and Michael planned to move at the end of the summer. She was busy taking her furniture and belongings out of the public rooms, which made it easier for us to make changes.

A friend named Brodrick Haldane came to stay. There was nothing he liked better than arranging rooms and he was dying to help us. He was older than us, a spindly, slightly-built man full of nervous energy but little strength. He would sit on a chair at one side of a room and decide that a huge chest or table would look better somewhere else. Peter and I would heave and shove 'just a little further' or 'forward a bit' as he waved his arm to left or right. Then we would all sit down and contemplate the new arrangement for a few minutes. 'No, no it was better where it was before,' was the usual verdict, and we would heave and shove it all back again.

Brodrick was brought up on the west coast of Scotland until his family inherited Gleneagles, an old family house in Perthshire. His father never reconciled himself to the huge hotel built nearby and insisted that any letter addressed to 'Gleneagles' should be delivered to him. Every morning he sat at his desk going through the mail, solemnly scoring out Gleneagles and readdressing it to 'Railway Hotel'.

Brodrick became a photographer. He had a good eye but knew little of the technical side of photography. He took photographs with a diffident manner that put people at their ease and he produced some excellent portraits. His connections helped him to become a society photographer, but his chief interest was architecture and old houses matched by an equal fascination for the people who lived in them. He observed human behaviour and all the minutiae of social life with a sardonic eye since he was 'a quiet little boy sitting in the corner of a room listening unobserved to adults talking'. Lord Haldane and Naomi Mitchison, the novelist, were among his relations.

He was fond of my spoilt cousin Pookie and was both amused and shocked by her outrageous behaviour. He told us that he had once photographed her at Ince in front of the lake. 'How beautiful you look,' he told her, whereupon she signalled to a gardener to fetch a mirror and soon a young footman came staggering out of the house carrying a full-length looking glass. One winter when he was sent to a ski resort by the *Tatler*, she arrived, uninvited, at his hotel and demanded a room. It was full up. The only way they could get her in was for her to pose as his secretary. She was given a room in the attic but after she insisted on non-stop room service and castigated most of the staff, he was asked to remove her.

Every year Brodrick went to stay in Lausanne with a friend who was a leading light of the tax exiles. Her circle included Marlene Dietrich, Noel Coward and the ex-Queen of Spain, one of Queen Victoria's granddaughters, whom he described as a frightening woman, trying to keep up her royal status while living in straitened circumstances. One day she invited him to a small tea party. She told her guests a story that involved a Mrs X who was known to be an impoverished widow. 'I am surprised your majesty knows poor Mrs X,' commented one of the sycophantic guests. To this the queen drew herself up and replied in a withering tone, 'I have royal blood and *we* fly very high, from where *we* look down everyone looks the same.'

Brodrick's conversation was fascinating but diverted us from our work. Once he left, we again concentrated on the house. We soon discovered that old used rugs and fabrics fitted in better at Traquair than anything new. We bought up carpets that had been discarded in London for being too worn. We were anxious to keep the 'lost in time' atmosphere of the house and to renew as little as possible.

We could see that we would have to add to the furniture. When Frank and Dolly inherited Traquair, it was sparsely furnished except for a few good pieces. Rumour had it that when her brother, the last earl, died, Lady Louisa moved into a wing and in her old age the butler sold off the furniture. Tommy and Ian's father made furniture for the Maxwells when they inherited. As the great-uncles had not believed in repairs, Frank and Dolly found much of it in a bad state. Dolly replaced sofas and armchairs and these were now being taken to her new house. When we finally moved in, the linen cupboard contained only vast linen tablecloths and piles of eighteenth- and nineteenth-century napkins. Many of the floors were bare as, being of an economical nature, she had even taken linoleum and old carpets off the floors.

From the beginning we did not think of the house or furnishings as our own. After several years we would ask each other, 'Does this belong to the house or is it ours?' We had brought up the furniture that I had bought at auctions when we first married and my parents had given us some more. We also bought things from the two Constable Maxwell sisters who were equally related to both Peter and myself. They ran an enticing antique shop, full of elaborate gilt mirrors and exotic furnishings as well as more everyday items, on three floors of a Georgian house in Edinburgh. Ursula, who also sculpted and painted, had brought back Chinese wallpaper from Hong Kong for her magnificent drawing room in Moray Place and was continually adding birds and butterflies to it. Her husband, Chalmers Davidson, was a cultivated Edinburgh man who knew most of the art and literary world. At one of their dinner parties I sat next to the author Compton Mackenzie. He was an amusing man to talk to and he began to tell me how much he admired Lord Mountbatten. 'He is so good-looking it prevents me from taking him seriously,' I commented flippantly. Monty lifted his head, turned his profile towards me and said sadly, 'That has always been my trouble.'

We had made friends with Geoffrey Hay, one of the Royal Commission architects, and he drew up plans so that we could make the old kitchen into a private sitting room, turn the back kitchen into a small dining room and convert the old bathroom into a modern kitchen. This would give us private quarters at the back of the house where we could use the back stairs to go up to our bedrooms. I was determined to live in an area that I could look after myself if need be. I did not want to be dependent on domestic help as my mother had been.

When I told an elderly friend of our plans, she threw up her hands in horror. 'My dear,' she said, 'what a frightful idea, living in the servants' quarters. You are just like my sister in Aberdeen who says how much she enjoys having meals in the old dog room. I find it quite ghastly.'

When it came to the kitchen, we met a stalemate between the Historic Buildings Council on the one hand, who said that a new window could not be introduced, and the local authority on the other, who said that a kitchen must have a certain amount of light. Fortunately, when it was realised that the back corner of the house had been altered in the nineteenth century, we were allowed to have a new small odd-shaped window made to blend in with the others and, best of all, convert the window in our new sitting room into French windows so that we could walk out on to a side terrace. It was the only private outdoor area we were to have. I planted climbing roses and filled it with pot plants and many happy times were spent there over the years, eating and drinking and entertaining friends.

Peter was anxious to get the library on the top floor into a fit state to show to the public. The cove of the ceiling was decorated with portraits of classical philosophers and writers whose names were written above each bookcase. It contained nearly four thousand books, some of them dating from the sixteenth century, and was formed by the fifth Earl of Traquair, the earl who closed the Bear Gates. Although he did not actually fight in the '45 Jacobite Rebellion, he was involved in its planning and after it was over he was condemned to spend a year in the Tower of London. After his release he was 'confined to his estates'.

The portraits were peeling badly, and it was soon discovered that this was caused by damp from the roof above which was in such a bad state of repair that both the sarking and slates would need renewing. Peter also discovered a flaw in the building that was to cause us endless expense and worry. In the late seventeenth century, when castles were being turned into country houses, the architect James Smith was employed to form the courtyard at the front and to landscape the rocky bank at the rear. He made a double terrace with ogee-roofed pavilions at either end. It was beautiful to look at but had become a recurring problem The water tended to seep into the terrace walls, and when it froze a bulge would begin to form and sections of the wall had continually to be rebuilt.

We found a story about the terrace in an old game book that had been assiduously kept by a great-uncle. Apparently, a gamekeeper who had come for an interview was being shown out of the back door that opened on to it. As he said goodbye he bowed obsequiously, took a few steps back and fell on to the terrace below. Unhurt, he picked himself up, bowed again and, apologising for his clumsiness, stepped back and fell over the next terrace.

Peter started on the laborious process of applying for a grant towards the cost of the restoration. Although we already had a large overdraft and a grant would be only a percentage of the full cost of the work, he managed to convince the bank that it must be done and if we could open the library to the public it would pull in extra visitors.

Peter was still taking tours round and was now joined by James Corrie, a gentleman who lived nearby. He was a poet, a dedicated Scottish Nationalist and a passionate fisherman. Although he had lost a hand and part of his arm in the Second World War while demonstrating, only too successfully, how to explode a bomb, he could still tie his fishing flies with one hand. He always wore a shrunken tweed jacket that had been immersed in the Tweed a few times and smelt accordingly. He literally stalked fish, and if he caught sight of a large trout he would walk straight into the water up to his armpits so that he could cast directly in front of it. He fancied himself as an orator and liked to compose his own scripts about the house. He would start his tours by grouping his party in the court-yard and then, looking up at the house, would proclaim, 'Look at this beautiful building, which has evolved gracefully over the years, and then compare it with that ugly monstrosity of Balmoral.' A short pause while he dropped his voice and changed to a mocking tone, 'And Queen Victoria wrote in her diary, "dear Albert thought of it all".' He threw out further anti-English remarks as the tour continued, which, if he was in good form, became longer and longer. When we received complaints from English visitors, Peter would ask him to tone it down a little. This would last only a few weeks and he would soon be back again in full flood.

I enjoyed talking to the visitors when I was serving in the shop or selling the tickets and picked up some useful titbits. We knew that the first Earl of Traquair had realised that the River Tweed ran too near the house and was in danger of undermining the foundations. In the seventeenth century its course was diverted by cutting through a bend. This stretch of the river, now several hundred yards away from the rear of the house, was still known by fishermen as the 'new water'. A crescent of water, called the Well Pool, fed by two springs, remained by the house. A wraith-like woman, a retired school teacher who used to make regular visits, told me that on an autumn evening the mist could easily be seen rising along the twists and turns of the old bed of the Tweed. Another visitor told me that her grandmother had walked barefoot across the hills from the neighbouring valley to be married in the Traquair chapel. She had carried her shoes all the way so that they would be clean for the wedding.

Visitors would chat with me quite freely if they thought I was one of the staff. We advertised the house as the 'oldest inhabited house in Scotland', which curiously seemed to prompt the question 'Is it still lived in?' I would explain that it was and they would then go on to ask, 'Who lives there?' I learnt to reply casually, 'the Maxwell Stuart family.' This would generally satisfy them but occasionally they would probe again and if they realised who I was, some of them would become embarrassed and break off the conversation.

Visitors having tea in the tearoom, especially groups, would react quite differently. Their priority was a good cup of tea and to have it served promptly, and they could not care less who gave it to them. I had never realised that making tea could be such a skilled task. 'That was a lovely cup of tea,' I would be told with a sigh of satisfaction, or, when I thought I had made it in an identical manner, 'Did you forget the tea bag, hen?'

I was helping out in the tearoom at the end of the season, hugely pregnant and trying to manoeuvre my way between the tables, when a woman put her hand on my arm and said kindly,

My parents and brother Edmund, with me as a baby. My mother was amongst the first women to go up to Oxford to read agriculture. My father was director of the LSE for over twenty years. Immediately after the publication of his book, *The Population Problem*, he was granted the chair of Social Science at Liverpool University.

Above. Water Eaton Manor, near Oxford. My parents found this house empty and neglected and obtained a long lease. They loved it passionately and lavished their care and attention on it. I had the happiest days of my childhood here before it was suddenly requisitioned by the army.

Right. My beloved Irish nanny Brigid McCormack. Her calm, contented nature was one of the biggest influences in my life. We kept in touch until she died.

Above left. With my brother Edmund in the garden at Water Eaton. He was four years older than me and took a long time to get over my arrival.

Above right. Young Thomas Pakenham, holding forth during a seaside holiday.

Below. A picnic on the beach on the Isle of Wight, 1939. From left: me, my brother Edmund, in front of him Antonia Pakenham (later Fraser), my mother, and Elizabeth Pakenham, who I admired enormously. My father told us it would probably be the last holiday until the war was over.

Above. Our family with the Strickland Constables in 1953 outside the barn near our house in Cumberland. From left: Lettuce, my brother Edmund, my mother standing behind Freddy and Robert, me, Lisbet, my father and my brother Nicholas. Three years later, young Robert was a page at my wedding.

Right. Peter and his nephew Michael Paterson. Michael was the youngest son of Joan, one of Peter's beautiful elder sisters. When we first met he asked Peter, 'are you going to marry that lady?'

16 Margaretta Terrace SW3

Above. Peter and me outside St Ethelreda Church after our wedding ceremony. The page boys were Michael Paterson and Robert. One of the bridesmaids, almost hidden, was god-daughter Felicity Leng.

Left. Our first Christmas card: my drawing of the house in Chelsea where we spent our first married years. It was the centre of the terrace. We lived on the top three floors and rented out the ground floor to a cousin.

Traquair brew house. After the death of Peter's father we moved to Traquair.
Soon after our arrival Peter resurrected the eighteenth-century brew house and started
to make beer.

Catherine's christening. After the christening we put Catherine in the old cradle which had been used by James VI of Scotland and I of England. She was the first baby to live at Traquair for over two hundred years.

Above. Pram outside Traquair. I had been instructed by the nurse to wrap Catherine up in three shawls and put her out in all weathers.

Below. We decided to have a King Charles Spaniel, without ever having seen one, as soon as we moved to Traquair. They were a rare breed then but their gentle nature soon made them very popular, as can be seen here with the latest brood of farmyard ducklings hatched out by Catherine.

Above. Family group on terrace with Peter, his neice Laura, me, Peter's mother Dolly, and Michael, holding his son Justin. After their marriage Kirsty and Michael moved to Lanarkshire.

Below. Belinda, our donkey, with Catherine and me. I soon learnt how obstinate donkeys can be.

Right. Doctor Johnson, played by Peter Woodthorpe. The BBC decided to use Traquair as Boswell's house, Auchinleck, in a documentary (their first in colour) about Johnson's tour of the Highlands. They wanted Catherine to play Boswell's daughter. When Catherine saw him in costume she needed a lot of persuasion to go near him.

Below. At Michael and Kirsty's wedding. Catherine was a bridesmaid.

Above. Catherine, Peter and Joseph Maxwell Stuart, Peter's first cousin, on the terrace. He often stayed with us and was like an elder brother to Catherine. He is now a successful artist.

Below. Peter and tourists. Peter enjoyed showing visitors round and liked to start outside so he could describe the different stages in the building of Traquair, which had not been altered since 1680.

Left. Swedish ball in 1967. We were invited to be guests of honour at a magnificent Scottish-Swedish ball in Stockholm. Many of the Swedes had Scottish names and had lived in Sweden for many generations.

Below. Catherine and me in the wagonette in which Robert Louis gave rides to the visitors. He lived with his family in the grounds in a gypsy caravan.

Above. The maze soon after planting in 1980. We decided to plant it at the back of the house where there had once been a *parterre* garden. John Schofield, who had a workshop in the grounds, designed the plan. My brother Nicholas supplied the fifteen hundred Leyland Cypress trees. A grid of stakes was first put in and then a wire nailed to them to mark the pattern. After losing a third of the trees in a hard frost it was partly replanted with beech, but despite many problems it finally became a perfect maze.

Below. The maze after ten years.

Right. Peter, Catherine and me in costume. Robin Crichton, of Edinburgh Film Studios, used our drawing-room as the set for Burns' introduction into Edinburgh society. We all took part as extras.

Below. Television studio in Virginia. The British Tourist Authority sent us on several trips to America, where we gave interviews on local TV stations and to news-papers. Peter ended up on a national network show, *What's my Line?*

Above. Felicity Leng and Peter, his cousin and god-daughter, on the terrace. It was our only totally private outdoor space and I had filled it with plants. Felicity was studying at the Slade and often came to stay.

Below. The Fairy Queen, a promenade play for children, performed in the grounds. The children were given 'magic juice' and then led away by a Pied Piper into the woods, where they saw good and bad fairies. It was very popular and followed by several more.

Mary Queen of Scots projected onto the house for a *son et lumière* display at Traquair for which the Borders Festival obtained sponsorship. It ran for five nights and was a great success. Other huge blown-up portraits were also occasionally projected onto the house.

'I hope it's a boy.' I smiled and thanked her, but I hated this British mania with inheritance and was annoyed to think that anyone could quibble over the sex of a child. It was so wonderful to be able to have one at all.

A Birth and Settling In

~

Our baby, a bouncing girl, cleverly decided to arrive in November 1964 on Peter's birthday. Although my mother had urged me to have her in a private nursing home which she would pay for, I was determined to have her under the National Health Service. At thirty I was considered a 'mature mother' and was eligible to go into a teaching hospital in Edinburgh where I had excellent treatment.

On our way back to Traquair, as I clutched the tiny parcel in my arms, I wondered how I would ever be able to keep this small being alive and was only too glad that I had accepted my mother's offer to pay for a 'monthly nurse'.

It was the custom among Catholics for babies to be baptised as soon as possible after their birth. It was thought that a baby who died before it was baptised would not be able to go to heaven but would remain happily forever in Limbo. Nowadays baptism is no longer considered a passport to heaven and Limbo has fortunately been abolished.

She was christened Catherine Margaret Mary in the chapel by candlelight a few days after our return, with only the Priest, Peter and me, Dolly, Michael and our King Charles spaniel present. Peter borrowed the silver punch bowl from the dining room to use as a font. This provided an anecdote that went down well with visitors later on. As we drank champagne in the drawing room afterwards, we watched the flames from the huge bonfire that the Miller brothers had lit at the end of the avenue. Catherine was to be the first child to be brought up from birth in Traquair since the family of the fourth earl in the eighteenth century.

We spent that winter living in the high drawing room while the builders banged away downstairs. This part of the house was built in the sixteenth century. Like many houses in Scotland of that date, the beams that run across the ceiling, and the walls, were enlivened by murals. It was then redecorated in the eighteenth century by Charles, the fifth earl, the eldest in a family of seventeen children.

He made a grand tour of Europe in 1717 and cunningly convinced his parents that this should be done in style. 'I am now consulting on the properest way to travel,' he had written from France, 'that is by common voitures, or by post, or hired horses or by having an Italian chaise. The first has the disadvantage that I must rise early and arrive late so that I have time to see nothing by the way, the second is much opposed by some of my friends perhaps too solicitous and tender about my health, and the going on horse back exposing me to the injuries of the season make them more apprehensive of it than I am and so advise me to have a chaise, which I find all computed will not increase the expense and which is by far the most convenient way of travelling. I am in a doubt whither I should take my servant with me but am afraid of the expense.'

After he inherited the house and married his heiress, Theresa Conyers, Charles decided to redecorate the room in the classical style. He covered over the beams with a plain ceiling and panelled the walls. The original large fireplace was replaced by a more elegant one that could hold only a small fire. Even if it was lit all day and helped by two electric heaters, it produced a temperature that was only just bearable, although probably warmer than it had ever been before, with the result that the panelling contracted, leaving large gaps through which an icy draught blew from the space behind.

Before she left, the nurse instructed me in baby care. I was to wrap Catherine up tightly in three shawls and put her out in her pram in the courtyard every morning. As she gradually began to focus, she could watch the two Miller brothers climbing up the forty-foot ladders to the roof. Bit by bit they stripped off the old slates, repaired the beams and left them covered with sarking ready for the slater. They worked all day, supported only by a plank that they secured horizontally across the slates.

My parents were spending more time in their house in Cumberland, and I took Catherine down to see them. She was their first grandchild, and my mother was in ecstasies over her. One evening, Catherine was lying in her cot and gave a sort of smile. 'Alec, Alec,' she called excitedly to my father, who was reading in the next room, 'do come and look at the baby.' 'I have seen her, my dear,' he replied patiently.

In February, we were determined to visit the Spring Gift Fair, which at that time was held in Blackpool. As I was still breast-feeding Catherine, we took her with us. We stayed in a bed-and-breakfast and took it in turns to visit the Fair. Unlike most fathers at that time, and much to his eldest sister's disgust, Peter enjoyed looking after Catherine. He had no hang-up about it being 'unmanly' and soon learnt to change her nappy or give her the odd bottle.

In Blackpool, where the Fair was held in halls and hotels all over the town, a collection of vehicles transported buyers from one venue to the other. We were quite amazed at the goods on offer. It was before the days of Conran and an interest in design, and it seemed that a gift did not need to be either attractive or useful. Gradually, we managed to sift out some passable bits and pieces, although generally these were imported and not what a tourist shop in Scotland should be selling. When the best Celtic jewellery turned out to be made in Birmingham, the choice was even more difficult. The salesmen were all pushy and determined to land us with huge orders, although their faces quickly fell when they heard that we had only a small seasonal shop in Peeblesshire, a county that they had never heard of or could even spell.

I was not convinced by their assurances that even if I did not like something it was certain to 'walk out of the shop'. I decided that I would buy only things that I liked myself. I would be selling them and would not be able to work in a shop surrounded by objects that I did not like. At the back of my mind was the thought that if something did not sell, I would be content to keep it. It was a gamble the first year deciding what to order.

The Millers had converted the temporary tearoom into a shop with pine shelves and good lighting. When the parcels we had ordered at the Gift Fair arrived, it felt like Christmas. Having been brought up not to be extravagant, a habit also shared by Peter, I started at first to put on as low a mark-up as possible, but I soon realised that tourists are not influenced by low prices – in fact, in some cases it puts them off. I loved working on the display and when we opened was intrigued to find that there were certain positions in the shop where articles always sold. I also discovered that my instinctive hunch had paid off and that anything I particularly liked myself was the first to go.

Getting the house ready at the start of a new season is always a hectic time, but it was particularly frantic that year after we had been living in the public rooms all winter. Our beautiful new kitchen and sitting room were only just finished in time. Their wide French windows opened on to the terrace and faced the old croquet lawn, with magnificent fir trees and the hills beyond. I was delighted with it and felt that we were moving into a new house that actually belonged to us.

I tried to keep the courtyard weeded and bedded out annuals in the spring. I was amazed by the Peeblesshire climate where frost has been recorded every month of the year. One year, the dahlias had just started to flower when they were killed by a frost in early September. A couple of straggling roses and ancient *Cotoneaster horizontalis*, full of spiders' webs, clung to the walls. I wanted to plant more roses and was intrigued by the Jacobite symbol of a white rose. I kept being told that a different variety was the real one, so the walls ended up covered with several varieties. I learnt later that the Jacobites were not particular and used any white rose as their emblem.

I had to find someone to look after Catherine while I was working and I asked Jean Hately, a hospital nurse who had rented one of the cottages in the grounds, if she would be willing to work for us for the summer. We got on well, but it took a little while to get used to her quirky sense of humour. A few days after she started, I heard Catherine crying in her pram and asked Jean if she knew what was the matter. 'I have no idea,' she answered, 'perhaps I have got the washing machine instructions mixed up with the baby's.' She loved the grounds around the house and would put Catherine to sleep by letting her lie on a blanket at the side of the Quair Burn.

Visitors were less impressed by the state of the grounds. There were only a few houses open to the public in Scotland at that time, many with huge estates to finance them or others that belonged to The National Trust for Scotland, which appeared to have limitless money to spend on maintenance. As we were opening the house only at two o'clock each day (wages prevented us from keeping longer hours) we received complaints from tourists who turned up in the morning and did not have time to wait. They had frequently 'come all the way from Australia'. We decided to sell 'grounds only' tickets so that they could at least walk around and see the outside of the house. This only led to further complaints. 'Rather than sell tickets to see your grounds you should be paying people to stay away,' wrote one irate gentleman. The green movement twenty years later inspired more approving comments. 'We love it here. It's so wild,' we were told. Or, 'I'm so glad to see nettles allowed to grow to encourage the butterflies.'

Traquair formerly had only a walled garden, a hundred yards from the house. Dolly made herbaceous borders nearer the house but after she left, weeds took over. We decided that for the time being we would concentrate on maintaining the fabric of the buildings and keep only a small area as a garden. I have never seen great merits in taming nature. We employed a full-time man in the grounds and a series of young relatives or friends came to work in the summer.

Michael Paterson was one of Peter's nephews and also his

godson. He had often stayed with us since he was a serious little boy with huge round glasses. Now he was up at Oxford and a strapping young man. He had spent most of a vacation digging the new Victoria Line for the London Underground so Peter got him digging in front of the house. It was said that when the first bathroom was being installed, the workmen had come across a chest buried in the ground. The factor had immediately telegraphed the uncles in Yorkshire to ask what should be done with it. True to form the answer came back by return: 'Put it back where you found it.' Peter was full of hope that it might still be there, and with valuables in it, but all that Michael came up against were the old pipes.

We did however find good evidence for Aunt Emily's story that the great-uncles would walk around the house every year poking at cracks with their sticks. If nothing actually fell down they would say cheerfully to each other, 'That's all right, it will last our lifetime.' They had left behind examples of their ingenuity too. When we were spring-cleaning and took up the passage runners, we were intrigued to find a square cut in the floorboards. This, we learnt, was their fire escape. The square of wood would give way when stamped on, making it possible to drop through the plaster to the floor below where a similar arrangement had been made and then on to the next floor.

Peter had a talent for making the house look 'lived in'. He left up-to-date newspapers and magazines in the rooms open to the public, and was adept at finding articles in the bound volumes of old newspapers that were appropriate to the current news. One season he decided to fill the Bristol blue-glass finger bowls in the dining room with water but forgot to mention this to the guides. An over-enthusiastic guide who picked one up to show to the visitors got soaked. Peter fixed up a cassette player in the chapel, which he hid under a back pew. It played continuous Gregorian chants quietly in the background. Later on, a friend showed me a copy of the Women's Rural magazine to which a member had written a letter describing her experience in the Traquair chapel. She had heard low voices singing and realised they were ghosts from the past.

Peter also spent a lot of time arranging articles in the museum, and my skill at calligraphy came in useful for writing the captions. Our museum had to be set up with the minimum expense. Our second-hand showcases contained few items of intrinsic value, but they displayed fascinating objects that had been used by the families at Traquair throughout their lives. One of these is Napier's bones, a small handmade calculator devised by John Napier of Merchiston, the inventor of logarithms.

One of Peter's crucial tasks at the start of each season was to wash the Amen glass. There are fewer than a hundred of these eighteenth-century Jacobite glasses in existence. This one was made specially for Traquair and is decorated with Jacobite emblems – a rose for the exiled James III and buds representing his two sons. It is inscribed with the following verse: 'God bless the Prince of Wales, The true born Prince of Wales, Sent us by thee; Send him soon over And kick out Hanover, and soon we'll recover Our old libertie.'

We put out everything of interest that we could find to give the visitors their money's worth but when we put out all the silver, most of which was plate, it tended to give the impression that we had infinite resources. In reality, if we had sold land or valuables, we would have had to pay a huge capital gains tax. If something had been exempted from death duties we would have had to pay the back tax as well.

After spring-cleaning we were proud of our efforts. When we opened on Easter Sunday the brass was shining, the furniture smelt of wax polish and the rooms were filled with daffodils. We had also had the benches in the courtyard repainted but had not realised that the paint was not completely dry. A young man sat down on one while his child played on the lawn, and when he got up, it was found that there was a dark green streak of paint across the back of his new shirt. He complained to Peter, who looked at it closely. 'All right,' he said, 'it's a nice shirt and we look about the same size. You send me the shirt and I'll send you a cheque.' He was often to be seen walking around in the shirt with the green stripe across its back.

The Millers had transformed the old Malt Loft into a larger tearoom. Under Geoffrey's instruction they raised the beams, put down a new wood floor and made eight fine pine tables. I bought chairs that were being sold off by a local school. With the help of a friend, John Claridge, I mixed up a tank of caustic soda. He had arrived to do this with an Italian business colleague who could not understand a word of English and whom he left sitting in the car. John told me later that he had not been able to explain why he had put on an enormous pair of black rubber gloves and then disappeared with me into a small shed. I dipped the chairs one by one to remove the old varnish and washed them down with vinegar before sandpapering them.

Peter's advertising skills were paying off. We distributed our leaflets widely. I was often irritated that we could never go out in the car without stopping to drop them off in hotels and visitor centres. Independent visitors, especially on Sundays, when at that time there were few other shops or attractions open, increased enormously. Regular coaches were booking to come once a week and others with annual outings of Women's Rurals, societies and schools. Many of them wanted a high tea or a cold supper as well and we could now accommodate them in the tearoom. By the time they had been round the house, had their meal and visited the gift shop, it would often be after ten o'clock at night but still daylight by the time they left. The light Scottish evenings made a very long day.

We soon noticed the difference between Townswomen's Guilds, who came dressed up in high heels, and even white gloves, ate their tea in near silence and bought little in the shop, and the Rurals, who were out to enjoy themselves, cracked jokes all the way, ate every crumb of their tea and spent recklessly. Many of them were farmers' wives who rarely had the chance to shop for pleasure and had been given a good dollop of spending money by their husbands. Schoolchildren also came armed with notes and a determination to spend every penny. 'I have still got this left – what can I get with it?' they would ask. I found myself telling them to keep it for another day.

Once Dolly had got over the excitement of settling into her new house she enjoyed walking over to see us. Occasionally, she would flag down a visitor on the way and ask for a lift. 'Take me to my son,' she would gasp dramatically. Indignant-looking visitors would arrive at Peter's office with his mother on an arm. 'I found this poor lady on the road,' they would say accusingly. Dolly would smile triumphantly and Peter, who had been trying to work in his office, would have to entertain her. On fine afternoons she enjoyed sitting in the courtyard scrutinising the visitors and would comment in a loud voice, 'Look at all those dreadful people.'

During our first years, we could seldom leave the house for more than a day at a time. London was more distant than it is now, with no motorways or cheap flights, and it even felt a long way off. When I listened to the news it seemed remote and less relevant. I was cut off from my life in the south and had to miss the wedding of Michael Maxwell Scott, one of Peter's cousins, and Deirdrie, one of my best friends, whom we had introduced to each other. Even when friends came to stay, I could never spend much time with them.

A young student named Cherry Jobson, who had taken a year out, came to help. She had never cooked before but together we turned out huge quantities of scones and sponge cakes, always the most popular items. Whenever we tried anything more adventurous it never went so well. She was helped by local schoolgirls who came at the weekends or in their holidays. They were fun to work with and, when she was old enough, amused Catherine by propping her up on a chair at the sink. 'Don't let anyone see her or you will be reported to the RSPCC,' my mother said in horror.

I was determined that everything should be home-made. My one lapse was gingerbread. I had found a make that seemed better than anything we could produce ourselves. I was helping in the tearoom one day and serving a family their tea. The mother turned to me and said, 'What delicious baking – you can tell it's all home-made.' Before I had time to answer, their little girl piped up and said, 'No it's not, look at all the gingerbread boxes over there,' and pointed to where we had hidden them under the stairs.

Fresh baking disappeared in a flash as girls did not have the same mania about keeping thin in those days. They also told me they would be quite happy to have false teeth. But they were fun and easy to work with and kept us in touch with what was going on in Innerleithen. They told us about the festivals that are held in turn in each Border town. At Beltane many of the inhabitants ride on horseback to inspect the 'marches', the borders, of the town. A week of festivities follows and in Innerleithen, on the last night, everyone goes up the hill to burn the 'de'il'.

I seemed to be rushing off to the Cash-and-Carry every week. I could not resist buying boxes of chocolate biscuits and other luxuries for ourselves, but I soon tired of loading up heavy bags of sugar and flour although I never tired of the journey. The road to Galashiels follows the Tweed as it runs through a fertile valley between the hills. I was constantly amazed by the beauty of the scenery. I got to know the countryside even better when Cherry asked us if she could keep her two horses at Traquair. On a spare evening it was a great escape to ride with her, or on my own, over the moors or to follow the forestry roads across the hills.

Each morning I checked the house and the flowers, and went into the garden to pick what I could find. I became adept at using small vases with a few wild flowers for the bedrooms, which proved popular with the visitors. When I hopefully put artificial white lilies on the marble altar in the chapel it did not meet with approval.

Having checked the toilets (I could now happily use this word without flinching) and often at weekends having to clean them, I would then replace items that had been sold in the shop, unpack any new parcels that had arrived and see what needed to be baked for the tearoom.

At the end of the afternoon, after the last visitor had gone, we had counted up the takings and given the girls a lift home, the sun, if there was any, would be shining straight into the courtyard. Peter and I would lie on the grass with Catherine and our King Charles spaniels, sipping our tea and eating up any left-overs from the tearoom. It was a busy but very happy life.

Meeting the Neighbours

〜

That summer, when I had time, I pushed Catherine around the estate in her pram and began to get to know some of the farmers and our neighbours. Dolly had impressed on us that we should call on everyone, but we had already met them at a party that she and Frank gave after our marriage. We knew they were as busy as we were and we felt shy about knocking on doors.

I met our neighbours gradually. The farm nearest the house was tenanted by Mr and Mrs Dalgleish. I called there one late September afternoon. A golden sun shone on the house. One son was milking in the byre and the other came in from cutting the hay. It felt like a scene from a novel as Mrs Dalgleish welcomed me into her kitchen and presented me with a bottle of wine made from a vine that she had grown from a pip. Mrs Dalgleish was brought up in Traquair and the first time she left the area was on her honeymoon.

The most remote farm on the estate was in the hills towards St Mary's Loch. The small picture-book house captures the imagination when seen from the road above and invokes an idyllic rural life. In reality, however, farming at a height of 1,000 feet is a hard existence. The land was farmed by Johnny Simpson and his wife, Agnes, who had grown up in a neighbouring valley. Agnes was a friendly, outgoing girl who adored the place. She had a small boy and a baby the same age as Catherine. We quickly made friends and now, over thirty years later, our grandsons are best friends at playgroup.

The farms were mostly tenanted by families brought up in the neighbourhood and many of them were related. The farmhouses were substantial stone buildings and each farm had several cottages to house farm workers but, since the advent of mechanisation, many of them were no longer needed and were let out. There was only one commuter, Ian Shaughnessy, living in the village who surprised everyone by driving all of fifteen miles to work every day. He and his wife had four good-natured sons who, one by one, came to work for us in their holidays.

The cottages were small, one-storey dwellings with thick walls and small windows, often with only two rooms. A kitchen and bathroom were tacked on in the 1940s. They generally had a chimney at either end, unlike the typical English cottage with just one in the middle. Originally there was only one entrance, a good arrangement to keep in the warmth but not convenient. The couple who lived on the road by the main gates had to walk out of their front door and through the gates to get into their garden or coal shed at the back. Many people still did not have a car so garages were not needed.

When I first arrived I used to hear people talk about Traquair village and it took me a while to realise where it was. I saw the sign on the road but after walking past a clutch of houses I was back in the country again. The village school lay off the road and the kirk was half a mile farther on. Behind the school stretched the Minch Moor and the old drove road that led over it that was used to take cattle over the hill to the Yarrow valley. I loved the countryside, with cattle and sheep grazing in the fields and the rolling hills beyond. In spite of the grumbles about tree-planting, I agreed with the intrepid eighteenth-century traveller Cecelia Fiennes who described the bare rock as having the 'disagreeable appearance of a scabbed head' and I preferred them clad with trees of any kind.

The schoolmistress lived in a substantial house near the school and was married to a large Swiss gentleman who kept house for her and hung the duvets out of the window in true continental style. We later discovered that he not only repaired furniture beautifully but was an able cake-maker. He was soon enlisted to do a spell of baking for the tearoom.

A large village hall had recently been built. Frank had provided the land and Lord Glenconner, on the adjoining estate of Glen, helped with finance. I was told that it had been great fun holding whist drives and coffee mornings to help raise the money but that now it was built there was less going on.

Mrs Bell, who was brought up in the cottage that we first lived in, ran the Post Office and the village shop from her front room. She would quote the *Bride of Quair* to me in her gentle soft voice and loved to talk about her happy childhood in the two-roomed cottage. She and her four bothers and sisters slept in a divided attic, her parents downstairs in the front room and all the living and cooking were carried out in the other. Their father would play to them in the evenings on a violin that he had made himself and which she still owned. They had free run of the grounds when the great-uncles were not there and the only blot was a constant feud with the coachman who lived next door.

When Mrs Bell talked about her childhood at Traquair, the past came to life. She told me about the spot on the avenue where, if you called out, an echo would bounce back off the house, and how in a hard winter the River Tweed had frozen over and she and her sister had been able to skate to Peebles. On her way to the village school she had always stopped to watch the blacksmith at work. She described the excitement of the arrival of the great-uncles and their staff, complete with the 'priesty man', at the big house each summer. Great parties had been held in the old kitchen. Another excitement had been the arrival of the 'flying circus'. A small plane would station itself in the field and offer flights for five bob a time.

Her shop was now the hub of the village. At dinner time the children ran down from the school to buy their sweeties. She knew everyone and relayed all the local news. But one day, when she was in her late seventies, a car stopped outside and a young man got out, pushed his way into the shop and held her up at gun point. She had the presence of mind to call out 'Jimmy! Jimmy!' to an imaginary man and the young man had fled. It turned out to have been a toy gun but this made it no less frightening for Mrs Bell and shortly afterwards she shut the shop and turned it back into her house.

I learnt from her how the small community lived together. 'The other day I bumped into Miss Nichols in Peebles,' Mrs Bell told me, referring to a woman who lived nearby. 'I've known her all my life; we went to school together but we never seem to meet. I said, "Fancy us bumping into each other here when we only live a few doors from each other." That's how we get on of course. We have a chat if we meet in the street but we don't go into each other's houses.'

A little farther on, Jimmy and Lizzie Alves had the cosiest house of all. The fire was permanently lit and the room smelt of fresh baking. In the summer their garden was a picture. They had a talent for making it look as if everything came up naturally. Until their old age they were a strikingly good-looking couple. Lizzie Alves had been in service since she was fourteen and spent most of her life at Glen, the house of the neighbouring estate, where she ended up as cook and her husband was head gamekeeper. She had been taken down to the Glenconners' house in London and attended their family weddings.

She could relate many a story about the young Margot Tennant who later married Herbert Asquith, the Prime Minister, and became a formidable political hostess. Margot was a wild girl, once riding her horse into the house and parading it around the large hall. One day, for a bet, when a shooting party was held and the guns were assembling outside the front of the house, she leant out of her window and emptied her chamber pot over their heads. Margot kept in touch with the Alveses, and in her old age, on her annual visit to North Berwick, Jimmy was regularly summoned for a picnic. They were a contented couple without a trace of resentment of their time in service. Lizzie compared life in the servants' hall under a strict housekeeper to a finishing school – she was taught good manners and given self-confidence. She remembered with pleasure the great round of roast beef that was the standard Sunday lunch in the servants' hall.

Many couples did not own a car. They were not necessary. Instead of going out to the shops, the shops came to you. They had vans that travelled around the country districts once a week on different days. Butchers, bakers and the Co-op grocery van called regularly, not to mention the laundry and the travelling library. We thought it the height of luxury when the baker's van stopped right outside the house, laden with iced cakes, breads with strange names like bloomers, various scones and jam tarts. We discovered the local delicacy, Selkirk bannock, round and fruit-filled, a cross between bread and cake. At Christmas black bun appeared, thick with fruit and covered in a thin layer of crust. It weighed a ton and was made to last forever.

We were living in a world of our own at Traquair, and I realised only slowly that I had moved to another country by talking to the staff who came to work in the house or on trips to Innerleithen. I was puzzled by some of the unfamiliar words that were used. To begin with, I could not understand why everybody was always getting and receiving 'messages'. I began to believe that they were all involved in a secret society and felt it would be impolite to ask what these messages were. Eventually light dawned when I heard a woman talk about her 'message bag' and I realised that messages meant nothing more then shopping.

Other commonly used Scots words were not difficult to understand. Many were influenced by French. 'Ashet', close to *assiette*, is the name for a large dish, and even the name Stewart began to be spelt Stuart because the letter 'w' did not exist in the French alphabet. But I was floored when a visitor said to me, 'The policies are looking well.' Was he talking about our forthcoming plans for the season or referring to a political agenda? No, I learnt later, 'policies' means the grounds around a house. The different use of language was more confusing.

When I asked someone where they lived they would reply, 'I stay in ...' I would then say, 'But where do you *live?*' and with a look of despair they would give me the same answer. People married 'on' each other, and Christmas was talked about like a birthday: 'I am getting ... for my Christmas'. Sometimes the use of words took on a different connotation. I was surprised one day when Tommy Miller, who was the politest man I knew, talked about my mother-in-law 'going on about' something. In England the phrase had an insolent sense attached to it, but this was not so in Scotland. Many of the Scots words had an extra descriptive quality: 'dreich' for 'dreary', 'puddock' for 'toad', and they often seemed more humorous.

The Social Round

~

I had already met two girls of my age in London married to Scotsmen who owned large houses in the Scottish Borders. The wives were both English girls and artists who, like myself, were faced with a change in their way of life. But while their husbands insisted on living in a formal style to which they were supposed to conform, I was lucky enough to have married into a family, similar to my own, who did not feel it necessary to keep up pretensions.

The Craigmyles lived in London but planned to spend holidays at the family house in the Borders. Donald Craigmyle's mother, a forbidding woman, still lived there. After their marriage she gave a cocktail party for the newlyweds and Anthea went to great trouble to buy a glamorous new dress such as she would have worn in London. Her mother-in-law, dressed in wool, met her at the foot of the stairs. 'You can't possibly wear that,' she scolded, and Anthea, reduced to tears, was forced to run upstairs to change.

Adrienne's husband, Dawyck, was the son of Field-Marshal Haig who, after the First World War, was granted an earldom and presented with a family house by grateful supporters. Dawyck was brought up to believe that he should live in state. He somehow managed to combine this life with being an extremely good painter. We all spent a happy holiday together sketching and bathing in the South of France. Dawyck was a charming man, but his upbringing got the better of him, and he asked me one day not to speak about socialism to his wife.

The dinner-party circle was a narrow one. We were invited to dine in houses that still appeared to be fully staffed and others where an elderly host would hobble precariously around the table trying to act as butler while mysterious hands passed dishes through from the kitchen. The men wore black ties and the women long skirts. If you sat on the right-hand side of an elderly gentleman, conversation could be difficult as shooting had rendered many of them hard of hearing. We could rarely accept an invitation to lunch, but if we did, we would often end with a walk around the garden in an icy wind while the hostess pointed out some rare but not very beautiful plants.

Social life in the Borders was rooted in the past. A friend who had invited us to a drinks party rang up afterwards to ask nervously, 'Do you think it went all right? It was the first time we have invited mill owners to the house.' It was strange, after living in London where you could choose your friends and people existed on their own merits. We found it hard to fit in. We did not hunt. Peter preferred the cinema to shooting. I was a socialist, and we were both Catholics. Added to that, we had both been brought up in England. I could not understand why so many of these patriotic Scots, who had excellent schools of their own, had been educated in England. Like the Scottish nobility who brought about the Union of 1707, they were obviously determined to get the best of both worlds.

There were some old families in the Borders living in magnificent country houses as well as descendants of industrialists living in baronial houses built by their forbears in the nineteenth century. It tended to create a society based on status. Living in large houses standing in their own grounds could isolate people until they felt safe only when mixing with each other. A discerning priest, Father Dalrymple, pointed this out in a talk to the Knights of Malta, an elitist Catholic group that tried to enlist us. He came from the same background as some of the knights and gently chided them for talking about their 'nearest neighbour' as the person most like themselves who lived near them, ignoring anyone else who lived in between.

There were many contradictions. While the men killed birds and hunted foxes for fun, they supported wild-life charities. They adored their dogs – often more than their children whom they did not hesitate to send off to boarding schools at an unnecessarily early age. Everyone was a Tory. For Peter's sake I tried not to be confrontational, but when I heard someone say 'we', meaning 'we Tories', in which I was supposedly included, I had to protest. In most cases I was able to ignore the remarks and some of the comments I received. The general opinion, I was amused to learn, was that my parents were socialists and that was how I had been brought up. The idea of a woman making up her own mind was still not to be considered seriously.

The wives did not work but devoted themselves to supporting charities and were successful in collecting large sums of money. We were constantly invited to various entertainments for good causes. When I first heard of a coffee morning, I imagined it would be like a wine-tasting but with different kinds of coffee. They sold tickets for splendid balls where it seemed incongruous to be swilling back champagne and eating an expensive dinner in order to help the starving people of a Third World country.

I was surprised by some of the conversations. I heard young people denounce miners who had 'large cars outside their council houses' and blame mill workers on short time for not working hard enough. The 'haves' were confident in their belief that some people in this world deserved more than others. The main topic of conversation among couples of our age was the choice of school for their children. I had had the misguided belief that the Scots were a democratic people and that the laird would send his children to school with everyone else. It was disappointing to find that this was not the case. Some little boys were still being sent off to boarding prep schools although it was becoming acceptable to send a child to a country primary school. Secondary state schools were out of the question for this so-called upper class in spite of the rising cost of private education. When I met a woman who had unexpectedly given birth to twins, she told me that her first thought had been 'How can we afford two sets of school fees?'

My upbringing, however, had turned me into a chameleon and I already had friends with very different beliefs from my own, although perhaps not quite so extreme. I can get along with most people so I made new friends and was very grateful for the generous hospitality we received. We repaid it by occasionally having a large lunch or dinner party in the main dining room. As the room was permanently on view to the public, we seldom used it during the season and it made me feel that I was dining out as well.

One day we were invited to lunch by Mrs Dalyell of the Binns. The Binns is an impressive seventeenth-century house overlooking the Firth of Forth in West Lothian. It had been in the Dalyell family for generations, but in 1944 Mrs Dalyell decided to give it to The National Trust for Scotland. After the war, other owners, thinking that they would never be able to maintain their buildings, also thankfully let The National Trust take over. Frank, my father-in-law, had consulted Mrs Dalyell when he felt that he might have to do likewise.

Although the National Trust is in theory a good idea – you give them the house and assets and they let you live in it while they look after its upkeep (in some cases the family still contribute) – in practice it does not work. I have yet to meet a past owner who is satisfied with the arrangement and many prefer to move out. This is a pity because houses are made to be lived in and a house without people becomes a museum. The Trusts, both English and Scottish, seem unable to understand that past owners have given away properties of great value and have done so because they care for them so much. They want them to keep the patina they have acquired over the years and for them to be cared for in the same way that they always have been. The Trusts, on the other hand, behave as if the last owner had no idea how to look after the house and they are doing them a favour by taking it off their hands. The staff often act with gross insensitivity. The young men and women who work for them, aptly described by one owner as 'the lovelies', behave as if the house belongs to them personally and will walk in and out whenever they feel like it, move furniture from one house to another and frequently make important decisions without consulting the family. The house soon becomes devoid of atmosphere and begins to look like The National Trust's idea of a country house, which is very different from the reality.

Peter and I had visited Oxburgh Castle, a National Trust property in Norfolk, where the guides were able to give us little information. When we visited the past owner, confined to a few rooms at the rear, she entertained us for over an hour with the complete history and amusing anecdotes.

Mrs Dalyell, who was of the same breed as my mother-in-law, was able to keep the Trust at bay. She lived in the Binns with her son, Tam, and his new wife, Kathleen. Kathleen has a sparkling personality and a good sense of humour and managed to live with her without friction. It was a relief to meet a couple I had something in common with. Tam was a Labour MP and Kathleen comes from a Labour Catholic family. I liked them from the start and we have remained good friends ever since.

The arrival of the Scott Moncrieff family at Traquair several years later brought me other compatible friends. George Scott Moncrieff was a writer whose first wife had died many years previously and he had recently married Eileen, a talented American girl a few years younger than me. They had both converted to Catholicism so the meagre number of churchgoers in our parish was increased, especially as they quickly produced a large family of good-looking boys. I loved visiting their house where, with small resources, Eileen and George had created a unique atmosphere. George wrote and Eileen painted or cooked delicious meals while their children milled around them. The boys and Catherine became great friends, and we had some wonderful Christmases together.

Peter loved Christmas and I started to go in for it in a big way. He would decorate a huge Christmas tree, arrange holly and ivy over the pictures and go to great trouble to find a piece of mistletoe to hang in a prominent position. We would have a party for our staff and close neighbours before the holiday started, have lunch on the day around a richly decorated dining-room table and have another party for all the children who lived on the estate a few days later.

The 1965 general election was approaching. Our Labour candidate had no office and was difficult to locate. His chances of success were nil. I spent a day canvassing for Tam in West Lothian although he felt I should be working in my own constituency. I knocked on doors with Kathleen while Tam followed behind. He had a formidable presence and made a good impression.

I was so much against the Tory government that I decided to vote tactically and back the new young Liberal candidate, David Steel. He got in with a small majority. It was a triumph for him as he was to be the youngest member of the House of Commons. He and his wife, Judy, came to live in the Borders. Judy was a refreshing MP's wife. We got to know them well and (except during elections) have had a lasting friendship. But Tam had been right, and I lived to regret my decision to vote tactically. After nearly forty years during which the Liberals have dominated the Scottish Borders both in local government and at Westminster, it is still, on average, the lowest-paid area in Britain.

Traquair House Ale

~

Traquair gives the impression of being a far larger house than it actually is. The massive front topped by a steeply pitched roof is just one room deep, and the wings, added in the seventeenth century, hold only a single line of rooms.

Various outhouses were built under this wing of the house – a stable, a cart house and a brew house. The occupants of most country houses built before the eighteenth century made their own beer. As water could be contaminated and milk could be the cause of tuberculosis, ale was considered to be the safest drink. It would have been given to all the servants and estate workers, and we even found an account for ale that had been supplied to a wet nurse.

Peter's father had always told him that he thought there might have been an old brew house in one of the outhouses under the chapel wing. Although he had so much to do – it was the spring of our third season – he could not resist investigating. From his earlier training in whisky distilleries, Peter knew that the first part of the distilling process was similar to brewing. When he penetrated through the rubbish stored there, which included a huge number of old champagne bottles left over from the great-uncles' days, he was amazed to recognise an old copper, a mash tun and cooling vessels not only intact but in good condition. It seems that after they were renewed in the eighteenth century, commercial brewing had started, making it easier to buy in the beer than to make it on the premises.

Shortly after we moved into the house, my brother Nicholas, who had dropped out of university to develop his own ideas, came to stay, and he and Peter were fired with the thought of putting the vessels to use and making a brew. While Peter was busy in the office, Nicholas and the Miller brothers cleaned the place out. I went down to see how they were getting on and saw Nicholas's head sticking out of the copper while he scrubbed the inside with Brillo pads. We were thankful that its existence had not been known during the war as there is little doubt it would have been removed for scrap.

While both Peter and Nicholas were dying to try out the equipment, they realised that the size of the vessels meant that a vast amount of beer would have to be made in one brew. They did not feel sufficiently qualified to try it out on their own. Peter sent Nicholas to visit a few breweries in the south of Scotland but there was little interest in the project until he arrived at Belhaven and met Sandy Hunter. Belhaven was a small family-owned business and Sandy was, as he said, 'a real brewer and not a chemist'. He enjoyed brewing and experimenting, and vowed that he had never made a bad brew. He volunteered to have a go. He warned us to be sure to get in touch with Customs and Excise to obtain a licence. A Customs officer promptly arrived. He asked for a duplicate key to the Brew House, told us that he could come and check it at any time and gave us dire warnings of brewers who had tried to put through secret brews and had ended up spending several months in jail. He also insisted that a wooden box with a lock and key be fitted into the Brew House to keep the book where the 'intention to brew' with the date must be entered and the strengths of the ale noted at each stage. The duty is estimated on the alcoholic content of the ale and in those days had to be paid before the ale was sold.

Sandy, rosy-cheeked and full of enthusiasm, duly arrived with his head brewer and all the necessary ingredients – malted barley, hops and yeast. The chimney was so badly blocked that we had had to install Calor Gas to heat the copper. Peter had filled the copper with water the night before, using a hose from the old lamp room, newly converted into a ladies' cloakroom above, and had got up at seven to light the burner as it took at least three hours to heat. By ten it had reached boiling point and was pumped into the mash tun. With the help of the Miller bothers, the malted barley was added and stirred around with old wooden paddles to make a porridge-like mixture.

The mash tun had been fitted with a false bottom to catch the wort and as a temporary measure this had been weighted down with old curling stones. At a critical moment the stones were accidentally knocked and the false bottom rose to the surface, releasing all the wort. There was a frantic rush up to the kitchen for my sieves and a slow hand operation was carried out. Once it was clear, the liquid was pumped up into the copper where the hops were added and it was boiled for several hours. Finally, the brew was run down wooden gutters into the flat cooling trays. The ale could not be run into the fermenting vessel or the yeast added until the ale dropped to a temperature of 20 degrees. So my jam thermometer was requisitioned and also Catherine's old nappy bucket for the hydrometer that Sandy had lent us. I was soon to realise that if anything was missing from the kitchen, I only had to go down to the Brew House to find it. It took a long time to cool the ale, and it was midnight by the time the yeast could be added, the fermenting vessels covered and we could all get to bed.

We still did not know how successful a brew we had made, as the ale had to be kept warm while it fermented over several days and began to produce a thick head of foam. Sandy told us that a dog had once thought the foam in his fermenting vessel was solid and had jumped into the vat but as he had begun to sink Sandy had managed to pull him out. 'What a terrible waste of beer,' I said. Sandy shook his head and laughed, 'Oh, it wasn't wasted.'

After several days the fermentation began to die down and it was exciting to find that we were left with a delicious rich brew with a strength of seven per-cent alcohol. The old

Memmel oak, full of natural enzymes, had given it a unique flavour. But we now had 150 gallons of it. Sandy arranged for it to be taken back to Belhaven and bottled, and Peter found an advertising agency to design a label written in Victorian copper-plate to add to its special appeal. As it was so strong, the duty would be high and it would have to be sold at an equally high price. At first Peter decided to write the number of each bottle and brew on the labels by hand to make it even more exclusive.

Within weeks, just before the end of September, crates of Traquair House Ale were delivered from Belhaven. All had gone so well up till then that it was disappointing to find that selling the ale was a different matter. We sold a few bottles to visitors before we closed at the end of the season, but although we had a tremendous amount of publicity, off-licences found the price too high – five shillings for a half-pint bottle – and the pubs called it a 'heid banger' and too dangerous to serve to customers.

Half a dozen brews a year were sufficient until in 1973 CAMRA, the Campaign for Real Ale, began to raise its head. Beer drinkers had become fed-up with the mass-produced fizzy drink they were being fobbed off with and wanted to return to the proper beer of former times. The campaign was one of the most successful private pressure groups in Britain, and soon our beer was in demand among specialist shops and off-licences. Peter started to brew more often. He still did most of the brewing himself, employing extra labour only to help with the mashing and to clean out the vessels after each brew. It was a long day, starting early if he hoped to get to bed before midnight. While the wort was boiling in the afternoon, he would emerge from the Brew House in his boiler suit, sprin-kled with the hops he had just been adding, and walk across the courtyard to spend a few hours in the office. Visitors took him for one of the staff while our smartly kilted head guide was believed to be the laird. The courtyard would fill with the cloying smell of malted barley which could be almost overpow-ering in the chapel just above the Brew House. 'The odour of sanctity' was how Peter described it.

Peter was good at making himself comfortable under any conditions, and during the long wait while the ale was cooling he was quite happy reading and listening to his transistor radio perched on the side of the mash tun. Our transistors never worked so well after he started brewing as, like his ballpoint pens, they often fell in and had to be fished out. I was surprised to see him paddling in the cooling trays in his gum boots during the cooling process, but he assured me cheerfully that the alcohol in the beer killed any infection. I was glad that the public did not see this part of the process or the collection of his old under-clothes torn into rags which he used to cover the bungs.

Despite using the same quantities of materials, different quantities of ale were always produced. While it was fermenting, readings had to be constantly taken and noted. The fermentation also varied, sometimes dying out altogether, when an SOS for more yeast would go up and I was asked to drive over to Belhaven to get it. At other times, generally on a Sunday when we were about to set off for church, Peter would take a last look and find the fermentation rising over the top and running all over the cobbled floor. He had to try to beat it down and was covered by the sticky liquid in the process.

The Customs and Excise officer liked to be present after the yeast had been added and the last reading taken. We were his only brewery. Before we had cooling equipment, he had to turn out late at night and in the summer often had to wait while the ale cooled. Peter got to know him well, and he would often lend a hand at stirring to try to hurry it up.

Gradually the ale was written up in beer guides and given top ratings in the *World Guide to Beer*, which eventually began to attract buyers from abroad. An American specialising in unique ales was anxious to import it, and this entailed a long-drawn-out negotiation and a special label for the American market. The American authorities did not like the words 'strong ale' on the label so these were eventually changed to 'Hearty Ale'. We were also obliged to add that it was 'dangerous for pregnant women'.

Our first export orders were followed by others from

Hong Kong and most countries in Europe, all in small quantities, and we acquired wholesalers in Britain. Not only did Peter brew himself but he also delivered it in a smart grey mini-van decorated with the Traquair coat of arms and 'Brewed by the Laird in the ancient Brew House at Traquair House' written underneath. If ever I borrowed the van I was amazed by the attention I received. Builders on scaffolding would wave as I passed and if I stopped at traffic lights there would be requests for samples from cars pulled up alongside.

Our brewery became a place to be visited by brewers from all over the world. Britain had led the way with real ale and we had been one of the first to make it, but micro-breweries were growing up everywhere, soon followed by 'boutique breweries' in America. Many visitors came just to see the brewery and, having seen our smart bottles standing in stylish shops, were often surprised to find that the beer had been made in a small country brew house.

Demand for our ale increased so much that Peter decided to take on a brewer. There were students at Heriot Watt University in Edinburgh, attending one of only two brewing courses in the country, who were available to work for a year after they left university. To justify employing a brewer, production had to be kept up and Peter was always worried that this might wear out the old vessels. The choice lay between brewing only now and then and leaving it as a museum or making it into a commercial brewery and replacing the vessels as they wore out.

We managed to get a licence to sell the ale in our shop. At that time it was illegal to sell alcohol on a Sunday, a rule that our foreign visitors found impossible to understand, especially as the Scottish Tourist Board constantly used the Brew House in its publicity. We received a lot of abuse from visitors who seemed to think that it was our choice not to sell it. I was serving in the shop one day when a large Swedish gentleman lent over the counter, deposited a roomy hold-all on the floor behind the till and said in a threatening voice, 'Put the bottles in.' I stood my ground. I did not want to lose our licence.

Selling ale in the tearoom also had its problems. No one, not even the police, could tell us precisely how much food must be eaten to comply with our table licence. In the early days, when we served only teas, it was a question of how many cakes or scones should be served with it. As this was not everyone's favourite combination, the customer often ordered these only to be able to drink the ale and resented having to do so.

Our ale is very strong and easy to drink, and many a man would indulge himself in the tearoom while his wife or partner went round the house. While he was sitting he would feel only exquisite wellbeing, but when he rose to his feet the effect kicked in. Worried that drivers might not realise the strength of our beer, I decided to put up a notice to warn them: 'Drivers Beware, our ale is two and a half times stronger than ordinary ale.' To my surprise I was accused of trying to advertise and encourage people to drink, so it had to be taken down.

One of the best methods of selling the ale is to take a stand at a food and drink fair. Our first experience of this was in the Food Hall at the Royal Highland Show at Ingliston, outside Edinburgh, a site that had previously been used for selling second-hand cars. The floor had to be washed to remove the oil, and then we set up our splendid stand, made by the Miller brothers, with a huge photograph of the house in the background. We sold chocolate, fudge and shortbread, which were made for us under our label, as well as the ale. There was an odd variety of stalls, including one selling nothing but filled rolls, another with punnets of strawberries and a couple with German wines. Next to us was an elegant stand called the Laird's Larder, selling delicious home-made jams. Feeling rather out of place, the lady owner welcomed us into the hall with open arms, saying, 'Thank God you're here and can help to raise the tone.'

Once the show started, however, we soon realised that it was not tone that counted. The crowds surged in, particularly when there was a shower of rain, and it was the tatty stands with the rolls and ready-made cheap food that did the greatest trade. Many people recognised Traquair and would come and chat. Others could not understand what we were – one woman, seeing the chocolate and the picture of the house, asked if we were a chocolate factory. If the shortbread was not selling, we would cut it up into minute pieces and hand it out as samples on a cardboard plate. If you looked straight at the customers, they would take a piece genteelly, pretend to taste it carefully and then make an excuse such as 'too sweet for my taste' or 'we will come back later'. If there was a small crowd, however, and you looked away for a second, fingers would swoop down like a flock of birds and every crumb would disappear in a flash. It was the same with the ale. Those who were merely wanting a free drink would make a good pretence of swilling it round in their mouth and talking knowledgeably about real ale before making an excuse not to buy it.

We gave out leaflets continuously and talked to people about the house as well as the brew house. On the last day of the show, huge school parties arrived and small boys of eight or nine who could hardly reach the counter would hold out their money, swear that they were over eighteen and try to persuade us to sell them a bottle.

It was a long four days. I was kept going by the Pernod stand opposite, who were very generous with their samples. First thing in the mornings the gentleman on the stand would sail across the aisle to us with a tray of neatly filled glasses. Whenever I felt I needed a pick-me-up during the day, I would catch his eye and be given another. For me the whole show passed on a cloud, but I do not think I have ever drunk Pernod since. Peter, having worked in the drinks trade, knew better and was much more careful.

Peter always swore he could do two or more things at once. He spent many evenings watching television and numbering up the beer-bottle labels, each with the brew number and a consecutive bottle number. My concentration was less good, and after my brother Edmund maintained that he had found two bottles with the same numbers I was banned from doing them. But Peter's faithful Miss F, who by then worked as his secretary, was given batches to take home.

Mr Boswell and Dr Johnson

~

In the spring of 1968 we received a call from the BBC who wanted to use the house for a dramatised version they were making of *Dr Johnson's Highland Jaunt*. Boswell's old house, Auchinleck, was unfit to use and they wanted Traquair to take its place. Patrick Garland was to direct and Peter Woodthorpe, who had been a member of the Footlights and whom I had met on my jaunts to Cambridge, was to play Dr Johnson. It was to be the first BBC drama in colour. They would film Boswell and Johnson coming down the avenue in a coach and being greeted in the courtyard by Boswell's wife, youngest child and his dogs. Patrick suggested that Catherine could play the part of the child and they would use our King Charles spaniels. There was also to be a scene in the dining room where during dinner Dr Johnson would take Catherine on his knee to demonstrate the gentler side of his nature. The only problem was that after a two-hour make-up session, Dr Johnson emerged with a repulsive pock-marked face. In his long wig and with a protruding stomach, he was not an attractive sight, and every time Catherine saw him she would clutch my hand and refuse to go near him.

I walked round with her for the couple of days while they were rehearsing and Peter Woodthorpe kept a packet of Smarties in his pocket hoping to encourage her, but it made no difference. The *Daily Mail* came to write a story about the production and focused on this angle. I soon had a telephone call from an anonymous woman. 'I just wanted to tell you that if your little girl is too shy, my little girl can take her place.' My pride as a mother was challenged. 'It's very kind of you to suggest it,' I answered, 'but don't worry, Catherine is definitely going to do it.' Shortly before the scene was to be shot, one of the make-up girls swooped down on her, told me to keep out of the way and carried her off. They dressed her in a long skirt and bonnet, and she sat happily on Dr Johnson's knee in the dining room. They ate a huge roast and used a line that I told them was always quoted at home when hot food burned the mouth: Dr Johnson was said to have spat out a hot potato and said 'only a fool would have swallowed it'.

After several seasons we gave up having guided tours except for groups who came outside normal opening hours. We decided, instead, to have guides in the rooms who could give information and also act as security. Our first guides were mainly students and school-leavers, supplemented by the children of cousins and friends who came to stay.

We had given Mrs Bell tea in the tearoom one afternoon and were sitting in the courtyard afterwards when the house closed for the afternoon. The boys came out in their sixties' garb. 'Is this your staff, Mr Peter?' Mrs Bell asked in mock horror. I had always been against uniform but her remark prompted us to think how much better they would look in white T-shirts and tartan trousers which could be made by the excellent Polish tailor in Innerleithen. But we had not realised how quickly boys grow. At the start of each season the trousers had to be altered and shuffling them around from one boy to another became a problem. We had extended our season, which was now longer than their school holidays, and had also started to find Coca-Cola bottles under the King's bed and sweet papers in the potpourri. We also realised that we needed to build up a more permanent staff who would increase their knowledge and return each season. So we decided to go to the other extreme and employ older men and women.

Most of the guides became very interested and dedicated to the house. They were always adding to our fund of knowledge and seldom wanted to leave. Age is no barrier, and we had one eighty-year-old who sat in the library. She would often have a little nap so a visitor suggested we put up a sign, 'Please do not wake the guide'. The guides did, however, want to have definitive information about the building and contents, and this was not always possible at Traquair. Experts were changing their minds all the time and new research was constantly turning previous information on its head. When we first opened the house, for instance, it was thought that most good furniture had been imported from England or abroad. It was not until Francis Bamford spent years tracing cabinet-makers in Scotland that it was realised how many important pieces had in fact been made here. Early Scottish portrait painters had not been well researched and the portraits were regularly attributed to a different artist.

When Andrew Brown came to work as a guide after he had retired from farm work he brought an authentic atmos-phere to the place. At fourteen years of age he had arrived to work on a farm nearby, bringing with him a wooden trunk that contained all his possessions. After marrying Jean, he moved to Traquair and for the rest of his life lived in the cottage at the top of the avenue where she had been born. He had enjoyed working with horses, and I remember standing next to him watching a tractor plough a field while he shook his head. 'They canna get round the corners,' he explained, pointing out all the land that was wasted.

When he reached retiring age, Andrew asked Peter if he could give him a job. Peter realised that he knew the place so well he would be an excellent guide. He was a small, neat man with a healthy, ruddy face and was as smart as a new pin in his gaiters and polished farm boots as he stood on duty at the front door. When the visitors left the main part of the house, he had to tell them that there were still the chapel and dining room to see. 'There's twae mair rooms tae see,' he would say in his thick Border accent. 'We don't want any tea, thank you,' English visitors were heard to reply.

As a young man Andrew had driven a pony and trap.

When the great-uncles were at Traquair he was employed to take the dirty washing down to the old wash house in the woods by the Quair Burn. After the laundry-maids had boiled it up and laid it out on the bleaching green, he brought it back to the house and took it up to the laundry room above the chapel to be ironed. The laundry maids rose at 5.30 a.m. and worked every day except Sundays. They made up for this by getting up an hour earlier on Mondays.

Andrew's other duty was to collect younger members of the family from the small railway station in Innerleithen. Peter's aunts told me that they used to travel the first part of the journey, from London to Edinburgh, third class and bought first-class tickets only for the short journey from Edinburgh to Innerleithen. The station master and Andrew, dressed in their best, would be standing on the platform where the first-class coach stopped and they did not like to disappoint them.

Andrew told us many stories about the old days and the 'grand ceilidhs' that were held in the loft above the coach house. He could point out the two springs that fed the Well Pool and could remember the dairymaids immersing their crocks of butter in the water to keep them cold. He had a great respect for the laird and was also very fond of Peter. It took many brews before we realised that the huge amount of water taken by the brewery left the cottages at the top of the avenue short. He never mentioned this, and it was only when a new neighbour moved in that we received a complaint. She had told Andrew that she had no water and he had merely answered, 'Och, we never have any water when the Laird is brewing. You'd best use yon pump across the road.'

Andrew was adamant that he had seen a ghost. On a hot July afternoon in the 1930s he had been working in an old joiner's shop on the avenue when he saw a lady in old-fashioned clothes coming towards him. Instead of opening the gate she had come straight through it. 'I was gey shocked: my hair stood on end,' he would say. She had then passed on through another gate and across the avenue. Andrew had known a woman in Innerleithen whose grandmother had made dresses for Lady Louisa Stuart. She was the sister of the last earl and lived alone in the house after her brother's death until she finally died at the grand old age of ninety-nine. The dressmaker had kept samples of all the dress materials, and Andrew recognised immediately the one that the ghost had been wearing. He also heard that Lady Louisa's favourite walk had been by the old joiner's shop.

Andrew's familiarity with horses was invaluable when our donkey mare, Belinda, went into labour. I could see that she was struggling and did not know what to do. Andrew was on duty in his usual place at the front door so I rushed up to ask his advice. He merely asked someone to take his place, followed me down to the field, gently eased the foal from the mother, washed his hands and went back on duty.

For a few years Andrew had a burst of writing verse and turned into a veritable McGonagall. He had a keen eye and a sharp sense of humour. The following is an abridged version:

The Big Hoose is often throng wi' visitors galore
But whiles I'm not so busy when posted at the door
I meet a lot o' pleasant folk their pleasure they express
But, what I'd like tae write aboot is their different
      style of' dress . . .

Some ladies may have on a dress that might have
      come from Paris
And whiles you see a good Scotch tweed that once
      was spun in Harris
We often see some Indian girls so lovely in their saris
And then we get the trendy folk wi' claes bocht frae
      the barras . . .

Noo, I'll have to draw this to a close if you'll excuse
      the pun
So dress ye up in what ye like and aye enjoy the fun.

From birth Catherine had loved animals, even toy ones, and had refused to have anything to do with dolls. She was soon able to sit on the donkey while I held on to the bridle. When I led her round the grounds the visitors were charmed by Belinda, the donkey, but completely ignored the rider. I watched a woman bring a bag of sweets out of her bag which she fed slowly to Belinda while Catherine looked on eagerly from the saddle without being offered one.

In the good weather I took her for rides on the forestry roads, but my favourite walk was by the side of the River Tweed. One grey winter's day we watched a large swan swimming majestically in the water, head erect and lord of all. We must have frightened him, as he suddenly flapped his wings, rose into the air and flew straight into a live cable that stretched over the river. There was a blue flash and in a second the splendid creature was nothing but a pile of white feathers floating downstream. The donkey reared and Catherine fell off with a thud. I picked her up and tried to comfort her but she would not stop crying. She kept saying 'on', and I slowly realised that she was crying because I had not put her straight back on Belinda.

Music and Needlework

~

Different aspects of Traquair and its contents introduced us to some remarkable people, many of whom were experts in their field. They were immersed in their subjects and willing to spend hours of their time in research with little desire for kudos. The harpsichord in the house introduced us to William Thomas and John Rhodes and the needlework to Margaret Swain.

The two gentlemen, who always referred to each other as Mr Thomas and Mr Rhodes, were the first to approach us. Both quiet, highly intelligent and knowledgeable in many fields, they reminded me of my father, although, unlike my father who could not boil an egg, their erudition was tempered by craftsmen's skill. They shared an enjoyment of music and had developed an interest in early keyboard instruments. After studying their construction, they built one themselves. They went on to build their own tower house on a cliff above the Firth of Forth, using mainly old materials. When an architect working for the Ancient Monuments who had listed all the old buildings in Fife revisited the county, he was shocked to see the building and wondered how he could have left it out of the inventory.

They were among our first visitors when we opened Traquair and they had immediately spotted the musical instrument in the drawing room and asked if they could come again to examine it. They identified it as a harpsichord made in Antwerp in 1651 by the celebrated harpsichord maker Andreas

Ruckers. They explained that it was unique in having remained in its original state. When music requiring a longer range of notes had been composed, most harpsichords of that date had had their keyboards extended.

We were excited to hear of its importance as Frank had taken a look at it and thought it beyond repair. 'All I can get out of it is woodworm,' he would tell visitors. Mr Rhodes was still commuting south, where he was working on protective material for spacecraft, so the work took several years. Each autumn they would arrive in their old Riley, take the harpsichord back to their workshop and return it in the spring. They not only worked on the mechanism but restored the case as well, even making a block to reproduce the pattern on a small area above the keyboard. When the actual instrument was finished they went over to Holland to study a Vermeer painting. On their return they made a copy of the stand on which the instrument in the painting rests.

We became very fond of these two men who spoke as one. Mr Rhodes did most of the talking, slowly and precisely, and when stuck for a word Mr Thomas would slip it in. They invited us over for lunch in their castle with its magnificent view over the Firth of Forth. It had a small lawn and garden a hundred feet below the building. They had developed the rocky slope connecting the two into a natural rock garden. Mr Thomas produced the meal and after tinned soup, cold ham and salad and tinned peaches, Mr Rhodes sat back with satisfaction and said proudly, 'Mr Thomas is an excellent cook.' Then came the speciality – Mr Thomas' fruit cake – which genuinely demonstrated his prowess in the kitchen.

To celebrate the completion of the harpsichord in 1966 we decided to have a musical evening. This turned into a mini-festival that ran for a week. There was Scottish dancing on the lawn, the front of the house was floodlit and French Baroque rococo music was played by candlelight in the drawing room. Elizabeth Seton gave a recital and Jean Campbell played the harp. The entertainment was followed by a light supper and a glass of wine in the tearoom.

On the advice of Mr Thomas and Mr Rhodes we had asked Kenneth Elliott, a professor of music in Glasgow, to play the harpsichord. Not many musicians enjoy playing old instruments as the keyboards are cramped and there is always the chance that a note will stick. He agreed to play but was not put at his ease by Mr Thomas and Mr Rhodes who sat in the front row bent in concentration as they watched every movement of his fingers, more conscious of the way the harpsichord was being treated than of the music itself. At one point a note stuck and Professor Elliott seemed on the verge of losing his temper as he had to hit it several times. I could see the concern on the two gentlemen's faces but the concert passed without incident.

The evenings were all fully booked as our largest room, the drawing room, could seat an audience of only seventy. The setting was attractively intimate and several other evenings followed. Unfortunately, they hardly covered their costs and as we became busier the labour of moving all the furniture and laying out the chairs as soon as the house was closed discouraged us from holding them regularly.

Harpsichords were suddenly in vogue, and we had numerous visits from musicians and musical-instrument makers who wished to examine our Ruckers. Several wanted to play it. Mr Thomas and Mr Rhodes believed that it was good for the instrument to be played, but only by experienced musicians. When in doubt we were able to consult them. When Gerald Gifford, a professor at the Guildhall School of Music who was making recordings of early instruments played in original settings, suggested making a recording on it, they agreed. As the slightest fluctuation in temperature affected the tuning, the recording had to be done at night. The sound recorder was set up in a bedroom on the floor above and wired to Gerald who played a selection of music including works by Babel, Handel and Purcell in the drawing room below.

It was a very good recording that was sold first on tape and then on CD. We played it continually in the shop, to Mrs Fry's irritation. 'I know every note of that music,' she told us with exasperation. Gerald said, 'I bet she doesn't really, I'll test her.'

He substituted a piece of music by Sweelinck and he was proved right. Mrs Fry, to her own amusement, did not notice. Later on, Peter had a spoken commentary on the drawing room recorded which would start to play when a visitor came into the room and trod on a pad under the drugget. Halfway through the music would come out from a speaker under the harpsichord.

Mr Thomas and Mr Rhodes continued to visit us regularly. They would suddenly appear without warning and, like parents visiting a child away from home, would give the harpsichord a quick check-up.

Through the needlework in the house we made another lasting friend, Margaret Swain. Margaret had also started as an amateur and become an acknowledged expert. When she first came to Edinburgh with her husband and young family, she took two afternoons off a week to study needlework. Over the years she lectured, advised museums and wrote many books on the subject. Like Mr Thomas and Mr Rhodes, she was generous with her knowledge and belonged to a generation more interested in the object of their studies than in commercial gain or making a name for themselves. Like them, too, she was occasionally used by younger would-be experts who wrote up her research and published it as their own.

Margaret was interested in the sixteenth-century 'slips' at Traquair. These dated from 1600 and were rows of animals and plants stitched on canvas which were intended to be cut out and appliquéd on to plain material. It was the simplest way at that time to decorate fabric. Some were long narrow lengths, obviously meant to be bell pulls. For some reason there were many in the house that were never used. Their colours were unfaded as they had been kept in metal trunks into which, according to Frank, his uncles dropped a few mothballs once a year and left them undisturbed. 'Just as well they were bachelors,' he told me, 'a woman would have wanted to use them.'

Margaret also identified some fine silk embroidery worked on paper as 'collifichet' work. Two of the daughters of the fourth earl had learnt this exacting skill in a convent in

France at the beginning of the eighteenth century. 'We have learnt the "colly fishes", they had written back to their mother. Margaret wrote a booklet on the needlework for love and made an inventory of the outstanding collection of vestments in the house. She explained that some of them had been made out of eighteenth-century dresses. A woman would donate her best dress, which often happened to be her wedding dress, to a convent in France where the nuns made them into vestments. It would have been banned in Britain during the Penal times when all signs of Catholicism were forbidden in Britain. My mother had told me that this had remained a custom among recusant Catholics families. As the church in Innerleithen was short of vestments and the priest at that time had an Italian housekeeper with an aptitude for dressmaking, it prompted me to give her my wedding dress, which had been made by Digby Morton out of west Cumberland silk. It gave me more pleasure to see it being used than stored away out of sight.

One thing tended to lead to another at Traquair and in 1978, when I was approached to put on an event to raise money for a charity, I thought of all the wedding dresses kept stored away and I decided to have a wedding-dress exhibition all over the house. I was able to borrow dresses going back to the early nineteenth century. They were of every colour, including one of brown silk, and I learnt that it is a comparatively recent fashion for brides to wear white.

With the help of three costume experts we managed to arrange them on models in different rooms of the house. In the chapel a whole wedding scene was set up. The exhibition created a lot of interest. When Border Television came to film them they insisted on the models being brought out into the courtyard. It was a windy day and a gust of wind knocked the bride and groom flat on their faces in front of the camera. As soon as we picked them up, they were knocked down again. It was used in their programme of the funniest clips of the year.

Hollywood Takes Over

~

Life in a house open to the public can never be boring but, as we were beginning to realise, it was a continual financial worry. We had now been open for six years. Although our visitor numbers were increasing steadily, our overdraft was increasing even more rapidly. The business would have been a thriving one without the extra capital expenses that continually hit us. The income we generated could not cover large repairs and, as Peter said, 'there was always something falling down'.

So, one June evening in 1969, when we received a telephone call from someone who said he was the art director of a film company and was searching for a country house to use in a major new film, our spirits rose. He had come to Traquair as a visitor that afternoon and thought it was just what he was looking for. We knew that film-location fees for a Hollywood movie could be substantial and when Peter heard that Ava Gardner was to star in it, he was even more enthusiastic.

My cousin Mary Weld Blundell and her solicitor husband, Antony Davis, were staying with their children at the time, and a contract was drawn up. As they wanted to shoot the film in July, when the house was open to the public, they could use only the exterior, although we were inveigled into letting them use three bedrooms in the house as costume stores and a dressing room for Ava Gardner.

The film was to be called *Tam-Lin*. It was a modern version of an old Border ballad in which a rich unscrupulous woman surrounds herself with beautiful young people and finally draws an innocent local girl into her web. One of the young men falls in love with her, with dire consequences.

Three weeks before the start of shooting, studio craftsmen arrived to work on the house. An extra projection was built on the top terrace with another flight of steps so that a dramatic descent could be made. The work was so expertly carried out, with the new wall matching the existing old weather-beaten harling and covered with reproduction moss, that even people who knew the house well did not spot the new addition.

On the lower terrace, where I had recently planted old-fashioned roses and alpines, everything was removed and the hired contents of a local nursery installed, including shrubs, herbaceous plants, fruit trees, small poplars and copper beech. They left them in their pots huddled together so that they filled the whole terrace. In the wood behind the house where the Quair Burn meets the Tweed they built a romantic wooden bridge. The courtyard railings were repainted black but picked out in gold. 'It's got to look as if a very grand lady lives here,' the painter told me. A few days before filming started a huge catering marquee with its own kitchen was set up in a nearby field.

The film was produced by Alan Ladd Junior, and Roddy McDowall, the famous child star, was going to direct for the first time. They had American backing and money seemed no object. The company settled into the Peebles Hydro Hotel nearby and many local people were taken on as doubles and extras. The High School had just broken up for the summer, and it was a gift for the teachers who all managed to get work. Ian McShane was a juvenile lead and Stephanie Beauchamp played the part of the innocent young minister's daughter who was to be corrupted. Several scenes had already been shot in a manse nearby where, according to one of the workmen, the incumbent minister and his family had ended up sleeping in a caravan in the garden.

Every limousine from far and wide had been hired for the producers and stars, and on the first morning a fleet of vehicles arrived with the actors, their doubles and the rest of the crew. I felt completely overwhelmed as the wardrobe people poured into the house. It was impossible to know who was supposed to be there and who was not.

Two of the young unknown actresses walked into the courtyard and asked if the tearoom was open for coffee. One of them seemed anxious to impress and asked me if I knew whether our neighbour, Colin Tennant, was at home. She said her name was Joanna Lumley. I told them sharply that the tearoom was reserved for visitors and they must use the catering tent.

Most of the filming took place on the terraces at the back. The grass beyond made a good spectators' area. The weather was fantastic for the whole ten days of the shoot. The beautiful young people, dressed in the latest sixties' fashions played Frisbee while they waited. On the second day we detected a nervousness in the air and discovered that Ava Gardner had arrived. We had been warned that she had just come out of a clinic and was very self-conscious about being overweight. She was forty-seven and the fact that she would be acting with a group of much younger, more glamorous women was a challenge for someone who had once been voted the most beautiful woman in the world. If anyone said that they thought forty-seven was old, Peter said 'absolute nonsense' as he and Ava happened to be exactly the same age.

Ava Gardner arrived with her male attendant and her little dog. She shook hands with us before disappearing quickly into the downstairs bedroom that she was to use in the daytime. She would not emerge until strangers were cleared from the set. The location manager was horrified when he discovered that Peter had tried to drum up trade by putting up a notice at the gate saying 'Filming to-day'. 'If she sees that,' he told us, 'she might take off for good.' The company ordered a huge bouquet of flowers to be delivered and I was amused to be asked to give them to her and pretend that they were a gift from us. Catherine, who had just learnt to ride around on her own, was asked to present her with a feather from one of our peacocks.

Every evening the wardrobe people came into the house and removed all the costumes which were cleaned and pressed for the following day. The cousins who were staying came back one evening to find that all their clothes had been removed as well.

There was a visit one day from the backers – two spivvy-looking gentlemen who, it was whispered, belonged to the Mafia. Everyone was busy being nice to them. There was a scene in the film when one of the characters hallucinates and sees the house in rainbow colours and we were told with much amusement afterwards that they had asked if the house was going to be painted.

I was very impressed by the total commitment that everyone gave to the film. During production, it was the whole company's entire life and they lived totally absorbed in their own world. It just happened that Neil Armstrong was simultaneously making the first landing on the moon and we were glued to the television set watching it. When I asked some of the crew who were waiting around if they would like to watch, they were not the slightest bit interested. When we marvelled at the amount of money being spent on the smallest detail, the actor Richard Wattis explained that excellence in every department encouraged actors to give their best as well.

An assistant director was anxious to use our peacocks and I told him that it might be possible to lure one into the courtyard. I did not realise, however, that he was under the impression that, at a word from me, the peacock would be obedient enough to perch on a pillar. The scene was set up, actors ready, cameras ready, and I was told 'Now make it perch.' The last thing any self-respecting peacock will do is obey an order to do anything. I said I would try clapping my hands but did not think it would work – and it didn't. Suddenly the furious voice of the director came through the megaphone saying that x pounds a minute was being wasted while the peacock strutted around, unconcerned, on the ground. The assistant director looked as if he was expecting to be sacked at any minute but eventually accepted defeat. The scene was temporarily postponed, to be repeated the next day with a pinioned peacock brought from a pet shop in Glasgow.

In the autumn Peter went down to the studios where the rest of the film was being shot and was amused to see the front door of Traquair opening into a modern studio set. The film had gone through hard times. The backers had changed and the writer had withdrawn his name. It was now called *The Devil's Widow*. For a year or two we heard nothing of it. Finally, we were told that it was to be shown at the Edinburgh Film Festival in the hope that it would attract distributors. We were given tickets and hired a bus for the entire staff to be driven up to Edinburgh. The staff included our gardener, Tom Pow, who said that he had not been to the cinema since silent movies. I went on ahead to meet them in Edinburgh and was touched to discover that Peter had made sandwiches for everyone to eat on the bus. It was a rather weird film, but we all enjoyed it although it failed to find a distributor.

Everything the film company had built was taken down and the house put back exactly as it had been before, but some of the plants on the terrace were left behind. We planted the poplars in a long avenue leading to the Tweed. They are now twenty feet high and a beautiful screen to a boggy area as well as being an interesting souvenir of the life of the house. Visitors admire them and only experts, trained by the book, say they are out of place.

So far we have not managed to attract another major film to Traquair although it has been used for several small scenes. In 1985 Robin Crichton, a friend who had built a film studio nearby, was making a series for Channel Four entitled *The Stamp of Greatness*. Each programme was a dramatised biography of one of the people who have been commemorated on a stamp. One of the programmes was about Robert Burns. Robin used our drawing room as Lord Monboddo's salon in Edinburgh, the place where Robert Burns was first introduced to society. He needed about a dozen extras to take part and in no time we had rustled up any craftsmen and staff willing to offer their services, including ourselves. Costumes were brought out and a make-up lady installed in a bedroom. Peter and all the men looked particularly handsome in their wigs and buckled shoes. At the end of the morning we were delighted to be asked to queue up to be paid.

On another occasion Robin was making a series for American television called *In Search of Other Lives.* He brought to Traquair a good-looking woman with bright orange hair. She was dressed in a black tunic with a silver belt and was convinced that she was the reincarnation of James IV. At that time, in 1513, most of the house had not been built and Robin wanted to see if she would try to go into the house by the old door.

Peter and I sat in the courtyard chatting with her while she waited for the lights to be set up, and she completely disarmed me by saying 'You must think I am very strange.' She went on to explain that the belief that she was James IV had come on slowly. In the winter in particular she would find herself walking with a man's stride. She had a *déjà vu* reaction to the places James IV had been to and experienced a sickening feeling when she went near Flodden. She told me that she bought her clothes at a Church of Scotland ministers' outfitters. While we were talking she asked Peter about the history of the house and he inadvertently explained the dates of the various parts of the building. She had no difficulty in finding the old door.

Hippy Days

~

My brother Nicholas used to come up from London on short spasmodic visits. He seemed to come from another world. He had always been fascinated by new inventions and hated conventional lifestyles. He admired the sixties' hippy values and had grown his hair long and sprouted a beard. With his dark hair and huge brown eyes he looked like an image of Christ in the Wilderness.

Nicholas had started to collect material for a book on hippy life in London which was also a practical guide to living differently. As he explained to a *Times* journalist: 'I want a viable alternative to the way people live now. I want people to express their personalities; I want a world full of eccentrics.' He gave advice on squats – he had friends who had been living in an abandoned embassy belonging to an obscure African state for several years. How to get cheap meals – sneak into an office canteen that is subsidised for its employees. You could also get to see half of an opera at Covent Garden if you mingled with the audience when they came out into the street at the interval on a warm summer evening and went back in with them. Much of his advice was on the edge of the law, and it was as well that my father, who had been scrupulously honest, did not live to read it. One of the few times my father was really angry with me was when I told him proudly that my rail ticket had not been punched, so I could use it again.

Nicholas was helped by a small team of friends. He published *Alternative London* himself and it became a cult book and a bestseller. He followed it up with *Alternative England and Wales*. The format was copied for different towns all over the world, but after several editions he got bored and passed subsequent editions on to a friend.

At this time he was living in a garden flat in Edith Grove where he replaced the outer wall with a piece of plate glass that left a gap of about nine inches between the bottom of the glass and the floor. He made a large pond in the garden and allowed the water to come in under the glass to form a small pool in his open-plan living space inside. A variety of tame ducks swam in and out. The only furniture was bean bags, and the flat became an open house.

On our visits to London he held dream parties for Catherine with the white floor sprinkled with Smarties and gold- and silver-wrapped chocolate biscuits. He kept Peter and me up-to-date with hippy life and would take us off to eat in mysterious dark cafés smelling of marijuana. Peter, who loved adventure, was intrigued by this new side of London life.

After a few years Nicholas grew tired of his flat being used as a doss house and was not unhappy when a Danish girl who had been meditating in front of a candle accidentally knocked it over and started a fire. The bean bags disappeared in minutes and then much of the floor and windows.

He had fallen in love with Neal's Yard, a small yard in Covent Garden, which was enclosed by high buildings built as warehouses, and invested the capital he had inherited in one of them. The building next door belonged to the Opera House and was used for storing costumes. He and his hippy friends would drop in through a skylight, dress up in the fabulous costumes and parade in their finery along the roof tops.

By chance the old Covent Garden fruit market was being moved and the Council were carrying out an innovative scheme on its site. The whole area was becoming a popular place to shop and was always buzzing with people. He made a flat for himself on the top floor and decided to open a wholefood shop below. Although not a wholefood addict himself, he admired those who were, primarily because they were going against conventional eating habits. He realised that pulses and vegetarian food were then obtainable only in health shops in small packets at high prices. He decided to buy such foods by the hundredweight and pack them in larger weights so that they could be sold at lower prices. Having carried out most of the building work himself, he opened the shop and it soon became a huge success. He had no trouble in finding dedicated wholefood addicts to work there.

He gradually acquired other buildings in the yard, and in the next ten years a flour mill, a co-operative bakery, a dairy and therapy rooms were installed. A shop selling lotions known as remedies also took off. He made a coffee house which roasted its own beans in Monmouth Street and let us use two small rooms with a shower and a cooker on the top floor. We put mattresses on old palettes and would wake up to the delicious aroma of roasting coffee. It was an ideal base for a few days in London and it was a joy to be only a few yards away from the West End.

Nicholas had noticed the growth of interest in alternative therapies. Many of his friends had trained as therapists but could not afford to rent a consulting room, especially in central London. He decided to make a row of cubicles on the second floor of his building to rent out. He installed a receptionist and, not being a great believer in alternative medicine himself, he insisted that the therapists gave a written account of their therapy and their training which should be shown to clients before they booked appointments. This did not go down well with some of the therapists, who can be even more arrogant than conventional doctors. Again he became bored with the administration and handed it over to an efficient woman.

Like myself, Nicholas was good on ideas and initiating projects but did not enjoy management. He helped finance the shops to get them going but it was the monotonous hard work that largely contributed to their success. Once they were on their feet he tried to get their owners to pay a fair rent. This led to strained relations as both sides believed their contribution was underestimated.

Nearly every time Nicholas visited us he would bring a new girlfriend, usually much younger than himself. I thought it was a bad example for Catherine and whoever else was staying in the house. Felicity, a young cousin of Peter's who had lost her mother, Joseph and other cousins stayed with us regularly. I told Nicholas that he would have to have had at least a six months' relationship before he brought a girl to stay. He thought this was very funny but it cut out most of his girlfriends, as few of them lasted that long.

On a visit to London I found him worried and depressed. He told me that Brit, a Danish girlfriend, was pregnant. Their relationship was over but he knew he must look after her. He went over to Denmark for the birth of his son, Kristoffer, and for a time rented a flat in Copenhagen so that he could learn Danish. He bought a house for Brit and their son in Denmark. Kristoffer came over regularly to stay with him in London, and he often brought him up to Scotland to stay with us. He was very proud of his son but had no idea how to be a father. This was not altogether his fault. He did not have the same memory of a happy childhood as I did. Edmund had always been sure of my mother's affection and I had had Nanny's, but he was born at the beginning of the war, when our mother was forty-six and our father fifty-eight, and although they loved him they had little time to show it. Fortunately, Brit was an ideal mother. Eventually she had another relationship and Kristoffer ended up in a happy family with three young half-brothers.

Kristoffer was sent to a Rudolf Steiner school in Denmark. It had its own system of education which Nicholas could not understand. When he asked Kristoffer's teacher which was the boy's best subject, the teacher thought for a while and then said, 'Playing. Kristoffer is very good at playing.' He began to understand this later when Kristoffer turned out to be the friendly extrovert boy that Nicholas himself had been before he went to Ampleforth. As the Rudolf Steiner school set no exams, Kristoffer had no idea if he could pass one and surprised himself by getting into university.

The four years that separated me from Nicholas marked

the start of a metamorphosis in society. While unable to change our own way of life, Peter and I were fascinated with his. I was impressed by the breakdown in class structure that was taking place and I admired Nicholas's vision of everyone earning their living with their own hands and helping each other.

In the Scottish Borders the sixties caught up with us slowly. One day I was waiting for petrol at the local garage when out of the car in front of me stepped two monks in saffron robes. Being curious, I asked them where they were going and they told me Samye Ling. They turned out to be monks who had been forced to leave Tibet and had been given a house at Eskdalemuir, a barren and exposed spot on a hillside above Langholm in the Scottish Borders.

Within a few years the house had turned into a thriving monastery, attracting disciples from all over the world, and an impressive temple with a gilded dome appeared on the landscape. The Dalai Lama has made several visits to the monastery and we have been lucky enough to be invited to hear him speak on two occasions. The first was in 1984 before the temple was fully completed and the second in 1993, when the temple, huge as it is, was not large enough for the thousands who came to hear him. An enormous marquee had to be erected nearby. Christian churches could learn from this shaven-headed man in his cotton robe and huge sandals who speaks in a gentle, hesitant voice. He laid down no rules but merely made suggestions. His message is similar to the Christian one – let peace start at home and spread out across the world. No one is excluded from Buddhism. We can take from it what we want and leave what does not suit us. On his first visit he told the monks that Buddhism should adapt to its surroundings and that the Buddhists at Samye Ling should be 'Scottish Buddhists'.

At about the same time, Colin Tennant, who owned Glen, the neighbouring estate, told us that he had let a row of farm cottages to a group called the Incredible String Band who were moving out of Edinburgh. They were becoming well known and had recently toured the United States. The Glen Christmas party that year was a colourful event, with long-haired members of the band and their hangers-on in hippy clothes interspersed with shepherds and their wives from remote cottages, all seated at trestle tables in the village hall.

From then on we rarely drove to Innerleithen without passing young hippy men and women in flowing dresses, sauntering in a trance-like state and smiling benignly. Even in icy weather, they refused lifts as they were 'enjoying the walk'. Gradually, as our farm cottages became vacant, their friends moved in and began to fill the place in the community previously occupied by farm workers. When their children were old enough to go to the village primary school they began to be accepted.

The Borders also attracted young people from Newcastle who wanted to try a different life and bring up their children in the country. Ian and Comrie Cameron came to live on the estate. Ian first worked on one of the farms and was then employed as an estate worker. He had as much hair as Nicholas and when he moved into a cottage next door to Mrs Bell she told me she had said to him, 'I know you're a hippy but you've got beautiful eyes.' She made a good judgement as Ian was the perfect neighbour and fixed up a bell for her to ring if she needed him. Later on he came to work at the house. Peter taught him to brew, and he has been the brewer and mainstay of Traquair ever since.

Every summer, Colin and Anne Tennant came up from London and Glen House was brought to life. The garden, which had been timed to flower in August, was a mass of colour and the house full of the scent of lilies and exotic house plants grown by a skilful gardener in the greenhouses. The guests at their house parties were equally exotic, and we felt we were miles away when we left the daily grind of Traquair and drove the couple of miles to visit them. Colin was a flamboyant host and his wife, Anne, a beautiful woman who was a lady-in-waiting to Princess Margaret. The 'Princess', as she was referred to, came to stay every year. Colin was reputed to have nearly married her and Anne had known her all her life. Nevertheless, they were obliged to keep up a sycophantic relationship that allowed her to order them about.

Princess Margaret had to be entertained all the time. Parties had to be given in the evenings and cabarets put on so that she could shine. Sometimes she brought her children. One year Anne gave a party on their private loch for all the children and their parents on the estate. The Princess seemed to like the idea of mixing with people but as soon as she thought someone was getting familiar, he or she was made to feel that they had overstepped the mark.

If the weather was bad and they did not know what to do with her, we would be rung up and told that they were on their way. One summer they brought her over with her two children who were about Catherine's age. Colin suggested that she took them round the house. Catherine was in the stable and furious at having to come out. She finally appeared looking grumpy with straw in her long unbrushed hair. I saw the Princess looking shocked – her daughter had a severe pudding-bowl haircut.

I feel sorry for the royal family. We have raised perfectly ordinary people on to a pedestal so that we have a focus for our class-based society. The Queen allows herself to be treated like a puppet and reads out a speech composed for her by the Government at the opening of Parliament each year. She is even obliged to change her religion when she travels north and in Scotland she becomes a Presbyterian. No wonder her family have begun to want lives of their own. It is a pity we have made them believe that they are unique individuals who deserve all the benefits of their royal status.

Our first encounter with the Queen in Scotland was at one of the garden parties that she holds at Holyrood each year. The Lord Lieutenants of each county draw up lists of those who should be asked and are allowed to present half a dozen couples to her personally. When we were new in the county, Peter and I were chosen. It was a boiling hot day and our elderly Lord Lieutenant had a bent back so that the sun caught the back of his head. Just as the Queen was approaching us, he keeled over and fell gently to the ground. The Royal Company of Archers, who are the Queen's bodyguard in Scotland, were supervising the affair and were all for lifting him up and getting him out of the way, but he refused to be moved. Peter and another guest hauled him up and supported him on either side while he carried out the introductions.

Two garden parties were enough as far as I was concerned. They were usually held when we were busy, the weather was often both cold and damp, and I hated the bother of dressing up for them in the middle of the afternoon. There was never sufficient marquee space, and after the year when the wind blew the tea out of my cup and on to my coat, I decided I would prefer to go and have tea with our friend Brodrick Haldane who kept open house on that day. Peter was quite happy to go on his own. After a while we ceased to be invited and a more deserving list of people was drawn up.

Peter's time in the army had conditioned him into having great respect for the monarch although he would have preferred to have had one who was descended from the Royal House of Stuart. He accepted an appointment as Deputy Lord Lieutenant. Much later, in the eighties, when the Queen was about to make a royal visit to the county, I was amazed to see these normally sensible men become as excited as schoolboys as they prepared for the visit. In the hall in Innerleithen, where a display of local interest had been set up for her to see, they spent a whole morning trying to gauge the number of footsteps she would take to cross the room and decide which one of them should accompany her.

Peter was as amused as I was when, after all the pompous talk and commotion, Mrs Beattie, the charming widow of one of the Traquair farmers, casually mentioned a few days before the visit that her brother, Sir Kenneth Scott, was one of the Queen's private secretaries. He had helped plan the visit and would be at her side all the way.

In the mid-seventies, a young couple, Robert and Vashti, who were trying to live a fairy-tale life in a horse-drawn caravan,

asked if they could move into the grounds. We thought that
their beautifully decorated caravan would be a great attraction
and we gave them a place behind our old cottage. The caravan
had a chimney and a small stove that enabled Vashti to make a
snug and picturesque home. She had been a singer and Robert
an artist who fell in love with horses. They already had one little
boy and Vashti was about to have another child. She brought
her tiny newborn baby girl out of hospital back to the caravan a
few days after she was born. Robert kept a Clydesdale mare to
pull the caravan and he was lent a wagonette that he later drove
and started to give rides to the visitors. Andrew Brown was
astonished at the combination.

I decided to move the antique shop into the front room of
the cottage where I could sell small pieces of furniture. In the
back room we made a snack bar. It meant that customers could
go into the shop without buying a ticket for the house. Vashti
agreed to look after it for me. The baby lay in an old wooden
cradle next to her and was much admired. She was surprised
at the end of the day to find coins in the cradle and learnt that
it was a Scottish custom to cross the newborn baby's palm with
silver.

Catherine loved having the caravan and Robert and Vashti
with their horses near the house. Like all the Maxwell Stuarts,
she and Peter adored animals and spoke to them as if they were
human beings. In spite of my childhood experience of animals,
I felt it impossible to live in the country without them,
although I was more interested in their decorative qualities.

When we first arrived at Traquair I bought a peacock and
two hens which soon multiplied. They had their bad points –
a tendency to trample over the garden nipping off buds and
yanking out small plants, a taste for home-baked scones that
they stole off visitors' plates and a habit of leaving huge
droppings on paths. But the incredible beauty of their colour
and their sweeping tails made up for everything. We also had
fantail pigeons in a high turret that had been made into a
doocot. They fluttered down when children threw them grain.
The gamekeeper hatched out a variety of white mallard ducks

who swam around the Well Pool. It did not take them long to find the tearoom, which they visited each day. It was quite a sight to see visitors standing back as the loudly quacking procession passed through the courtyard gates and waited outside the door noisily demanding crusts. Having swallowed them down with appreciative noises, they would progress out again. Many of the animals seemed to be aware that they were on view to the public and posed accordingly. Our two King Charles spaniels would sit like china dogs in the courtyard. The far from beautiful Muscovy ducks would try to copy the peacocks and perch elegantly on the tops of pillars and walls. The cat would take up a decorative position on the chaise longue in the drawing room or frighten the life out of visitors who saw the bedcover start to move as she woke up underneath and tried to get out.

An interesting girl called Pamela who had been living at Glen came to live in the next-door cottage. She dressed in black and belonged to a sect called the Divine Light Mission whose guru was an Indian boy of fourteen. She agreed to work as a part-time cleaner in the house and, as she was oblivious of the days of the week, was willing to work on Sundays which pleased the rest of the staff. She moved around the house polishing and dusting as if in a dream. She also volunteered to work in the Cottage Snack Bar. Towards the end of the summer she heard that her guru was coming to London and she was desperately hoping to get down to London to meet him. She was worried about the cost of the fare and taking time off. Out of the blue, two days before he was due to arrive, she started to chat with the chauffeur of a hired car that had brought a rich American family up to Scotland from London. The family decided that they wanted to go back by train. The chauffeur was asked to take the car down empty and meet them at the other end. He offered Pamela a lift. We put it down to the power of the guru.

Lessons from America

~

In 1974 an exhibition entitled *The Destruction of the Country House* was held in the Victoria and Albert Museum in London. It consisted of a series of photographs showing country houses that had once been the pride of their owners lying abandoned in various stages of disintegration. It brought the problem of maintaining an historic house to public attention.

Lord Montague of Beaulieu was prompted to set up the Historic Houses Association. The aim was to bring the owners of historic houses together to represent their interests and to lobby the Government. It would provide general advice for all members and practical advice for owners trying to turn their houses into viable enterprises. Subscriptions were levied from houses already open to the public, and Friends of the HHA were enrolled to give extra support. Peter was one of the first to join. I attended the first Annual General Meeting with him, which was held in London in the autumn. When a separate HHA in Scotland was set up, he sat on its committee and later, after his death, I was asked to take his place.

As any house owner knows, the cost of maintaining a property increases continually, and this cost is multiplied many times for the owners of historic houses. In many cases it is far beyond the income that can be generated by the house, however hard the owners try. There are many historic house owners like ourselves who live on the edge, perpetually dreading the appearance of cracks in the walls or the sight of furniture in need of repair. Minor repairs are often neglected, which only aggravates the problem later on.

I believe that historic houses should be looked after by their owners. If the houses have been inherited through many generations, they are the people best motivated not to break the chain and to work long and hard to keep the houses going. Moreover, they can do it more economically than any public body. A comparison with the National Trusts – constantly beneficiaries of large bequests but still unable to make all their houses self-financing – proves this point. The HHA works to bring these facts to the Government's attention and to lobby for tax concessions. For example, why is a new building not liable for VAT but restoration work on an old building is?

Although I am totally in agreement with the aims of the HHA, I have on occasion felt uncomfortable sitting among some of the richer members of society who, like ourselves, have an above-average lifestyle, and hear them pleading poverty and asking for Government handouts.

In 1989 Nicholas Ridley, the Secretary of State for the Environment, was invited to address the HHA Annual General Meeting. He believed that historic houses are 'safer and better run in private hands' but it was of little importance to him whose the private hands are. If the *anciens pauvres* could no longer afford to maintain a house, they should put it up for sale and give the *nouveaux riches* a chance. He pointed out that 'many families who pride themselves on having always lived in a house, in fact married into it, bought it or stole it at some point in their murky history when they were robber barons.' The view of this Tory minister came as a shock to his listeners. His family pile had been inherited by his elder brother and there were mutterings from the audience that it was the 'typical rant of a younger son'. I felt he had made some good points but would there really be many buyers?

One of the solutions seldom discussed in Britain might be to change the method of inheritance. Estates in France, which are by law divided equally among the members of a family, are generally held up as an example of the evils of splitting an estate. In some cases the contents of the house are sold and the house left empty, but there other cases where the children manage to work out a compromise and divide the pain of maintaining the house with a share in the pleasure of living in it.

The attitude of owners has changed enormously over the years. In the past, for example, opening hours were set to suit the owners and not the visitors. It needed a mathematician's brain to work out a tour taking in as many houses as possible in a short time – 'open Wednesdays and Thursdays, closed Saturdays in August, closed Friday afternoons in September'. When this was brought up at an HHA meeting, the chairman answered that owners had to accommodate their children's school holidays. The visitors' school holidays were obviously of secondary importance. The new generation of owners has learnt to be far more accommodating.

At Traquair we had followed Frank's system of closing on Fridays but as we became busier we spent so much time turning away disappointed tourists that we decided it would be less trouble to stay open. We were surprised when we calculated how much money we were making by opening daily and we gradually extended our opening hours to the morning as well.

In the early days of the HHA we attended some enjoyable conferences. One summer we stayed first at Christchurch in Oxford where we dined in the great hall. The following evening a banquet was held by the Duke and Duchess of Marlborough at Blenheim Palace, a memorable setting with flower-filled rooms, candlelight reflected in the gilt mirrors and a glamorous duchess to complete the picture. Our final stop was Chatsworth in Derbyshire where we were given lunch. By the time the self-effacing Duke of Devonshire had taken us on a lengthy tour of the treasure-packed house, I was becoming overwhelmed by great houses. I was desperate to leave and to go and pick up my mother from her old farmhouse in Huyton, but the Chatsworth security had locked us in and we had great difficulty in sneaking out without setting off alarms. There must have been some lectures and discussions during the two days but I can only remember the splendour of the surroundings. We thoroughly enjoyed ourselves, but I could not feel that the visits were in any way applicable to our own problems.

In 1979 a more practical course was run by Lord Montague at Beaulieu. He was one of the first owners to recognise house-opening as a business, although it must be said that his visitors were more interested in the Motor Museum than in the house. The course was run by his manager and we sat in the museum while we were given detailed information on how to turn house-opening into a successful commercial enterprise.

It is important, we were told, to separate visitors from their cars before they learn the price of admission. If they do not have their cars nearby, they are less likely to change their minds and get back into them. We should realise that people like spending money so we should help them to do it. Gift shops should not contain too many items as customers will waste time browsing. A few selected gifts standing in a glass case with a code number is sufficient display.

We were urged to increase our admission prices. It had been worked out that as a costing of entertainment per hour, a visit to an historic house was good value. We were warned not to print the price on the ticket so that the entrance fee could easily be altered. If we wanted to have a fleet of buses in our car park we must make it worthwhile for their drivers – a special room with a television and a good tip was the least we could do for them. We knew this was true. When the mill shops started to give the drivers ten per cent of their passengers' purchases, tourists complained that all they saw of the Scottish Borders was woollen goods.

The course was attended by administrators who enjoyed getting together to discuss their problems, the greatest of which was their employers. 'They want to have their cake and eat it,' was the most common complaint. 'They worry about the detrimental effect of thousands of feet on their Persian carpets and then freak out at the price of a scone in the tearoom. They will even decide to have a party in a room that has already been booked for a group. At the end of the season they will ask us why the opening has not been more profitable.'

One of the administrators who never criticised her employers was Helen Fairbank, who worked at Scone Palace. Several years later when she wrote to say that she was leaving we decided to try out the difficult owner/administrator relationship with her and between us we managed to make it work.

The following year we were invited by the British Tourist Authority to go on a promotional tour of the United States to advertise its new season ticket which gave a reduced entry into historic houses. A tour of newspaper offices and television interviews had been set up for us, and we toured the studios and went on chat shows. The atmosphere was much less formal in America and the interviewers less stiff than they were in Britain at that time. Peter was asked to wear full Highland dress, which he borrowed, down to the socks, from one of our generous guides. I was asked to bring an object from the house so I chose a very small eighteenth-century brass dog collar. It was near Hallowe'en so there was generally a question about ghosts. As we progressed, a story developed that the collar had belonged to a dog who had appeared in the grounds as a ghost.

We ended up in New York where Peter was booked to appear on *What's My Line?* a popular television panel game that was shown across the States. A person with an unusual job was chosen to go in front of a panel with two 'impostors'. The panel had a limited number of questions to ask each competitor, at the end of which they had to make up their minds who was the real one. Peter was billed as a 'Brewing Laird'. A young Scots businessman in Highland dress and a British Airways pilot who had hired his too-short kilt at a theatrical costumiers were the impostors. The panel consisted of elderly actors and actresses. Peter was warned that their one aim was to keep their faces on the screen as long as possible so they often asked for a question to be repeated or asked them in a convoluted way. I had fun watching from the wings and was impressed that Peter managed to win, bluffing his way through and pretending to be as unfamiliar with the technique of brewing as the others were.

At the end of this trip we flew down to Virginia to visit Williamsburg. The Rockefeller Foundation has restored this small town and returned it to the eighteenth century. Houses are all furnished in the correct style and the guides are dressed in costume that varies according to the time of year. A replica of the Governor's Palace has been built where candlelit concerts are held. Horse-drawn vehicles travel the cobbled streets – no cars are allowed. Small shops sell the produce of the time, and skilled craftsmen can be seen at work, using only tools of the period.

The town had a special meaning for us as it was here that Christina Stuart, the daughter of the sixth Earl of Traquair, settled after she married Cyrus Griffin in the eighteenth century. We even saw the white clapboard house researchers had decided was theirs. Cyrus was the son of a Virginian tobacco planter. Financed by tobacco money, he was sent to study at Glasgow University and met Christina through her brother. After their marriage they went back to America where he became the President of the last Continental Congress, the body that governed the colony before it gained independence. Christina walked with a limp, and this led to the romantic story that she had jumped from a window at Traquair to elope with Cyrus. Unfortunately, after reading letters in the archives in Williamsburg we found that the story was far more prosaic. Christina's father reluctantly agreed to the marriage and Cyrus was disappointed to find that he had not married an heiress. He wrote to her father continually, asking for money, even using her disability as a reason for him to be compensated for taking her off her father's hands. We found both their graves in Bruton Parish Churchyard.

The fact that the direct Stuart line died out in 1875 and the house then passed to Maxwell cousins also encouraged romantic fantasies. When we were first living in the cottage, I was crouching by the fire on a stormy day when a woman blew in, sat down opposite me and said she must speak to Peter, who happened to be out. After a while she broke her silence and in a confidential manner informed me that, according to her research, the last Earl of Traquair had been married secretly in Coldstream. Although she had no concrete evidence – apparently the page was missing from the parish register – she had worked out that her father was descended from this marriage.

Even before her appearance, Peter's father, Frank, was approached by an elderly American named Stuart Linton (Linton was the courtesy title of the Earl of Traquair's eldest son). He also claimed to be a descendant of the last Earl of Traquair and said that his family possessed a portrait of Christina Stuart. He had shown Mr Pine of *Burke's Peerage* the earl's marriage certificate and was told that if he could prove that his elder brother was no longer alive he could claim the earldom. As Stuart was a bachelor in his sixties, he said that he was not interested in doing this. Frank treated the whole story as a joke as he was never actually shown the marriage certificate and thought that Pine had seen it only after a good lunch. He took a liking to Stuart, however, who was generous with his hospitality, and later, when he returned with an elderly bride, arranged for Aunt May to present them at court in London.

Peter and I visited Stuart's apartment in New York and saw Christina's portrait, which he promised to leave to Traquair when he died. We went back to see his widow after his death and found her in a sad state. She had tried to drown her sorrows and told us that she had put the contents of the apartment in store but had overlooked paying the rent and everything had been sold. Neither Peter nor the Williamsburg authorities have ever been able to trace the portrait.

We were particularly interested in the way that Williamsburg has been presented as a tourist attraction. It avoids a museum atmosphere and is alive without seeming phoney. We were impressed by the craftwork going on in the town, and when we returned to Scotland it gave us the idea of turning the old abandoned buildings in the grounds into workshops where modern-day craftsmen could work and sell their wares direct to the public. There was a stable, a tack room, a grain store and a coach house as well as 'Bachelor's

Hall', a one-roomed bothy with a chimney which still contained an old washstand and basin. It was last occupied by an Irishman who worked in the grounds in the 1940s.

Some of the hippy couples in the area were starting to make things and needed outlets for their goods. Ray, a young potter from Stoke-on-Trent, had set up a pottery locally but had gone bankrupt and was living in Innerleithen. He was keen to make a pottery in the old stable and was prepared to install a kiln. He and his wife, Cath, moved into a cottage in the grounds and she also helped in the house. The pottery got going slowly as Ray seemed to be disaster-prone. His kiln either over-baked or he bought the wrong kind of clay or the lorry that delivered it knocked down a wall. It took a while for his work to be an attraction to visitors but he finally settled in and produced handsome ironstone ale mugs so that both the mugs and the beer were made on the premises.

A young English couple who had been attached to the Incredible String Band had been living in Glen Row and wanted to move away. John had taught himself wood-turning and started to make beautiful cradles and high chairs. They too came to live in a cottage and set up a workshop in the loft.

Within a few years a potter, a woodworker, a candlemaker, a silk-screen printer, a tapestry-maker and Silvia, 'the artist', an old friend from art school days who had come to live in one of our cottages, were all installed in workshops in the grounds. There were no craft communities in the south of Scotland at that time and visitors had not become bored with the endless 'crafts' on sale. We maintained the exterior of the buildings and the craftsmen looked after the interiors. We charged no rent and took no percentage on their sales but wanted them to be in their workshops on a regular basis so that we could adver-tise them in our leaflets and thus attract more visitors into the grounds. It sounded like a simple plan, but I soon began to sympathise with Tolstoy when he complained that the only thing that prevented his schemes to benefit the tenants on his estate from working was human nature.

Artists and craftsmen choose to work on their own and do

not like to work set hours. If the weather is good they want to take the day off. Tourists, on the other hand, expect to get what they see advertised and complain if they don't. The craftsmen also found it difficult to have people watching them while they worked. They were bombarded by questions that often had nothing to do with what they were doing. 'Where is the nearest B and B?' or 'Is the house worth visiting?' If they had developed a talent for executing an object quickly, say throwing clay for a mug, they would hear people commenting, 'It only takes him a few minutes and look at the price he is charging.'

They also found that their large pieces were difficult to sell and had to resort to small quickly turned-out items that were boring to make. The wood-turner found himself turning out spurtles by the dozen and the potter started producing lumps of clay that looked like small animals. As they were inclined to be nocturnal in any case, some of them preferred to work at night, and it was irritating for us to see the lights on in their workshops when there was no one around and the next day to have visitors complaining, 'Why is the x shop closed? We came all the way to see it.'

On the other hand, it was promoting a way of life advocated by Ernst Schumacher in his book *Small is Beautiful* and one that Peter and I would have preferred to have lived ourselves. The craftspeople gave a creative energy to the place and it was a pleasure to see their children playing in the grounds. We did not enjoy organising staff or attending endless meetings and seminars with the constant pressure to join committees. Peter did his bit by becoming a member of the county council and serving on various tourist committees or attending meetings connected with the estate such as the fishing. As we were always short-staffed I decided that my time was better spent working at Traquair.

Fishing meetings become a bit of a joke between us. As we owned a stretch of the River Tweed, there were regular meetings with the other proprietors. They were held in the evening in Peebles, which then had a cinema. If the meeting ended early, I knew that Peter could not resist dropping in there on his way home. One evening, a Women's Rural branch had booked a visit and I had promised to open up the house for the guide who was to take them round. To my horror I found that the main key was missing and guessed that Peter must have taken it by mistake. I went straight to the telephone and rang the cinema. 'Yes, Mr Maxwell Stuart was seen going in.' They flashed a message on to the screen and he arrived home with the key in the nick of time.

Catherine had reached the top of Traquair school. It was a couple of miles from the house but too near for her to be eligible for the school bus so I usually took her in the car. It took children from the age of five and they stayed until they were ten when they went on to a primary school in Innerleithen. There were fewer than twenty children in two classrooms with one full-time teacher who lived in the school-house nearby. The older children helped the younger ones and extra teachers came in once a week for music, art and PT. In its idyllic setting it was the perfect start for country children who, at that time, rarely left their homes before they went to school. If the weather was fine, they were taken up the hill on nature walks. Lunch was brought up from the school in Innerleithen in a heated van and a little bus took them down once a week for swimming. The cost per head to the council must have been more than the fees at any private school and there were constant threats that, if the numbers fell, it would be closed. The numbers could fluctuate suddenly by one large family coming or going. The school-teacher rejoiced when she heard of a pregnancy, and I am afraid I was a disappointment to her. We had made inquiries about adopting a child but had been found unsuitable. The adoption worker had concluded that the only reason we wanted to adopt was to give Catherine a brother or sister. 'Probably the reason that most people have a second child,' remarked a social-work friend when I told her.

Traquair School actually struggled on for another twenty years or so, the numbers diminishing all the time. Whenever there was an attempt to close it, there would be strong protests. But as life in the country became less isolated and many of the children went to a nursery school in Innerleithen anyway, there was no problem in sending them straight down to the larger school there. It had more facilities and gave them a chance to widen their outlook and make more friends. Gradually it was the local residents, for whom the school was actually designed, who decided not to use it, and it was incomers from farther afield who drove their children up each day. The final demise came when the numbers went down to six and it was regret-fully agreed that the village school belonged to the past.

The Fun of the Fair

~

In 1976 when we had five craft workshops in full swing, I decided to try holding a Craft Fair. There were plenty of craft workers in the Scottish Borders and tourists were interested in what was being made. I had heard about these fairs from friends in Norfolk but, oddly enough, there was none at that time in Scotland. We needed a covered area that would hold at least a dozen stalls so I took a gamble and hired a marquee that we erected in the old walled garden. I wrote to all the craftspeople we knew and asked them if they would rent a stall over the weekend. Peter was so worried that we would be left with a huge debt on the tent that I made them promise to contribute if we made a loss. The weather turned out to be fine, however: we more than covered our costs and the craftsmen were satisfied with their sales. Our tearoom had extra trade and, surprisingly, our gift shop did as well.

Peter felt confident enough to let me make it an annual event. I had become involved with Theatre Workshop in Edinburgh and at the next Fair they agreed to come down and put on some street entertainment. Nicholas had also told me of the new movement for putting on country fairs in England and had taken Catherine, now aged fourteen, to the Albion Fair in Norfolk. She spoke to the organisers, who were encouraging and passed on addresses of groups who might come and perform. One of these was Cliff Hanger. They consisted of three men and a girl who dressed in a variety of costumes and mingled with the audience, acting out different roles. They would sit in the tearoom and start talking to visitors about their problems and no one knew if they were acting or not. Two of the men dressed in uniform and dark glasses and behaved like CIA agents, walking around the house saying authoritatively in American accents that the building was a danger and should be pulled down.

Their main act was a ballroom-dancing spoof where they dressed up in white ties and tails and danced solemnly with a life-size puppet partner in front of the house. They became good friends and returned several years running with a new act and helped us to find other entertainers. The leader of Cliff Hanger was called Pete McCarthy. One year he asked if I knew anywhere where he and his girlfriend, Becky, could stay for a week afterwards as he wanted to do some writing. I said they could stay in the house. Later he began to work as a presenter in radio and television. His first book, *McCarthy's Ireland*, was a bestseller and he has repeated his success many times.

In the early days the Fair was more craft-orientated. We tried to keep the standard up by asking to see examples of craftspeople's work before renting stalls, and we encouraged demonstrations. Gradually the entertainment increased and almost swamped the crafts. The popularity of the Fair slowly spread and began to develop a cult-following while still appealing to people of all ages and different tastes. Every year, the entertainment became more expensive and the numbers of visitors grew. We held it on the weekend before the Edinburgh Festival began in order to attract Fringe performers and street theatres on their way there. It always turned into a really happy joyful weekend. As long as we covered the costs, I was not concerned with it being a money-making venture, although we did hope to build up a sum that would carry us through a year when it might be rained off. It was a great pleasure for me to be able to create an event that just gave enjoyment without any pressure to make a profit.

Knowing how draining it is for parents to have to keep shelling out money, we decided to have one entrance fee at the gate and everything else would be free. It took a while for the public to appreciate this. It seemed a large sum at the gate but it was no more than the price of two tickets to a Fringe event at the Festival. Once they learnt to come early and spend the whole day going from one entertainment to another they seemed to realise what good value it was.

Preparations started during the winter, booking entertainers and the marquees, renting out the stalls and thinking up new ideas. Peter and I worked at the publicity all through the year and whenever a journalist came to write about the house or the beer we always pushed the Fair.

Watching the weather in the weeks before the Fair was a nail-biting time. In my convent schooldays I had learnt to offer up a small sacrifice if you wanted something. In the days when I smoked, I would give that up, and then had to think of something else. My prayers were answered as we never had a total wash-out – and August is not the driest month in Scotland.

The night before the event, we had to check that we had the right number of tents, tables and benches and put them in position. Early the next morning we had to name the stalls and tell everyone where to go. When the gates opened, we would be on constant call as a mass of small problems needed to be sorted out and the toilets inevitably blocked or water ran out.

Peter and I began to find that it was getting too much for us. On the other hand, the craftspeople began to resent not being involved in the organisation so we decided to turn the Fair into a self-supporting charity and let the craftspeople take it over. We attended regular meetings merely to keep in touch with the programme. A secretary and a treasurer were elected who were to be paid and everyone was to get an hourly rate for the work they put into it. They each contributed an individual talent.

Peter and I were still backing it financially, but we handed the book-keeping over to the treasurer. Each Fair became a larger gamble as we aimed to use the gate money to cover all the expenses, which were now running into thousands. If it was rained off on both days of the weekend, we would be liable for a huge loss.

During the two days of the Fair each committee member was to have a particular job. It took a while for them to get into it. When the potter who was supposed to be allocating the craft stalls had not appeared on the Saturday morning, I had to go to his cottage and get him out of bed. After a year or two, with extra energy and new combined talent, the Fair grew and took on a more professional format. For the first years it kept the same atmosphere. It was a relief to have the organisation taken off our hands, and our own staff were glad to hand over the building of stages and the installation of extra electricity and water points on top of everything else they had to do.

We tried out new entertainments each year and brought back the popular ones. We developed the Fair to suit the grounds, which seemed purpose-built for each entertainment. We had archery on the avenue, croquet on a colour maze on the croquet lawn and a busking competition outside the pottery. There was mask-making, kite-making, puppets, magicians and storytelling for children in another area. Chess, yoga and samba-dancing workshops for adults each had a turn, as did clog-dancing and Scottish country dancing in the court-yard and Northumberland pipers and baroque music in the chapel. Food stalls were dotted around the grounds and street performers did their acts in any available space. A feature of the Fair were the gas-filled balloons that we sold or gave free to children under five. Children had to take off their shoes to enter the colour maze and a line of small shoes with balloons attached to them would be lined up at its entrance.

For many people Traquair Fair has become an annual meeting place. A woman I met on a train once told me, 'I met a man and fell in love.' When Catherine was travelling in India, she met another traveller who said he must get back to Britain in time for Traquair Fair. Many years later a couple who farmed locally and had attended every one asked if they could celebrate their marriage in the old garden just before the Fair opened. Instead of a party they gave all their friends tickets to enjoy the day with them.

We marvelled at its success. By the mid-eighties it was attracting over 6,000 visitors and bringing a lot of trade into the area. We kept wanting to make it bigger and better. We passed the peak of the perfect Fair without realising it. The music groups we booked began to insist on a sound system and we gave up having acoustic music. One of my favourite groups, Pookie Snackenburger, played acoustic music the first year but the next time they came they wanted amplification. They needed a three-hour sound check and their music lost its charm. Groups could no longer survive by appearing live at fairs and needed to make recordings or appear on television.

In 1984 we had a young Polish sculptor, Joanna Przybyla, staying in the house for the summer. She was making an installation on the avenue into which she incorporated any scrap material she could find. It took a while for everyone to appreciate her work, but we were all impressed by her dedication and concentration, and we gradually began to understand what she was doing. We gave her the space below the coach house as a studio. I was irritated that her work was going to be interrupted by the Fair. It had been arranged that her studio space was to be used as a café and a marquee was to be set up where her installation was being made. She had to move everything.

That year we had Hank Wangford and K. D. Laing on a music stage in the avenue and an alarming number of visitors crowded into the grounds. It was one of K. D. Laing's first appearances in Scotland and she was a huge success. After a brief meeting, Joanna told me, 'KD and I recognised each other as strong women.' They made an instant friendship and wandered in the grounds all night before KD's roadies came to take her away.

Meanwhile, our own finances were far from healthy. Appreciating that I had contributed so much to the house, Peter did not insist on taking money from the Fair's takings except as compensation for loss of house admission tickets. It was impossible to arrange for visitors to go into the house without going through the Fair first, so they had to pay for both, and not many did. Apart from that, the house received no benefit and yet had costs to bear – each year equipment would go astray, our staff would find themselves working for the Fair committee and the grounds would be damaged.

Peter and I were also very conscious that the Monday after the Fair was the peak of our tourist season and we were anxious to get the place looking as good as it had before. Committee members tended to do a bit of clearing up and then collapse in exhaustion, so our own staff were given even more work. Few workshops were open or had anything left to sell.

When a large marquee had been left standing on the avenue for several days and the site was urgently needed by Joanna, Peter, his cousin Felicity and I started to dismantle it. I watched Peter, looking tired and exhausted, helping to lift the tent pegs and I realised in a flash that the Fair could not continue, certainly not in the same way.

The committee members were taken by surprise and shocked, but we both knew that we had taken the right decision. The spirit of the Fair had changed and it was now seen as a vehicle for making money. The treasurer was unable to keep proper accounts and although the committee kept talking about giving money away, they decided to pay themselves a generous hourly rate as well as expenses. It was never suggested that anything be given towards the upkeep of the house. In spite of the very large takings, there was not enough money left in the bank to cushion a loss. It was no longer a Fair we could be proud of and we felt a break might eventually allow us to start again. We gave it a rest for three years.

Calling a halt had good consequences as well as one strange one. The committee members had gained local credibility and were no longer considered to be irresponsible hippies. The treasurer was adopted as a council candidate by the Liberal Party who did not bother to inquire into his background. He was duly elected and even became chairman of the education committee.

The Maze and Everyday Life

~

We realised that in spite of the secret stairs and an old swing and a seesaw out of doors, we lacked entertainment for children, so Peter created a 'spooky cellar'. He filled one of the ground-floor cellars with any strange object he found in the house and did not know what to do with – a carved wooden head, oddly shaped glass bottles, cracked mirrors, old clothes and an ancient wheelchair into which we placed a figure made of stuffed cotton half-hidden under a black veil. One white gloved arm hung limply at the side. Over all this he spread synthetic cobwebs bought from a theatrical supplier and lit the space with a low-watt coloured bulb. The ghostly atmosphere grew as natural cobwebs appeared. When I added several large papier-mâché heads that a friend and I had made for a children's fancy dress party, mice began to nibble at them and they became more gruesome every day.

We had always thought it would be fun to have an active ghost in the cellar, and when my art-school friend, Silvia, was staying she volunteered to play the part. She sat in the wheelchair in place of the dummy, hidden by the veil with only her gloved arm showing. The hole in the door was just large enough for one person to look through it at a time. When she heard a couple outside, she would slowly move her arm when the first person looked through. 'It moved,' the visitor would gasp. 'Let me have a look,' the second would insist, and Silvia would keep quite still. Great arguments ensued: 'It moved, it did, I'm sure it did,' the first would say. 'You are just imagining things, dear,' the second would answer. Two nuns were sure they had found out how it worked: 'It's when you put your foot on this bit of the floor, sister.'

I was upset when I received a telephone call from an anxious mother saying that her daughter was having nightmares after looking into the cellar. What could I say to help her? There was little I could do apart from offering to take the child in with a bright light and let her see the objects close up.

Parents of young children often asked if we had a playground. Apart from the swings and the seesaw, I was against having a playground in the country where I felt children should not need that sort of entertainment, but in 1979 I had another idea. I was standing on the terrace at the back of the house one day, looking down on to the rough grass below trying to imagine the *par terre* garden that had once lain below. Lucie Stuart had written to her mother in the early eighteenth century, 'I am sorry to hear that your *par terre* has been flooded.' There was not a trace of it left but Peter had discovered an old plan of the ground at the back of the house showing fountain heads. We could not possibly afford to make another garden, but the idea of a maze suddenly came to me. A maze would repeat the idea of looking down from the terrace on to patterns below and would not only be attractive but fun for visitors of all ages.

Knowing how long it would take for hedges to grow I wondered if we could use dry-stane dykes instead. These walls, built of local stones, are skilfully balanced in such a way that they hold together without any mortar. I heard that a dyking competition was being held in Kirkcudbrightshire and went over to get a view of the experts. It was fascinating to watch. Every dyker was given a pile of stones and told to build a few yards of wall. In spite of the similarity of the materials, each wall was completely different. Each dyker picked out different stones and had his own style of building.

When we discussed the maze afterwards, it was pointed out that the enormous amount of stones needed to build a maze would be hard to find, and where could they be placed within the reach of the dyker while the building was going on? We realised that we would have to settle for trees. Peter and I then visited the maze at Hampton Court, but we decided that the hedges were too high and seemed to create a claustro-phobic atmosphere. We then went up to the only maze in Scotland at that time, at Hazelhead in Aberdeen, which we preferred.

We went to the Botanic Garden in Edinburgh and asked for advice on the sort of trees we should use. We wanted a fast-growing tree that would form a good hedge. They suggested the Leyland cypress. I was all for buying large ones, but we were told that the shock of transplanting a larger tree slowed them down and that smaller ones, which transplanted easily, ended up growing more quickly. When I mentioned Leyland cypress to a friend from the south of England, he said, 'Don't have them – they will grow so quickly you'll never be able to reach the top to cut them.' It was not a problem encountered in the freezing north.

My brother Nicholas was enthusiastic about the idea and generously agreed to pay for the trees, 1,500 of them. John Schofield, who had the wood-turning shop, offered to make the design. It would have four sub-centres that had to be visited in turn before reaching the middle. The ground was duly prepared and a grid of stakes driven into the ground. The pattern was marked out with string. It covered a quarter of an acre.

In the spring of 1980 we invited the pupils of Traquair School to come and plant the first trees, and the very first one was planted by Anna Vaughan, the youngest girl in the school, whose parents happened to have the silk-screen workshop. We generated good publicity for the opening, as it was only the second maze in Scotland. A photographer sent up by *The Sunday Times* rang up from Innerleithen saying he did not know where he was but he had been told to photograph a maze.

After the children returned to school, the birth of the maze was well celebrated with Traquair House Ale. We contemplated how the rest of the trees should be planted. We had hoped that visitors might be invited to plant a tree, but Bill Robson, who worked on the estate, insisted that the planting should be done properly. It turned out to be a particularly dry spring. We became so worried about the young trees drying out that we appealed to the Innerleithen Fire Brigade to have a fire practice over them to give them some water. The next problem was weeds that grew so high they nearly smothered the trees. The final disaster was the icy winter of 1982. It was so cold that the village water supply froze below the ground for six weeks and the best present you could give anybody was a container of water. The following spring we saw to our horror that the trees, now about three feet high, were brown. 'They will green up in the spring,' we thought hopefully but by the summer we had to admit that two-thirds of them were dead. We learnt that the Leyland cypress was a relatively new hybrid and had probably never experienced such low temperatures.

We removed the dead trees and replanted with beech. As they grew, the two varieties of tree knitted together well. We let visitors go round the maze throughout its growing period. It was cut and cared for by Jim Baird, who, in spite of a sight impediment, managed it with skill. He had an uphill task. Although we had made a quick way out with a 'Fool's Gate' for those who did not wish to walk round the whole maze a second time, there were still some people, mostly children, who insisted on pushing their way out through any weak spot. Jim would frequently find damaged trees, and he asked me once, in desperation, whether he could block the gaps with barbed wire. I had every sympathy with him, but we decided that it would not be 'tourist-friendly' and he persevered with plain wire. It took twelve years before we felt that we had the perfect maze. When I heard John Julius Norwich give a lecture on country houses and saw him show a slide of the 'Elizabethan' maze at Traquair, I crowed with delight.

From our new small dining room, which we squashed into for meals – however many relatives, staff and friends were there – we could look out and watch visitors walking through it. Men with children on their backs, push-chairs, prams and wheelchairs, all moving determinedly in different directions. We would hear parents calling their children and voices from the interior answering, 'We can't come, we can't get out.'

During the season Peter rarely finished lunch without being interrupted. Salesmen, tradesmen, journalists, television crews, visitors with inquiries they felt were urgent – all felt they could call in at any time without making an appointment. Having an office in the house gave a less formal atmosphere but it was hard to live a private life. When I cooked, I would often be called out in the middle, leaving saucepans boiling on the stove and returning to burnt-out pans and a smoke-filled kitchen. We were also aware that we needed to be available for the occasional complaint from a visitor – that a peacock had scratched his car, his child had been stung by a wasp or had his head stuck through the courtyard railings. In the last case the Innerleithen Fire Brigade again came to the rescue. A member of staff would find it far harder to pacify a complaining visitor whereas the sycophantic British public tended to collapse completely if Peter or I appeared.

Tea time, just after the house closed, was the most sociable time. Old friends would suddenly appear and we would end up having endless tea parties. On one occasion, when our sitting room was so crowded that neither Catherine nor I could get to the door, an unknown American girl took over and prepared tea for the next batch. It seemed that we were living in a perpetual party and needed little social life outside the house.

The brewery was still attracting much attention. After it was written up in numerous guides, brewers started to appear from all over the world. Two Americans, from famous breweries at the opposite sides of the States, were astonished to meet each other for the first time in our old Brew House. Some visitors were shocked at what they saw. A French family once rang the office door and demanded their ticket money back. They had bought our stylish and highly priced bottles of beer in Paris and were convinced that the beer could not possibly have been made in the two cellar-like chambers with their uneven flag-stoned floors and ancient equipment. They were convinced that it had really been manufactured in a modern brewery somewhere else.

Our ale was also a great attraction to journalists. Local television appeared immediately if we sent out a press release mentioning the beer. Peter had started to make several special brews in limited editions. They were extra-strong, were bottled in engraved glass bottles and were usually bought as collectors' items. The first one celebrated the Hundredth Brew and another was for our silver wedding. It happened to fall in 1981, the same year as Prince Charles's wedding. When a journalist rang up and asked Peter if he was making a special brew for the Royal Wedding, he said, 'Certainly not. I'm making one for our own silver wedding.' This prompted his newspaper to come up with a heading: 'The Royal Wedding is small beer at Traquair'.

Advertising had become very expensive and we were well aware of the value of the media in getting free publicity for the ale and the house. In comparison with a small costly advertisement, a piece in the paper or an item on television was seen or read by many more people and did not cost us anything. Added to that, the public tend to believe what they read in the newspapers. Peter, who drank little, found himself drinking beer with mock relish in front of the camera over and over again. 'You can see he's not a beer drinker,' a cameraman commented. He enjoyed talking to journalists and they found him unusual. They liked an eccentric laird whom they might first meet walking across the courtyard carrying packets of lavatory paper to replenish the public lavatories. The Scottish Tourist Board had us high on their 'places to visit' list and camera crews from all over the world would appear, often unannounced.

The British Travel Authority, while it existed, did what it could to help us. One of their executives, Dick Thomas, who was full of creative ideas, was put in charge of their 'British Weeks' which were held overseas to promote British goods. A store in Japan had shown an interest in the Stuarts, and he brought two of the store's directors up to stay for a night. They could speak only a few words of English so we asked Patrick Cafferkey, a cousin of Peter's who could speak Japanese, to come and stay. All seemed to be going well, although we did get the impression that they were hoping that Peter was the direct descendant of the royal line. Peter and Dick managed to deflect them from probing too far, but they caught me alone before dinner and produced a genealogical tree of the royal house of Stewart. 'Where Mr Stuart?' one of them asked. I waved my finger vaguely over the page but they were not convinced.

We did later have a trip to Japan where, at a reception in Tokyo, we were greeted with a model of Traquair carved out of a block of ice. We took Catherine off school, thinking it might extend her knowledge of the world, and went on to visit Peter's nephews, Michael and David Paterson, in Hong Kong and the Philippines. I realised we had made a mistake when, as we waited in Michael's car in Manila, she turned to me and said sadly, 'I wish I was at Traquair.'

I also did my share of talking to the press on radio and television, although as the years went by I began to resent giving up so much time to journalists. If the house was closed, we would have to open it up specially to show them around, and by the time we had locked up again and probably given them coffee, the morning would have gone. If we had to pose for photographs more time was lost. When I saw how many photographs a professional photographer took to obtain one publishable shot, I began to think we could all take good photographs if we did not mind wasting so much film.

Occasionally we would have to go off to a studio. Our local television station was based in Carlisle, a couple of hours' drive away. One of my first interviews was a half-hour programme with a friend, Silvia McCosh, who owned Dalemain, a beautiful house in Cumberland. It had belonged to her family and she was confident of her right to own it. I was less secure in my new role so I tended to answer questions with one or two words. The interviewer became desperate, and I remember her asking frantically 'And what about the toilets?'

One of my most painful interviews was on French television. My French had deteriorated badly but I was persuaded by a charming presenter to go in front of the camera. He had told me that he would be asking me about the house, which I knew I could manage, but halfway through he started to ask about the political situation in Scotland. He asked questions that I would have had to think hard about in English, let alone in French, and I tried to stumble through but eventually gave up and told him I could not do it. 'Continuez,' he smiled encouragingly, as only a Frenchman can, 'J'adore la petite hésitation.'

I have never forgotten the good advice a public relations woman gave us on one of our visits to America. She accompanied us as we travelled round the television stations and newspaper offices. 'After an interview you will always wish you had said something else or wish you had said something differently, but forget it.' It was only too true. I sometimes wonder how it is that actors are rehearsed before they speak while members of the public are supposed to give long interviews extemporarily.

We always had a good relationship with journalists and were reasonably satisfied with what they wrote. I have no time for people who use the press for their own purposes and then criticise what they write. People – and I am not talking about those who have been propelled into the limelight against their will by some tragedy – can refuse to give interviews and thereby avoid press attention. If you do talk to journalists you must realise that it is their job to get a story. They write what their readers want. I once tried to explain to a journalist that Peter and I did not live a life of feather-bedded luxury and that we had to work to keep the house going. She said she quite appreciated that it was not what her readers wanted to hear. They wanted to read about people who lived a more glamorous life than they did themselves.

I have also been on the other end and have written pieces for the press now and again on any interesting subject I have come across, including a farmer making sheep's cheese, a

French castle with a Scottish connection and a visit to a nuclear arms protesters' camp outside the airbase at Greenham Common. I am interested in the spin-off an article can have. Many are picked up by other papers or radio stations and lead to further interviews. The strangest broadcast I did was for BBC News. After the Indian government commemorated my cousin Madeleine on a postage stamp, a piece that I had written about her for *The Scotsman* several years before must have been filed away and was resuscitated. I was rung up by the BBC and asked to go to their studio in Edinburgh to be interviewed. I drove up on a summer evening and arrived at the building, totally deserted except for the doorman who let me in. He told me to go into the empty studio and put on the headphones. I was then spoken to by a voice in London and told to stand by. It was odd to be asked about Madeleine by a voice from far away, but I felt more at ease than I did when I am interviewed face to face.

Overnight Visitors

~

We had become accustomed to requests from young men or women who wanted to come and talk about an 'exciting project'. Inevitably the project would turn out to be about bringing exclusive groups of rich Americans to dine or stay in historic houses. In the British mind, America is entirely populated by rich Americans dying to come to Britain. In fact, only a small percentage of Americans ever leave their country and very many cannot afford to. The would-be agent would want to be shown around the house and told what we could provide. Usually we would never hear from him or her again. I often thought it a perfect way to get a personal free tour of all the great houses in Scotland.

One enterprising young man, Hamish Cathie, did manage to start up an agency to bring groups to Scotland and it ended up being one of the most successful travel agencies in Edinburgh. His first contact with us was not encouraging, however. He told us that he had met an American woman who wanted to bring six rich widows (or divorcées) to make a tour of Britain, staying in country houses and ending up in Scotland. Each host was to give a dinner party for them and would have to find some men to make up the numbers. A large fee tempted us to take up the offer. At that time we did not have six bedrooms in good order, so we decided to do up a large bedroom on the second floor and install a shower in its small turret alcove. The panelled room had a four-poster bed. A narrow passage ran between the wall and the panelling and the floor was uneven, so the furniture stood at an angle. New curtains were hastily made for the bed and the chaise longue re-covered. Peter and I had slept there at different times and we thought it had a cosy atmosphere, but to others it could seem like a set for a horror movie.

The work was completed just before the great day. A cook was hired for the dinner, and I accomplished the most difficult task, which was to rake up spare men from different parts of the county. Peter kept in touch with several of the houses in England where the American ladies were staying on their royal progress north and he kept being informed that another one had dropped out. English country houses evidently could not give them the comfort to which they were accustomed and their dinner guests had not been sufficient compensation. When he rang up Sir Everard Radcliffe at Rudding Park in Yorkshire he was told that only two were going to make it to Scotland. 'You have not missed anything,' Sir Everard said abruptly. 'They have no idea how to behave and have not tipped the staff.'

Finally, two exhausted ladies arrived whose only wish was to have early night. I was relieved I did not have to put one of them in our 'atmospheric' bedroom as I could tell at once it was not their style. I cosseted them with extra electric heaters and hot-water bottles, and after a pleasant but low-key dinner I escorted them to their rooms, leaving our gentlemen guests with Peter to be rewarded with some port. In due course we received the full payment for the whole group.

Not long afterwards we were approached by an agency that was looking for venues for overnight visits in special houses. Having cut our teeth on paying guests, we decided to put ourselves on their books. We were to have one or two couples at a time and to act as if they were our personal friends. Money was never to be mentioned. The agency would forward a cheque after their visit. They would expect a dinner party and hospitality guidelines were laid down – two drinks before dinner, wine with the meal and a drink afterwards. We were also told of a couple's particular interests. The agent came and stayed a night to vet the premises and told us in a pompous way that 'most people do this sort of thing to keep their staff occupied'. It was patently obvious that this was not the reason in our case.

If there was no one else who could do it, I cooked as much as I could beforehand but always needed someone to be in the kitchen. One day, in desperation, I persuaded the new keeper's wife to help. She was very nervous and said she could not cook. I took no notice and bought a crown of lamb. 'It will just need half an hour in the oven,' I told her, neglecting to say that it should be a very hot oven and our stove took a long time to heat up. The lamb appeared, looking completely raw. I looked at it in horror, wondering whether to serve it or not, when a French friend saved the day by saying, 'It's wunderfool to see lamb properly cooked.'

The couples who came to stay were all American but, nice as they were, after a busy day it could be very tiring entertaining strangers, 'ships that pass in the night,' as a friend described them. The friends whom we asked to dinner to meet them sometimes found it hard work and joked that they should get a cut of the proceeds.

We once had a couple whose main interest was said to be 'conversation', so we prepared ourselves for a lively evening and invited suitable guests. To my surprise, the pleasant middle-aged American who arrived sat quietly at dinner, listening to the talk going on around him and seldom joining in. After the other guests had left and we were having a final drink before going to bed, the husband told us that it had been a very enjoyable evening but he guessed that we must have been as misled as his previous hosts. Their interest was 'conservation' not 'conversation'. 'I am the original strong, silent American,' he apologised.

Most couples came for one night only but occasionally stayed on for a second day. We did not have to give a dinner party on the second night. After a long evening, when we were dying to go to bed, one couple started to discuss where they should go the next day. Should they look at the Borders or should they go to the Trossachs. Peter got out the map and began pointing to the Highlands. 'But that looks a long way. We don't want to get back late,' they protested. 'Oh, don't worry about that,' Peter insisted with feeling. 'It doesn't matter how late you are.'

Gifts and Antiques

~

By the mid to late seventies all seemed to be going well. The house had achieved a reputation as one of the important houses in Scotland. Visitor numbers had risen steadily every year. The two tills that had been installed in the gift shop rang incessantly and Peter was dispatching beer in small quantities all over the world. But the overdraft was also on the increase.

Catherine was enjoying Peebles High School, which had become a comprehensive. It was an improvement on the old system in which only those who had passed an exam at the age of eleven could go to it and the rest stayed in Innerleithen. I had been torn between my democratic ideals and a wish not to upset our relatives. I had always thought private education was the most divisive element in our society but should you make your children fit in with your own beliefs? We were both in total agreement about not sending her to a boarding school. Nearly all our friends and relatives sent their children to private schools and would not consider allowing their child to have a state education. In fact, some parents were making huge sacrifices to pay the fees.

Bowing weakly to outside pressure we decided to send her to St George's, a highly-thought-of Edinburgh school for girls. Although there was the choice of a Catholic school run by nuns, I had not got over my dislike of convents and was not convinced that segregating children from different religions was a good idea. I borrowed some money from my father's trust in order to buy a small flat so that Catherine and I could stay in Edinburgh during the week and Peter would come up when he could.

I soon realised that we had not made a good decision. We both disliked living in Edinburgh and I travelled down to Traquair most days. St George's was not the right school for Catherine, who seemed to live in perpetual terror of her class mistress. I realised how like my mother I had become when I found myself protesting at having to buy, as part of the uniform, an expensive overcoat that was to be worn only during the summer term. After a year we gave Catherine the choice of staying on at St George's or going to Peebles High School, and she chose Peebles.

She was much happier at a local school where she already had friends. Every morning she mucked our her pony while listening to Terry Wogan on the radio and then bicycled up to the top of the avenue to catch the school bus that took her to Peebles.

She joined the Pony Club, and in the holidays I took her to rallies where I often sat in the car with the heater on while robust Scottish mothers sat outside in all weathers. When it was time to get the pony back into the trailer, I dreaded being watched by these experienced Pony Club women. [Peter told me that if he went to collect her he had no trouble as it was all done for him.] Lilly Cockburn, a horsewoman whose husband worked as a shepherd on one of the farms, took Catherine in hand and gave her lessons, which inevitably led to going to shows. Many Saturdays were spent travelling around the countryside with the pony in a trailer hitched on behind, trying to find the remote locations where the smaller shows were held. The smaller the better as far as Catherine was concerned as there would be more chance of winning a rosette. My one dread was losing the way as, like Nanny's niece, I found it hard to turn. Once when I ended up in a cul-de-sac we had to detach the trailer from the car and turn it manually.

Peter's young cousin Felicity was now at the Slade School of Art and often invited fellow art students to stay. An amusing young man named Jeremy appeared, a rotund figure with a shaved head who clad himself in a white silk robe when he went out. He was a treasured guest as he enjoyed cooking and sewing. One day we combined taking him to an art exhibition with first dropping off Catherine, dressed in jodhpurs and hairnet, at a rally. She pleaded with me to make sure that Jeremy did not get out of the car.

Catherine progressed to larger shows and finally qualified for the Highland Show, held at Ingliston, outside Edinburgh. Her pony was a gelding that had been cut late and how he performed on the day depended on how he was feeling. That was not one of his days. It felt like a triumph, however, when he was moved up from the bottom of the line to change places with the pony that had beaten him most of the summer.

Looking after a pony taught Catherine more self-discipline than any boarding school. While her bedroom was often in chaos, the stable was always immaculate, and she would get up at five to get Gamester, her pony, groomed and plaited for a show. She learnt to accept failure and to keep persevering, a quality that she inherited from Peter.

The rest of the holidays she helped in the shop or tearoom or, as I was horrified to discover when she was only ten, secretly give riding lessons to visiting children with her friend Katy. She could always find school friends to help. Packing fudge into cartons was a popular job. It was amazing how many blocks were reported broken and unfit to sell. Our Davies cousins came to stay most summers. Marny, aged fourteen, was soon able to take individual visitors who came out of hours around the house. When we were trying to create an atmosphere for an American group, her elder brother, Ben, played the harpsichord in the drawing room while Simon played the harmonium in the chapel. Most summers we managed to sneak off in turn for a few days to stay with them in their beautiful villa above Cannes.

With a grant from the Scottish Tourist Board, we had moved the tearoom into our old cottage in the walled garden. It was now self-sufficient, and it was a great relief not to be told in the middle of the afternoon that more scones were needed or find at the end of the day that all the milk in our fridge had disappeared. It was doing better but still not making a profit. No one could believe that it was not a paying business until they tried to run it, and we had plenty of requests to take it over. They tried self-service and waitress service. On a wet day there was still not enough room inside. We longed to enlarge it but, like so many potential improvements, we simply could not afford to do so.

The main problem was not knowing how many to cater for on any particular day. Coaches were asked to book in advance but would often turn up unexpectedly, sometimes disgorging forty or so foreigners at lunch time who could not speak a word of English and had only foreign money. We had been able to make French windows that opened on to the old walled garden and we had seats and tables outside. One of my greatest delights has always been to eat out of doors and I liked seeing people eating their lunch or tea, sitting on the terrace or under the old apple trees.

I still did all the buying for the gift shop. I tried to get as much as I could reproduced from papers and articles in the house. We had old recipes and cures printed on cards. 'Cure for the bite of a mad dog. Take a table spoonful of common salt, add as much water as will make it damp, apply it like a poultice every six hours and it will be sure to stop the hydrophobia.' How to prevent contagion: 'A piece of sulphur rolled up in cotton, and constantly worn about the person is said to be an effectual preventative of every kind of contagion; care must be taken to renew the sulphur from time to time.' An interesting prescription for the fourth earl gave the following instructions: 'Every morning his lordship at getting out of bed, the earlier the better, should take two teaspoonfuls of the bitter elixir in a drink of ale. Sometimes in place of it my Lord may take his ordinary bitter brandy but the elixir is better because it keeps the belly open. After breakfast my Lord should get into his coach or much rather on horseback and continue travelling till dinner.' It finished: 'If my Lord can be persuaded to drink wine and water it should be much better for him than malt liquor of which he certainly drinks too much. What wines he takes should be of the strongest kinds such as sherry white Lisbon or Madera, but always dashed with water.' Jean Hateley, the retired nurse who had looked after Catherine when she was a baby and was now a guide, used to ask the visitors to try to guess what he had been suffering from.

I also arranged with the Royal School of Needlework to reproduce some of the old needlework designs and make them into packs for people to work themselves. I had The Gardener's Monthly Directions from a seventeenth-century *Art of Gardening* book reproduced. It was a change from the prosaic prose of modern gardening books and waxed lyrical at the start of every month. April begins: 'In this month your garden appears in its greatest beauty, the blossoms of the fruit trees prognosticate the plenty of fruits for all the succeeding summer months unless prevented by untimely frost or blights. The Bees now buzz in every corner of your garden while the sweet nightingale tunes her warbling notes in your solitary walks.'

I started to make potpourri. It was not so widely sold in those days and I dried the rose petals in the linen cupboard and bought a specially blended essence, a neroli oil substitute from a professional scent maker. It is the base of eau de cologne and has universal appeal. I sold it in cellophane bags with a special label in the gift shop. If sales were down at all I merely sprayed a little extra neroli into the bowls of potpourri in the house and I would always be told that sales had gone up that day. I received orders and telephone calls from overseas. I gathered our own petals and friends brought me theirs but as demand increased I soon had to buy in ready-dried imported petals. After a while potpourri was sold in every gift shop in Scotland so I decided to bottle up the essence with instructions on how to make your own.

Now that I had an efficient manager who had retired from running her own shop in Peebles, I had to work in the gift shop only in an emergency. I had always regretted not having a shop window to decorate and not being open for the Christmas market, so when I saw a tiny bow-fronted shop for sale on Peebles High Street, I decided to buy it. Peebles is a busy holiday town. We could sell our own label products and our ale there, and it would be a good advertisement for the house.

The fudge boxes were suddenly causing us a problem. We had started to have the fudge made and packed in Orkney. Our newly designed boxes, decorated with the Traquair coat of arms, were sent there for filling. In Scotland, coats of arms and all such matters are dealt with by the Lord Lyon and his Court. When Peter and I were living in London, his father sent us a tape recording of an interview with the late Lord Lyon talking about the origins of Traquair. He had a wavering, high-pitched voice and that, together with his title, conjured up images of a strange beast.

A member of the Lyon Court, on holiday in Orkney, visited the fudge factory where he caught sight of one of our boxes. He noticed that the coat of arms related specifically to the earls of Traquair. It had supports to which apparently only an earl is entitled. The title was granted by Charles I, who took great care to make sure that his lords remained loyal by ensuring that titles he gave could not pass to less friendly branches of a family. They could only be passed to a son, so with the death of the eighth earl of Traquair, the title died out and with it the coat of arms, which Peter was not eligible to display. In fact, the Lyon Court had powers to fine him for so doing. This led to Peter being obliged to have his arms redrawn and registered, a huge expense and not one that gift shops selling fudge usually have to bear.

Obtaining a licence to sell the ale in our Peebles shop was not as easy as we had expected. Protests were lodged by other off-licences and the police, and we obtained it only the third time round. But for a few years our shop was the only gift shop in the High Street and business boomed. It was an awkward shape, deep and narrow, and when it filled up with school kids, it was difficult to prevent petty shoplifting or 'buying without paying' as I had heard a social worker describe it. But I had Betty, a pretty, professional woman who belonged to Peebles, to run it, and she kept a wary eye in spite of little help from the public. 'I was disgusted last time I came in to see a woman slipping things into her bag,' one of the customers told her, having said nothing at the time.

I found, as I had hoped, that the takings on the days before Christmas were the largest ever. But we had to balance the good days with those that followed. There were public holidays when the shop was closed, and after people had spent their Christmas-present money, business for the next two months was dead. There were occasional red-letter days, such as when the Scotland-Wales rugby match took place at Murrayfield. Peebles was flooded with Welshmen who got no nearer to the match than the television sets in the local pubs. Having had a good time away and wanting an equally good reception when they returned home, they rushed into the shop to buy presents.

We had now moved the antique shop at Traquair from the cottage into three pretty, intercommunicating rooms on the top floor of the house. These rooms had been left empty since they were used by Peter's great-uncle Charlie for his hobby of cutting precious stones, mainly sapphires, which he collected from all over the world. He had become such an expert that a well-known Bond Street jeweller asked him to work for them, but the idea of having anything to do with trade was sharply dismissed. He enjoyed designing and giving small pieces of jewellery to his friends. My own grandmother, Clare, received a beautiful brooch in the shape of a 'C' as a wedding present. After his death, his brothers were so embarrassed by his collection that, according to Dolly, they waited till the London season was over and everyone was out of town before quietly putting it into a saleroom where it drew as little notice as possible.

Having the antique shop inside the house meant that visitors had to buy a ticket to get into the shop. Fortunately, it made no difference to our sales and made the shop more secure. It also meant that we had a member of staff on the top floor. It did discourage me from buying large or heavy objects.

Above. Peter waiting to welcome a coach-load of tourists. We tried to encourage regular coaches to visit but as we were not on a main tourist route we did not get as many as we wanted.

Below. Traquair Fair, which I started as a small craft fair in 1979, is now two spectacular days of enjoyment for children and adults of all ages. Theatre of every kind, dance of every nationality, music and crafts all come together and fill the grounds on the first weekend of August.

Thank you for fertilizing the garden ~ you will be remembered with flowers.

Top. Music in the old walled garden at the Fair. Food stalls and a special Fair Ale are also on sale to add to the enjoyment.

Above left. Lady Christobel and butler. She acts the Lady Bountiful with her butler Scrotum. They are regular favourites.

Above right. Notice for lavatories at the Fair. Providing enough lavatories was always a problem at the Fair. Felicity designed green loos and Nicholas wrote this notice for them.

Above. Ferris wheel at the Fair. Every year there are different amusements.

All the staff at Traquair, including me and Catherine. After Peter died, we made every effort to keep Traquair a lively, happy place and had huge support from everyone who worked there. We used this photograph as a poster.

Above. The High Drawing Room. This room, in the sixteenth-century part of the house, spans its width and has windows on both sides.

Below. The King's Room. On the first floor of the original twelfth-century Peel Tower, it was used by Mary Queen of Scots when she came as a guest to hunt.

Above. The Library was created by the fourth and fifth Earls of Traquair between 1700 and 1740.

Below. The Dining Room is situated in one of the seventeenth-century 'modern wings' which were the last addition to the house.

Left. Mandi Mackenzie, our resourceful book-keeper, with llamas standing sentinel outside the front door. She had invited the llamas to Sheep and Wool Day.

Below. The event is devoted to sheep and wool with shearing, carding, spinning, weaving and sheepdog demonstrations.

Catherine and John Grey. I was overjoyed when they got engaged. John was a design consultant who latterly worked for *Media Natura*, an environmental charity. Our friend Brodrick Haldane took this photograph of them as guests at another wedding.

Left. Taking a breather during the Fair. Catherine with Isabella, aged one, and Rob. These are the busiest days of the year for him, and an anxious time for Catherine.

Below. Christmas lunch. From left: Felicity, Michael, Nicholas, Peter, Sylvia, Joseph, Kirsty and Catherine. We always had our Christmas lunch in the main dining-room.

Above left. Peter's Australian cousins, Ruth and Wayne Manley. In 1993 I spent a very happy month visiting the family in Australia after Peter died. We drove up from Sydney to New South Wales and I went on to Brisbane and stayed on Brampton Island.

Above right. Maeve in our sleeper on the Trans-Siberian Express. We started in Moscow and ended up in Beijing. From there we travelled across China in the far less luxurious Chinese trains where the lavatories often leaked down the corridors.

Left. Francis Vallat, married to a cousin of Peter's, making friends with Pearl, my Vietnamese pig.

My brother Nicholas. He was very close to me and here he is after meeting Anya, looking happier than he had ever been.

Above. Camping in the Ante-Atlas with Nicholas. We slept in double tents and the Moroccans set up a large one for food. They chose the sites, which had to be near water.

Below. Our camping group. On our route, we were able to visit small villages impossible to reach by road.

Right. Kristoffer and his mother Brit. Nicholas's son was brought up in Denmark by his mother but visited Nicholas most holidays and often came up to Traquair. Nicholas asked me to take his place at Kristoffer's confirmation, pictured here, as he was unable to go. He had not realised what an important occasion it is in Denmark.

Below. Nicholas's burial in spring 1995. He was killed in a car crash in South Africa, where he had gone for a few days to research a book. His close friend Nicholas Albery, who had started the Natural Death Centre, arranged his very moving 'green' funeral.

Above. Catherine's wedding to Mark Muller in 1999. Her first husband John had died two years earlier. It was the best news I could have had when Catherine, who had known Mark since her LSE days, told me they planned to marry. It seemed that everything was falling into place.

Below. With Robin Crichton after filming the Meskwakie Indians in America. After eight years on my own I met up with Robin, whose wife had recently died. He was a film maker and invited me to go to this Indian settlement for a month to make a follow-up documentary about this small, private tribe. We fell in love and married quietly at Traquair a few months after Catherine and Mark.

Above. Family group. Catherine, Mark, Isabella Stuart Grey (standing in the centre), Louis and Charlotte Muller Stuart.

Bottom. After our marriage, with our grandchildren. Robin is holding Natalie and Keiron and I am holding Isabella.

When I rashly bought a load of books at an auction, Peter hitched up a large basket on a rope and lowered it out of the window. I filled the basket at the bottom and he hauled them up.

Although a friend had helped with some of the buying and my mother still occasionally appeared with a box full of bric-a-brac, I gradually found that it was easier to do it myself. I knew what had been sold and what was needed. Every season there seemed to be a new trend in customers' taste. I got to know several dealers who gave me good prices, and I went off to auctions and antique fairs. I combined short visits to friends with buying trips. Like most dealers, I always felt that the grass was greener in another area. It also put a stop to the occasional visitor who would say, 'I saw her buying that for so much and look at the price she is charging.'

I was always afraid of having too much money tied up in stock. I bought carefully at the start of the season, but usually by August I would get an urgent SOS that much more was needed. Customers always bought more when the shop was full. I was also lucky enough to have the perfect sales person. Mrs Grey was an attractive older woman who had never been a saleslady in her life but took to the art like a duck to water. She loved most of the objects in the shop and also loved people, so putting the two together came easily to her. The customers were charmed by her and trusted her implicitly.

It always interested me that visitors in the gift shop would look at an article, decide if they liked it, ask the price and make up their mind to buy it without needing reassurance. The antique shop was different. There they were obsessed with getting good value. 'How old is it?' 'Is it perfect?' were the standard inquiries. An old antique dealer I knew with a handsome, lined face was so sick of being asked this question that he would answer, 'Look at me. I am old but I am not perfect.'

The more you handle antiques the more you get a feel for them. It is not a difficult trade to learn. When our local auction mart started to hold sales of furniture as well as livestock, the

porter who had been selling cattle and sheep soon acquired a
feel for an interesting or valuable object. When they made a
house clearance he was adept at dropping a 'good yin' into a box
of old junk he wanted to get rid of.

We tried to make it clear that we were not selling bits and
pieces from the house but people seemed determined to
believe that we were. It is impossible to know the exact date or
history of a lot of bric-a-brac, but Mrs Grey soon discovered
that she could talk her way round any query, and her charm
and sincerity gave the buyer confidence. When another woman
who had tried working there left because she felt she did not
have enough knowledge to answer questions, Mrs Grey
exclaimed, 'Surely she could have invented a wee storie.'

One day two Dutch ladies, with little English, came into
the shop and started to point to a 1940s' sampler that had been
mass-produced by a women's magazine to celebrate the
Queen's wedding. This one had been stitched and framed. The
two women pointed at it and talked to each other excitedly.
'Your queen?' they asked, and Mrs Grey nodded. After further
discussion, one of the woman indicated that she wanted to buy
it. As she left the room clasping her parcel, she turned to Mrs
Grey and said triumphantly, '*Our* queen, *she* never sell
anything.'

Clocks, whether they were working or not, always seemed
to attract men. They were a good bait to get them into the shop
as husbands were inclined to stand outside and tell their wives
to hurry up. One day a German reluctantly followed his wife
in and started to examine a clock, nearly taking it to pieces. He
finally made up his mind to buy it while making it plain that
he thought the price was too high. A few weeks later Mrs Grey
got a postcard from Germany. 'It is good,' it read, 'send more
clocks.'

The Jacobite Cause

◡

Felicity, who had taken her degree at the Slade School of Art, had been travelling round Europe and had ended up in Paris where she became fascinated by a bookshop near the Ile de la Cité run by an eccentric elderly American named George Whitman. He had opened his bookshop when he came to Paris as an ex-GI after the war. After the death of Sylvia Beech, the American poet, he tool on her mantle and called his bookshop after hers, *Shakespeare and Company*. George had philanthropic ideals and besides letting the shop become a meeting place for writers and artists, he allowed backpackers to bed down for the night among the books in return for an hour's work in the shop the next day. He had made it into an attractive, inviting place, 'the sort of bookshop that Americans expect to find in Paris but never do,' he told me.

George, who did not believe in comfort, lived in a cramped space above the shop and before long Felicity had moved in with him. George dispensed iced tea, home-made chocolate brownies and a bread pudding made from bread saved from waste bins. He had acquired a huge Alsatian that was fed on scraps from the local restaurants collected by Felicity each evening. When I visited them I slept on a sofa while he gnawed on the bones all night and I wondered whether when he had finished them he would start on me.

Felicity still came to see us regularly and on one visit told me that she was pregnant. I went over to see the golden-haired baby whom they called Sylvia. When she and George decided to get married, Felicity's father, David, her sister, Leonora, Peter, Catherine and I all went over for the wedding bearing a cake I had made. We followed Felicity, looking picturesque in a long green dress, with Sylvia in a pushchair before her, through the streets of Paris to the *Mairie*. George went separately on his motorbike. The Mayor read out the formalities and finished with an evil smile at George, then in his seventies, that they should return in twenty-five years' time for a special silver wedding ceremony. As time went on, Felicity found it impossible to bring up a child in the bookshop and after a few years she took Sylvia to live in Norfolk. Most summers they came to visit us.

By the early eighties we had an excellent staff and a band of experienced guides who had been with us for several years. They were interested in the house and able to pass their knowledge and enthusiasm on to visitors. Two of the guides, Frances Waldie and Winifred Vallance, have been guiding for over twenty years and even return voluntarily during the winter to treat the bindings of the books in the two libraries and make new catalogues. The last catalogue was handwritten in the eighteenth century and was listed shelf by shelf.

They are good at picking out books or items that amuse the public. The huge bound volumes of old newspapers make interesting reading. The advertisements give a good picture of the life of the times. The following from the *Star* of 1792 is a favourite: 'A buxom widow of Ramsgate turned of 40 of an irreproachable character, and who has decent competency, wishes to end her days in the arms of a single gentleman (if an Irishman the more agreeable) of a fortune superior to her own who may prove a parent to her three fatherless daughters, and a loving serviceable husband to herself. To prevent all impertinent enquiries, the Lady's constant and decided preference for the marriage state has caused this abrupt mode of application. NB None but persons whose characters will bear the strictest examination need apply.'

I still worked in the gift shop if someone was ill. I also

enjoyed an occasional half day in the ticket box, particularly before a telephone extension was installed. It was the most peaceful place to be. I would watch the cars approaching, huge expensive ones gliding in with condescending drivers asking for tickets and the smaller, jollier ones crowded with children. 'Tickets for two adults and one child please, the other is under five,' a driver declared one day (we did not charge for under-fives). 'I'm not *five*, I'm *six*,' came an indignant voice from the back.

The visitors were at ease sitting in their cars. It was as though they had brought their houses with them. When you met them wandering around later they often seemed more nervous. Some sophisticated picnics took place in the picnic area. Peter maintained that the best way to find out what sort of day it had been was to look in the refuse bins. Sometimes there were champagne bottles.

I still had to do the flowers, an oddly time-consuming job. Traquair was a house that needed fresh flowers to make it look cared for and lived in. We had several displays by Floral Art Clubs which were extremely popular. They spent hundreds of pounds on the flowers and did their arrangements as they were taught. I could hear the ladies asking each other 'Have you got your horizontals in yet?' Arranging flowers, like decorating your house or planting your garden, has been turned into a complicated art. When one club left stones, shells and pieces of fabric by their arrangements, Peter could not bear it. He went round the house after they had gone, collected all their artistic bits and pieces and when they arrived the next day asked innocently if they had lost anything.

Catherine had blossomed at Peebles High School. She had gone on to take A levels at a tutorial college in Edinburgh so that she could go to an English University. We thought it would be good for her to get away from Traquair for a time, and I was delighted when she took up my suggestion of applying to the London School of Economics, with which my father was so strongly connected. Once she had got a place she worked at various jobs both at home and in London and was then determined to go to India. We were naturally both anxious at the thought of her going away so far on her own, and we eventually managed to find her a voluntary job in the Cheshire Ryder Home in Dar es Salaam. I saw her off in January at Heathrow, with spiked peroxide hair, baggy cotton trousers, heavy leather boots, straw hat and a huge knapsack on her back. As we went up an escalator, we caught sight of the immaculately dressed buyer from Harrod's lingerie department, where Catherine had worked at Christmas, pointing her out to a friend.

I missed her at home and devoured her letters when they came. They were designed to soothe her parents and we learnt the true version only when she returned. After working in Dar es Salaam, she took off with a friend to travel around India. This she loved but she had to survive some awkward incidents. Peter could not share her enthusiasm for the country where he had spent an unhappy time during the war, suffering from malaria and dysentery. When she finally came home with a pierced nose and proudly produced a squashed box of Indian sweets from her knapsack for us, he took one look at them and said, 'When I was there they were always covered in flies.' 'They still are,' she answered cheerfully.

When Catherine departed for London University I began to be attracted by the Open University, which had recently been started. I would be able to work at home except for the one week when students had to attend a summer school. Course literature was sent through the post, a tutor was appointed and we could attend a monthly tutorial. There was also a weekly radio talk and a television programme. There were twelve essays to write and an exam to sit each year which gained a credit. Six credits were needed to gain a degree. I studied humanities, the Age of Enlightenment and the twentieth-century novel, which I enjoyed but always wished I had more time. My essays were only ever finished the day before the deadline, and I often had to rush down to Innerleithen to get them off by the last possible post.

I chose York University for my summer schools. It is an

attractive modern campus with shallow pools incorporated into the concrete. Ducks waddled all over the place. Good food was served in the canteen and for us older students it was a joy to be away from our distracting, ordinary lives and to be able to concentrate on our work. For most of the women, it was also a luxury to have ready-cooked meals for a week. Amusing telephone conversations could be overheard on the public telephones – wives talking to abandoned husbands instructing them how to make strawberry jam or how to entertain their kids. Not surprisingly, many affairs took place. Suddenly, husbands or wives found themselves on their own, sharing common interests with members of the opposite sex and plenty of opportunity to explore these friendships further. After three years and having gained half a degree, I decided I had done enough. I wrote a piece for *The Scotsman* on the joy of giving up the Open University – no more staying up half the night to finish an assignment or trying to keep awake while watching a television programme. Neither did I have to go away at the peak of the tourist season. But it had taught me to concentrate and to study a subject. It also encouraged me to act as a guide at Traquair.

I had learnt no Scottish history and felt out of my depth as the house's own history spanned nine hundred years. But now I read as much as I could, and after listening to Peter taking groups of visitors around, I felt able to do it. Peter had an easy manner with visitors and knew how to entertain them. He often started by saying, with a smile, 'I will first tell you why you are not listening to a belted earl,' which made them laugh and led into the family history. He was patient with people and never made them feel foolish, even when they asked which sport the chalices on display in the Priest's room had been won for, or if they picked out the one modern article in a room and asked how old it was.

I soon realised that most of the visitors were more interested in the upkeep of the house, and any detail about 'the family', past or present, went down well. I learnt to sum up a group early so that I had an idea what aspect would interest them most and how much history they could take. I also learnt to keep a distance from them. If you responded, even with a few words, to a chatty person in the group, she (it was nearly always a she) would try to keep up a dialogue all the way round. Early on I had a homesick American lady who kept close by me all the way, telling me about her house and family back home. There would often be a know-all in a group who would try to give her own commentary as you went around and had to be kept quiet tactfully. Knowledgeable people never gave instant judgements.

Primary school children were a joy. They were lively and interested in everything. They had usually been told about the secret stairs and could not wait till we reached them. Fortunately, they were the last item on the tour. When we reached the Priest's Room I would explain that during the Penal times Mass had been said there in secret. I would show them a cupboard where the altar had been and the old white vestments that could be disguised as household linen if the house was ever searched. I would then pull back the door of another cupboard where the bottom shelves had been removed and push the false back to reveal the old stairs, and the children, screaming with joy, would make their way down the three flights to the ground floor.

Taking older children around could be a less enjoyable experience, especially if their teachers had not prepared them properly. Some teachers would take themselves off to the tearoom and leave the children to us. The kids would stand with their hands in their pockets, looking bored. It was obviously not cool to show any interest.

For several years we had regular tours of French school children. Although we had one group who stripped the shop and anything in the house they could lay their hands on (all safely returned by the warden of the hostel where they were staying), they were generally more interested and could make useful comments. The bed in the King's Room, which Mary Queen of Scots is supposed to have slept in, appears to be too short for her height. A French boy explained that in the sixteenth century people did not like to lie flat in a bed as this was thought to be the position of death. They always liked to prop themselves up. I was reminded of an eccentric relative who had insisted on sleeping in a chair at night as she maintained that people only died in bed. 'It's not that I mind dying,' she said, 'it's just that I don't like changes.'

The only people who could get my back up were the ones who thought they were special and should have a private tour or who would come when the house was normally closed. I was plagued one winter by a woman who took individual connoisseurs around Scotland in a chauffeur-driven limousine and liked to pretend that she knew all the owners personally. I told her that there was no heating – it was usually colder inside the house than out – and that most of the interesting things had been put away. She finally got a mutual friend to plead with me, so I weakly gave in. She arrived with an American couple, the husband dressed in a thin suit and the wife wearing an unlined raincoat. I started my tour, taking them into the Still Room and on to the cellars without receiving a word. When we arrived in the drawing room they stood there silent and shivering. 'Is there anything special that you are interested in?' I finally asked, my breath clearly visible in the air. 'Do you really *live* here?' was the wife's reply. 'Yes I do,' I snapped, 'but I am sure it's too cold for you. I know what I'll do. I'll give you a guidebook and you can read it when you get back to your hotel.' I swept them out of the room, thrust a book into their hands and led them to the front door.

It was when I began to go through the papers in the archives with Peter that I really began to take an interest in the history of the house and those who had lived in it before us. I read family letters and could see the people who had written them in their portraits so I began to feel that I knew them. Their priorities were not very different from ours today – nearly every letter referred to money and health.

Since the time of the first earl, who was Lord Treasurer of Scotland, their religion has barred the Stuarts of Traquair from holding public office. After the Union of 1707 their neighbours of equal birth ran hot-foot to London to gain lucrative posts, but as Catholic landowners the Stuarts could survive only by keeping a low profile. Their main hope was to champion the Jacobite cause. Wealth was brought into the family by the acquisition of a rich wife. Until the time of the last earl, who did not marry, each laird had pursued this course. When the Jacobite fifth earl heard of a marriageable English heiress, Theresa Conyers, he decided that it was more important to woo and marry her than to take an active part in the 1745 rebellion. The estate started to suffer financially when the last earl and the Maxwell Stuart great-uncles remained bachelors.

The wives were forceful women and the main correspondents. 'My lazy lord will not make a scrape of the pen,' one complained. The widow of the second earl withstood the power of the Kirk after her husband's death, refusing to let her son be taken away to be educated as a Presbyterian. Mary Ravenscroft, the seventh earl's wife, was adamant that her interfering father-in-law should leave Traquair and take his daughters with him before she would agree to move in.

I read all I could about the Jacobite period. I learnt that the word 'Jacobite' means a supporter of James II. I was soon convinced that the so-called Glorious Revolution of 1688–89, when William and Mary were brought to the throne, had in fact been the dethronement of a rightful king. His son, James Edward, and his grandson, Charles Edward (Bonnie Prince Charlie) were the lawful heirs. I was shocked that Jacobite history is not taken more seriously. Too much romantic fiction has been woven into it – Hanoverian propaganda has done a good job.

The reality of supporting the losing side was brought home to me by a letter from Catherine Stuart, a daughter of the fourth earl who was living in Dumfriesshire when Prince Charles Edward made his attempt to gain the crown. At the best of times it was an anti-Jacobite part of the country but then it was in uproar. She wrote to her mother in desperation: 'I wish to God I were so happie as to be with you and to be

more plain I do not think myself quite safe in staying here . . .
I beg with greatest earnestness you'll send for me for if I was to
stay much longer I'm sure I would lose my health and I believe
break my heart.'

I was particularly impressed by the letters from Winifred
Nithsdale (née Herbert), wife of the fifth Earl of Nithsdale, to
her sister-in-law, Mary Traquair. Winifred had left her small
daughter at Traquair while she journeyed to London by coach
and horseback in the midst of a hard winter. Her husband had
been taken prisoner after the 1715 Jacobite rebellion and was
awaiting execution in the Tower of London. She was determined to rescue him and managed to engineer his escape by
disguising him as a woman. It was a remarkable story of loyalty
and bravery, and I thought it would be a good subject for a
book.

Research became a fascinating part-time occupation.
Peter and I visited most of the places where Winifred had
lived. She was brought up in Powis Castle, a magnificent castle
in Wales now famous for its terraced garden, and then went
into exile in France with James II's court at Louis XIV's former
palace of St Germain-en-Laye. On her marriage to William
Nithsdale, she went to live in his castle, Terregles, in Scotland.
Having saved her husband from execution, she accompanied
him into exile, this time to the Jacobite court in Rome where
she spent the rest of her life.

As I became interested in the Stuart cause, I wanted to
know who the present Stuart claimant was and to find out
more about him. I had been told on good authority that it was
Prince Albrecht of Bavaria, but as he was then in his eighties,
his son, Prince Franz, had taken on the role. He lived in the
Nymphenburg Palace in Munich but kept a low profile and I
had never read anything about him. I wrote to ask Prince
Franz if it would be possible to have an interview with him,
which I might submit to a newspaper. After several letters and
telephone calls I was asked to sign an agreement that I would
submit any article to his office before it was published and an
appointment was duly made to meet him. I had sold nearly

every piece I had written and was confident that this one would be of interest.

Peter had been wanting to go to Munich to meet some brewers, so we decided to go together and make it a brief holiday. On our arrival I was taken out to lunch by the Prince's private secretary. He answered my questions politely. He told me that the Prince acknowledged his claim to the British throne but was not at all keen to become a catalyst for Jacobite sympathisers. I was then taken to the palace and left in an ante-chamber with the Prince's personal secretary, a German lady who, it turned out, had been at one of my old schools, St Mary's Convent, Ascot. She was much more forthcoming about the Prince's claim to the British throne and quickly whipped out a copy of his family tree to show how it had come about. As Prince Charles Edward had no legitimate children, the line ran from Charles I's sister, Elizabeth, who had married Philip Duke of Orleans. Following a complicated route, it was through Queen Marie Thérèse, née Archduchess of Austria-Este, the wife of the Bavarian King Ludwig III, that the Stuart claim came into the family.

The secretary lamented the fact that Prince Franz was not married and that his heir was his first cousin, Prince Luitpold, who lived in Kaltenberg Castle outside the city and had his own Kaltenberg Brewery. His beer had been promoted in England, and I remembered seeing a poster in the London Underground in which he was featured drinking ale in his castle cellar surrounded by busty barmaids. 'Is he married?' I asked. 'Oh yes,' she answered. 'No children then?' 'They have two.' 'Surely that's all right then?' She shook her head. 'His wife is a commoner,' she moaned, 'and that will not do.'

When I was finally taken in to see the Prince, he was sitting on a small sofa in his study. He asked me to sit down. He was a good-looking man in his fifties and talked pleasantly and openly while keeping a dignified presence. He was more interested in talking about the role he plays in Bavaria than discussing the subject of the Stuart claimancy.

He was proud of the fact that his family, the Wittelsbachs,

were asked to stay on in 1918 after Bavaria became a republic. In fact, the new socialist republic never asked for a formal resignation. Together, the family and the state worked out a plan for the future of their vast estates and art collections. Two Wittelsbach foundations were set up, leaving the family a certain amount of control. Other properties were given outright to the state and others still remain in the hands of the family.

'I have offices here in the Nymphenburg Palace,' he told me, 'and I am addressed as Your Royal Highness and am invited along with the Mayor to official functions.' 'Do you have any political influence?' I asked. 'With the growth of extremism my family are of prime importance. We are always neutral. We get to know the members of both political parties and are able to keep a balance between them.' 'How is this done?' 'When people are at their wits' end they will appeal to me and one telephone call can often defuse a situation.' It was evident that the Prince is a cultured man. He is an internationally acknowledged art connoisseur and serves on many art commissions. He is building up a contemporary art collection and is encouraging other Bavarians to do the same.

When I finally brought up the subject of the Stuart claimancy, he was cautious. 'It is a tradition that deserves respect,' he said, 'but I leave the proof of the validity to the historians.' He admitted that it involved him in a large correspondence with Stuarts all over the world. Before I left I could not resist asking, 'How do you get on with our Queen?' 'We are on good terms and I visit her when I am in London,' he replied evenly.

While I was in the Nymphenburg, Peter had contacted Prince Luitpold, a lively and very friendly young man who greeted Peter as his cousin. He suggested that we should meet and follow him to his castle for supper. We followed him blindly in the dark as his sports car raced ahead at breakneck speed. At one time we found ourselves bumping along as we crossed a ploughed field. Finally we ended up in front of a huge building, the brewery, at the back of which stood his smaller castle. 'Just the opposite of us,' we told him. 'Our castle is bigger than our brewery.' He showed us around and took us back to meet his attractive young wife who gave us supper. He laughed about his royal lineage but told us that although he had been allowed to advertise his beer widely in England, he had not done so in Scotland in case his Stuart connection was discovered and he embarrassed Prince Franz.

During the meal Prince Luitpold told us an amusing story about a medieval monastic brewery that started to brew a special beer for Lent. It was actually stronger than their normal beer. 'Did the Church allow it?' I asked. 'The abbot was a bit worried when they first made it,' he answered, 'so they sent one of the monks off to Rome with a sample. He had to walk most of the way, and when he finally arrived, months later, it had completely gone off. The Pontiff had one mouthful and spat it out. "That will be perfect for Lent," he said, so they have been brewing it ever since.'

I was surprised to have the interview rejected by *The Scotsman*. They did not want anything to do with the Stuarts, I was told. Another paper told me the same thing. The article was finally published in the *Stuart Society Magazine*. Ten years later it was unearthed and I was approached by a popular newspaper to write about the Stuart claim. Perhaps this is a reflection on the changing attitude to the Hanoverian House of Windsor.

A Glasgow Writer

~

Peter and I received a large post every day from many diverse people. Occasionally we would get a letter that gave me a warm glow. I particularly remember one from a man who said he wanted to tell us that he had been feeling low and depressed while recovering from an operation. He had visited the house, sat in the chapel and walked in the grounds and come away with a renewed strength.

One Christmas we had a card inviting us to Holyrood Palace. It was signed 'Mary Queen of Scots' and scrawled underneath were the words: 'It will be quite informal – just roasting chestnuts on the fire.' I soon guessed who this was from. Before the local authority fulfilled the need, Father Dalrymple had started a house in Edinburgh for women who had found themselves homeless. It was run by a remarkable woman, Vivian Ethridge, who made the house of discordant women seem almost like her own home. I occasionally went to help in the kitchen and had met among the residents an aristocratic looking lady who behaved in a regal manner and was convinced she was the Queen. When she heard that Martin House, as it was called, was in need of funds, she went straight to the local branch of the Bank of Scotland and asked to see the bank manager. He was ordered to transfer ten thousand pounds (which she did not have) from her account to Martin House. She then returned and told Vivian with a reassuring smile that she did not need to worry any more.

Another letter I received came from Margaret Thomson

Davis in Glasgow. She enclosed her autobiography, *The Making of a Novelist*, and asked if she might come to Traquair to carry out research for the novel that she was currently writing, set in Edwardian times. Having little time for reading during the season and knowing that the Edwardian era was not relevant to Traquair, I left it unanswered for several months. When I did finally read her book, I was so impressed that I invited her to come over.

She replied that she had now finished that novel and was working on another. I suggested that perhaps she could get an idea for a book from reading some of the archives in the house. She is a small, pretty woman a little older than myself, and we took to each other at once. She was brought up in a tenement in Glasgow and had a difficult childhood. In spite of an unhappy marriage, she committed herself to writing, one book after another. She sent them off to publishers, starting at the top of the alphabet and proceeding to the bottom. Her books were continually rejected. She started again with the A's, and Allison and Busby wrote and offered her a contract. They also agreed to publish the six books that they had originally refused. At the last count, she has had twenty-eight books published.

We became great friends, and I began to visit Glasgow and learnt how different the Glaswegians are from the Edinburghers although the two cities are only forty miles apart. I found them more relaxed and easier to be with. With their kindness and hospitality goes a great sense of humour.

One day, when I had arranged to take Margaret to a bookshop where she was to give a reading, I left the house in a hurry and without my handbag. Worse still, I got completely lost in Glasgow and ended up in a cul-de-sac where the only sign of life was in a scrapyard where I saw a man lying under a car. I told him of my predicament and asked him if he knew where Niddrie Square was. He shook his head but got up slowly and said not to worry, he would find out. He led me into a shed with a telephone, wiped his hands on an old rag and rang a friend. In a few minutes he had the full instructions written down. I thanked him effusively and apologised that I could not even offer to pay for the call as I had forgotten my bag. As I was about to drive away, he leant through the car window and said in a concerned voice, 'Do you want a loan, hen?'

Before the iron curtain was lifted, Margaret had gone on holiday to the Black Sea. While she was there she met a member of the Writers' Union and generously offered to give hospitality to the Russian writer. The following year Violetta came to stay with Margaret. She was Lithuanian. Under Soviet rule, as she wrote poetry and plays for children, she was an officially approved writer and was allowed to travel abroad on speaking tours. Margaret brought her over to Traquair.

Several years later, after Lithuania regained its independence, Violetta invited Margaret, me and the cookery writer Catherine Brown to stay with her in Vilnius. She lived in an old block of flats that, under the old regime, had been allocated to approved writers who received preferential treatment. Now they were suffering as much as everyone else. They had electricity for only a few hours each day, the shops had little food in them and money was very short. One first-class restaurant was open, serving delicious meals, which to us, with sterling, seemed incredibly cheap but for Lithuanians was quite out of the question. When we took Violetta and a friend there for a meal, we were told that the bill was equal to a teacher's salary for a month. On the other hand, seats at the opera and ballet were cheap, and museums and galleries were in excellent condition.

It was my first experience of an ex-Communist country. The streets were always thronged with people. 'Of course they should all be at work,' Violetta told us, 'but they are taking time off.' We had been queuing in a post office for half an hour one day and had just reached the top when the woman at the counter told us abruptly that she was tired and was going off for a rest.

Margaret and I have formed a strong friendship over the years. I have seen her gain a well-deserved reputation as a writer and speaker. I admire the way she teaches and gives unstinting encouragement to all aspiring writers – even though she becomes snowed under with manuscripts while trying to write her own books. She gave me the impetus to carry on with my biography of Lady Nithsdale, and when I was feeling despondent she built up my motivation.

Past the Peak

~

By the mid-eighties the number of visitors to historic houses began to fall. It surprised us when our numbers, which had steadily increased each year, levelled off and then began to go down. It was blamed on many factors, most of all on the Scottish Tourist Board for lack of promotion and advertising and on the local tourist boards for their misguided priorities. Most of their budgets were spent on increasing staff to police new rules and regulations in the hope of improving standards. Those of us in tourism were all anxious to upgrade our facilities but needed the income from an increased number of visitors to enable us to do so. We wanted the STB to concentrate on aggressive marketing that would bring in more tourists and enable us to give visitors the facilities we knew they wanted. We knew that they did not want a country with so much variety in its culture and landscape to be beaten down into one featureless unity where every bedroom has to contain matching bedside lamps and tea trays.

The first to suffer inspections were the bed-and-breakfasts. If an owner's décor did not conform to the STB's collective taste, they were demoted. Wallpaper and fitted carpets were the rule long after polished wood floors and plain walls were the fashion. No one wants to stay in a dirty or run-down bed-and-breakfast or hotel, but the décor should surely be the owner's choice.

The irony is that, however much the STB spends on staff and inspections, there is no way that sub-standard hotels and bed-and-breakfasts can be eliminated. There is no law that compels bed-and-breakfasts and hotels to join their local tourist boards. If an establishment happens to be in a popular area, it will do just as well without the STB's help.

Grading was an STB obsession. This has already been done by many commercial guides but none has had the Tourist Board's inspirational idea of grading visitor attractions by the quality of their lavatories. We were warned that historic houses were next on the list. By threatening not to give grants or allow signposting, the STB was in a powerful position.

I have to admit that the STB was not alone responsible for the drop in tourist numbers. We now faced huge competition. Unlike the earlier days when houses were one of the few attractions open on Sundays, now everything was open, including many shops and garden centres (which have the advantage of being free). There were also new destinations – Europe and beyond were opening up, air fares were cheaper and people were more adventurous. The public's idea of recreation was changing. Now people wanted to have an activity and not just to sightsee. In comparison to many other countries, because of its weather and short season, Scotland can also be expensive.

I felt that the excitement of having a snoop around someone else's house had long since disappeared. The pressure to be more professional has meant that houses can seem like museums. I have visited a large number of houses over the years but only two stand out in my memory and that is because each of them was a personal experience.

Catherine and I were driving up from London one summer and, as usual, wanted to take in a visit to an historic house on the way. We looked through the guide and found one that sounded interesting. It had Catholic connections, a moat and a rose garden. It was a pouring wet day as we located what we thought must be the house. The moat was a bad-smelling ditch and the rose garden a few struggling rose bushes. The door was open and we went into a low drawing room where a guide was taking round a handful of visitors. The owner, he told us, was ill in bed upstairs. There was the strange atmosphere of a house which had once been a home but which was now falling into decay. When we reached the dining room, a beautiful rosewood table in a window alcove was being ruined by rain dropping on to it from above. I mentioned this to the guide but he took no notice. A year later I wanted to take Peter to see the place. We could find no mention of it in any guidebook. It seemed to have disappeared.

The second house was also in the north of England. It was an eighteenth-century manor house standing within a high wall. The young woman owner appeared to be alone except for a clutch of screaming young children. She sold us tickets and proceeded on the tour, clutching a baby in her arms. Every now and then she was interrupted by a toddler telling her that he was hungry. She gave us an amusing description of the house and told us how a nervous housemaid had dropped half a Worcester dinner service down the stairs.

During the winter months I had the unfortunate habit of thinking up new ideas to bring tourists in during the season – unfortunate in that I never foresaw the time and effort it would entail putting them into practice. Peter and I were well matched as he immediately threw out half of them as impractical but could pick out the one or two that might work. One year I thought it would give us a good start if we had an Easter Egg hunt and he agreed. I fondly imagined families taking an Easter afternoon walking around the grounds and every now and then coming across a foil-wrapped egg.

I managed to get 10,000 bird-sized chocolate eggs at half price. We advertised the event widely and got coverage on local television. A couple of hours before we opened, Catherine rounded up some friends to come and help, and we all started to hide the eggs. Well before opening time and before the ticket collector was on duty, we were amazed to see adults with large carrier bags walking round collecting them. We decided to put the rest in the maze where they would be safe. A long queue of children and parents assembled outside the gate, panting to start. We let adults with younger children in first. The parents were in competitive mood, determined that their child should have the most. Even if their child found a few eggs, they resented seeing other children with more. It was not quite the peaceful afternoon I had envisaged.

We made sure that we kept eggs back for any child who came out empty-handed, and on the whole the children, who seemed less competitive than their parents, had great fun. We had the odd complaint that there were not enough eggs, but the children who lived in the grounds were able to find some the next day. We have continued to hold it every year and have improved the organisation. It must be counted a success as Easter Egg hunts have now become a feature of many tourist attractions in Scotland. All our initiatives seemed to be matched by a corresponding lack of imagination elsewhere. Every new venture we started was inevitably followed, a couple of years later, by a pale imitation not far away.

Open-air theatre has always appealed to me, so when a writer, Howard Purdie, came to see us with Charles Novoselski, the director of an Edinburgh-based theatre company called Theatre Alba, and suggested putting on a play for children in the grounds I was enthusiastic. We looked around for a suitable place, and the magical walk through ancient yew trees by the side of the Quair Burn fired their imagination.

For several years running, Theatre Alba produced a promenade play specially written for children. The first year they won an Arts Council grant. Charlie was brought up a Catholic and as a boy served at the altar. The drama of the old high Masses, with the sumptuous vestments and dramatic stage management, must be a reason why so many Catholics or ex-Catholics are attracted to the theatre.

Although Polish by descent, Charlie was determined to produce plays in Scots. Howard Purdie was commissioned to write the first one for Traquair. Rehearsals went on for a week beforehand. Howard and Charlie stayed in the house, and the actors and stage manager rented a cottage nearby.

The language they used was a mixture of Border Scots and Lallans. Even Charlie admitted it had probably never been a real dialect. To any English person it was only just comprehensible, but this seemed to give the words an added humour. The audience started off in the garden after being given a coloured drink – the magic juice – and were then led by a musician with a guitar into the 'magic wids'. After being given a message by the 'guid fairie', they met the wicked magician. The effect of seeing a wicked magician in a real wood made some children so frightened that they had to be taken away, yet those same children would probably watch a crime movie on television without blinking an eyelid. The actors did two performances each afternoon. They retired to our sitting room between performances, often coming in soaked. While they tried to dry out their costumes I fed them coffee and filled rolls.

Some of the actors' families came down to visit them. Gordon Dougal's small son was quite unmoved by his father's transformation into a Pied Piper character singing and playing the guitar as he led a long procession of children through the woods. He followed his father at a close distance, asking persistently, 'Dad, where did you put my football boots?' As the week went by, our room began to resemble a cross between a second-hand clothes shop and a roadside snack bar. Peter was very long-suffering, but I was glad that he had to go down to London for a meeting mid-week.

In 1995, Richard Nisbet, who had started a successful small theatre company in Peebles, asked if they could perform a Shakespeare play as a promenade performance in the grounds. Richard had been at school with Catherine in Peebles and then went to the Guildhall School of Drama in London. He is a talented director and performer, but he chose to return to Peebles where his day job is that of manager of a department store and his evenings are devoted to theatre. The first play was *A Midsummer Night's Dream*. The company was very professional in their approach and rehearsed outside in all weathers for weeks beforehand. They were rewarded with perfect balmy evenings. The betrothal took place in the courtyard. We then moved to the croquet lawn, and as night began to fall the appearance of Titania and Oberon had a truly dream-like quality.

It was so popular that Richard has put on a different Shakespeare play each year ever since. They use different areas of the grounds for every scene and the audience moves with them. The actors are mainly untrained but have natural talent. Their rapport with the audience seems to make the productions closer to the way such plays were performed in Shakespeare's time. Not only does Richard draw large audiences but he fosters a love of the theatre by involving many children and young people behind the scenes.

Death

~

People often asked me if I found it difficult having the public walking around the house. To start with, the answer was 'No'. I liked to feel that the house was being used and even found it gloomy in the winter when it was closed. As my whole life revolved around its opening, I did not feel any loss of privacy. I was always aware that the upkeep of the house was dependent on visitors.

But I am not an extrovert, and after over twenty years, when I was able to do most of my work in the mornings and have the afternoons free, I began to yearn for a life away from it all. I hated being watched while I was gardening, sketching or sitting with friends outdoors. Sometimes I wished I could be invisible and be able to go in and out of the house without a chat with a guide or bumping into a visitor, although, as Peter discovered one day when he went to empty a wastepaper basket, a visitor might turn out to be the actor John Hurt (his father happened to be the Episcopal Minister in Innerleithen). I began to develop an unattractive habit of walking past people without acknowledging them.

I wished that Peter and I could live a more normal life. Peter wanted to do more writing and I wanted to start painting again. I asked Peter once if he ever regretted leaving his job in London, and he admitted that sometimes he did. It is much more pleasant to be your own master when you are young and everything is going well. I felt that Peter was tired. He seemed to be suddenly ageing, although he never admitted to feeling ill.

He hated people to question his health, and he always had a standard phrase, 'my iron constitution will pull me through'.

My mother, who was now in her nineties, had suffered a small stroke and had been living with us for a while. She missed being in her own house and tended to criticise everything I did. While Peter was unceasingly kind to her, I was finding it difficult to have her with us all the time. If I ever went out in the car, even to rush down to buy something urgently in Innerleithen, she wanted to come too. She never wanted to go to bed, so we developed a habit of watching the news and then rising to our feet and saying it was bedtime. We would take her down the corridor to her room and then return to have the rest of the evening on our own.

At Huyton, where she had made a flat in her old farmhouse, she felt needed. She organised her ground floor as an unofficial youth club, and the house vibrated three times a week when a band practised there. Her neighbours often called in, and she recounted with amusement how one afternoon two little girls had knocked on her door and offered her a bunch of flowers that they had obviously just picked in her garden. 'We have been told to be kind to old people,' they told her.

She finally left Traquair to return to her house in St John's Vale in London. She had persuaded a nun she was fond of to leave her convent to live with her. I had scoffed at the idea when she first mentioned it to me. 'How do you think a Reverend Mother will let one of her nuns go to live with you when there are hardly any nuns left in the convent anyway?' I asked. But times had changed, and my mother had a forceful personality. After a proposal that Sister Carina and my mother would start a House of Prayer which would also be a refuge for anyone in trouble, Reverend Mother agreed. Besides helping others, it was a great interest for my mother. She enjoyed the company of the people who came to stay and Carina looked after her. When her health deteriorated, it seemed like a miracle when another nun, Maisie, who had been trained as a nurse and was waiting to be accepted into the Dominican order, asked if she could join them.

I seemed to be constantly on the road to visit her in St John's Vale. One evening she begged me to sleep in her room. I agreed, feeling that she was near the end, but the next morning she sat up in bed and asked for some coffee. A few days later Carina rang me to say she had died peacefully in the night. I drove straight down. Edmund was arranging the funeral. My mother had never forgiven the Catholic diocese for pulling down the Pugin church that her grandfather had had built at Huyton and erecting a modern one in its place. He had built the church as 'fire insurance', she told us, explaining that the insurance was against the fires of Hell. She wanted to be buried in the old crypt, which was now under the entrance to the new church – it would cause great inconvenience and be a final retaliation. We hoped that now she was in Heaven she would change her views, and she was buried above the house next to my father in St John's Church graveyard.

Both at the funeral and the memorial service that we held later in Huyton I was amazed by the number of people who came up to me and told me how she had helped them. She had particularly cared for anyone whom priests had not considered respectable. If she had not been my mother and I had not had 'baggage' from the past, I too would have had only admiration for her.

I was anxious about Peter. To add to his troubles, a crack had appeared on the north gable wall of the house and he was having difficulty in obtaining a grant to restore it. I had little capital left and realised with a shock that all the money my parents had given me, which would have enabled us to retire, had disappeared into the proverbial 'bottomless pit'.

Our administrator, Helen Fairbank, who had been a great prop, had reached retiring age and although she would have been willing to stay on, we could no longer afford her, so I suggested that I took over her work. I had learnt to use the computer, a boon in a small office. All day we had interruptions – queries from visitors or staff – and it was difficult to concentrate while counting up cash. Peter dealt with the estate, the house restoration and the brewery. I took the bookings, organised the art exhibitions and started a new event, Sheep and Wool Day.

As the Borders are famous for their woollen goods and also for their sheep, I thought it would be an interesting project to show them both together. The mills were no longer thriving and there had been many redundancies. A number of uniquely skilled men and women had been made redundant and were trying to start up their own small businesses. Some were weaving for Jean Muir and other well-known designers. We had demonstrations of shearing, spinning, weaving, crochet, knitting and sales of woollen goods. Rare breeds of sheep and llamas were on show on the avenue. A sheepdog demonstration was held in the afternoon. The following year we had a fleece spun and knitted into a small sweater in one day. I had great co-operation from everyone who took part, even from the farmer who lost a sheep, but none from the Wool Marketing Board.

A few months later Peter started to feel a pain in his side. The doctor thought it could be a pulled muscle. As we were both exhausted at the end of the season, we went to stay with Silvia in Cyprus for a few weeks. Peter was unusually low and the pain got worse. By December he was admitted to hospital for a biopsy. Ten days later he had an appointment to see a specialist. It coincided with a tourist promotion that our group was holding in Perth. Catherine had just returned from South America and was learning to take over the administration of the house. I asked Peter whether I should go with her or go to the hospital with him. He told me to go with her, but I have always regretted that I did. When we returned he was sitting in the semi-dark of our sitting room. He had been told that he had liver cancer and that it was too late for treatment. He would have only a few months to live.

I was told that this was the 'modern way' to give a patient the news that he had terminal cancer. I felt it was like casting an evil spell. I was sure that he should not have been told so soon. It would have been kinder to wait for a second visit when

I was with him and he was feeling less well. Although I later learned that the Macmillan nurses had an office further down the corridor, he had not been put in touch with them but had been sent home without any further help. He had had to wait for us to return and repeat to us what he had been told.

It was a terrible shock. He was sixty-seven and had always prided himself on his health. I had believed implicitly that, like most of his family, he would live well into his seventies. But it seemed that he was going to die younger than most of the previous lairds of Traquair. He wanted to carry on as long as he could and did not want anyone outside his family to know how ill he was. I was pleased that the house was closed and we were alone. I always tried to manage with as few domestic staff as possible during the winter. He just wanted to be with me and Catherine who was living in the old gamekeeper's cottage in the grounds.

Everyone faces death in their own way. Peter and I didn't talk about it. We had been together so long that there was no need for words. I slept with him in our half-tester bed every night and for the last ten days, when he was bedridden, often climbed into bed and lay by his side during the day. All the time I was on the verge of tears. It was painful keeping them back, but I tried to seem optimistic and was frightened that even if I cried on my own he would notice. We remained calm. We both had the same belief in an afterlife and a kind God waiting for us somewhere when we died.

The doctor often called and two sensitive district nurses took it in turns to come in to wash him. I also contacted the Macmillan nurses who are trained in cancer care, and they told me to ring them at any time. Although the doctor had told me to do the same, I did not want to disturb him. My friend Helen, who was now back in Britain and whose husband had died a year earlier, came all the way from Somerset to visit us. She brought an alternative cancer treatment that had helped some patients but unfortunately did not suit Peter.

During his last days, Sister Maisie, the nun who had nursed my mother, came to help. He had to take so many pills that I was terrified of getting them muddled up and worried when they had an adverse reaction. Peter was sedated and said he felt no pain. He was being given morphine and I felt he was gradually detaching himself from this life and was contemplating the next phase serenely. I even thought I detected a hint of excitement. He had always had a sense of adventure and said that he would not be frightened to die. Catherine and I lay beside him as Maisie said the rosary and he slowly stopped breathing.

The house filled with relations, and I was touched by all the friends who offered help. The funeral in Innerleithen was full to overflowing and he was buried in the Maxwell family crypt at Terregles in Dumfriesshire where his ancestors lay beside him. It was a long dreary drive following the hearse, a journey I had made with Peter for his father twenty-eight years earlier. When we got back to the house, we found that Rob, without being asked, had prepared a dinner for us.

I was completely devastated. In spite of all the kindness and help I was given by friends and neighbours, I could think of nothing but Peter not being there. He was dead and I would never see him again. I had not cried since I was at school but now I sobbed continually. Tears would well up inside me and, like a safety valve, would let out the emotion. Nicholas took me to stay in Portugal for a week. By an extraordinary coincidence, staying at the hotel where we spent the first night was Deirdrie Maxwell Scott with her aunt. Deirdrie's husband, Michael, had died a few months earlier. It made a huge bond between us. Nicholas and I went to stay up in the hills and we walked and talked. I could not get out of my mind that Peter's death was somehow my fault and I went over and over our life together. In the evenings I insisted on a large glass of whisky and Nicholas, who used drugs but drank little, was worried that I would take to the bottle.

When I got back to Traquair, Catherine had started to open the house for the new season. Friends from all around had offered to come in to clean and polish. The fact that Catherine had been away from home and was now taking over the administration distracted her from her grief. Newspapers assumed that she had inherited the house and were wanting interviews and photographs. I was only too happy to let her talk to the press. I felt that my belief in the house and estate had only been to support Peter and now that he had gone everything seemed pointless.

I carried on mechanically, getting ready for the opening. Peter had always set up the Museum Room himself and hidden away most of the valuable items in the winter. It was a game of hide-and-seek trying to find them. Gradually we discovered everything except the Amen glass. I asked Peter where he had put it. Shortly afterwards I looked in a cupboard and opened an old biscuit tin. There was the glass, wrapped in cotton wool. Peter had always found things for me in his lifetime and now he was dead it made no difference. He continues to do so till this day.

The evenings were the hardest. I persuaded my dear cousin Mary who was recovering from depression to come and stay. She was still feeling low so we had no need to put on any forced jollity with each other. Grief comes in waves. It is difficult for people to help you. My only consolation was that when I sank to my lowest ebb, I knew I could go down no further and would gradually come up again. I prayed endlessly and visited Father Ronald Walls, an Anglican priest who had converted to Catholicism. He had become tired of preaching about poverty and had chosen to live in it instead. He had found a disused bowling pavilion in a run-down mining district outside Edinburgh. He and two friends lived in huts in the garden in total discomfort. He was always happy and exuded holiness. 'You can still go on loving someone after they have died,' he told me. He convinced me that it was my duty to try to be happy.

Once the house opened I had to start taking some of the groups around. Many of the regular tourist guides had seen Peter looking perfectly well the year before and were staggered to hear that he had died. Catherine and I were upset when they kept inquiring about how he had died and wanted to know every detail of his illness. They talked as though death was not a normal occurrence and seemed to imply that Peter had failed in some way. I knew they were only thinking of their own mortality. I felt much better when a genial gentleman who brought a group said in a matter-of-fact way, 'Life is like a conveyor belt. We are all heading in the same direction and some of us get there sooner than others.' Many of our American visitors were widows and showed their sympathy sensitively. When I went shopping in Innerleithen, women I hardly knew would pat my arm.

Mrs Grey, who was working in the antique shop, was a tremendous help. She had been widowed with four children when only in her thirties. I felt ashamed to be reacting as I was. She told me I must help myself and that no one else could. I realised that I did not want to stop grieving because this would be admitting that Peter had really died. I had always had a fear of death. I tried to draw comfort from the fact that Peter had not. 'Think how much worse it would be if people didn't die,' he had once told me.

It was a consolation to have the chapel in the house. I was wondering how I could make a memorial for him there when, by chance, as I was sorting out his dressing room, I found an old bit of needlework with a portrait of St Peter holding his keys to Heaven. Peter must have found it in the house somewhere and intended to have it looked at. I showed it to Margaret Swain. As it had a small handworked loop at the top, she thought it might have been made by someone for their private devotions. I had it framed and hung it in the chapel.

Lighting candles took on a much greater meaning, not only as an aid for meditation but as a form of prayer. I bought a candle stand for the chapel and kept candles available for people to buy and light themselves. There is scarcely a day in the season when there are not at least half a dozen burning. 'Just like a birthday cake,' one of the guides told me.

Catherine listened to me endlessly. She took to her job like a duck to water and settled at Peter's desk. We set to work to clear up the office. Peter had always worked with his desk piled high with papers, but he knew what was in each pile and could find something instantly. He had hated me touching anything. During the last months the piles had got out of hand. He had been a great hoarder and among important letters there were newspaper cuttings and forms to fill in for bargain offers. One drawer held a collection of ancient objects from around the house that he was waiting to identify. We found packets of painkillers everywhere.

There was no entail on the house and in view of the finance I had contributed to the house, Peter had left me nearly everything, with no strings attached – I would actually have been free to sell it all – but I felt no sense of ownership. Most of my own money was locked into the house. I had never wanted to take anything from Traquair, but now I was beginning to realise how much it had taken from me.

A few years before Peter died, we had taken on a new young factor who brought in a friend as our lawyer, and I had 'taken against' both of them. Cancer is an insidious disease, and for several years Peter had not been his usual self. He had lost his drive and found it difficult to concentrate. I had been profoundly hurt by the way they talked to him. Catherine and I made up our minds to change all our professional advisers. We gradually ended up with an able accountant who specialised in estate work and a new factor who was known locally. Not only did we have confidence in them, but they also became friends. Our last change was to a new lawyer, also an expert in his field. They began to sort out our affairs, which was a long, expensive business.

Saving Traquair

~

Looking back, I realise that I was lucky to have had so much to think about in the years following Peter's death. I could be distracted from my grief although I would still occasionally find myself in tears. I no longer felt any pleasure working in the house, but it made me feel that I was still doing something for Peter.

Our financial problems and dealing with the crack in the gable wall were our first priorities. Our old friend Geoffrey Hay came to my help and directed us to an architectural firm well known to Historic Scotland and skilled in the technique of obtaining grants, a definite plus in their favour. Our architect was to draw up a schedule of the work and get an estimate of the cost. He would then have to negotiate with the Historic Scotland architect who would make her own assessment. It was a long-drawn-out affair as Historic Scotland, like most government departments, appeared to answer letters only once a fortnight.

While there was so much going on in the house, I heard from the Borders Festival Committee, of which I was a member, that Scottish Power had agreed to sponsor a *son et lumière* at Traquair. The Festival, which had been started by Judy Steel, took place every second year. It was an ambitious event, with theatre, music and drama productions taking place in towns and villages all over the Scottish Borders. Peter and I had always thought that Traquair would be a perfect subject for a *son et lumière*. We had seen productions in England,

France and even Egypt and had been struck by the way that lighting effects and sounds could illustrate a story. The problem had always been the prohibitive cost as well as the light Scottish evenings at the time of year when most people are about. The festival, which was held in October, was now attracting substantial sponsorship as well as large potential audiences.

All the expertise that was required for it was available in the Borders and everyone was enthusiastic. Mike Casey, an experienced lighting man, dealt with the technical side. Michael Scott Moncrieff wrote the commentary, which was recorded and spoken by Ian Briggs and other Border actors. Catherine and I produced it. It took place over several nights at the start of the Festival after our season was over.

Instead of the golden autumn weather we usually have, that October was appalling. While the sound and lighting system was being set up, there were persistent showers and a cold wind. It continued during most of the week that the production was on.

A large audience assembled on the Wine-Glass Lawn and watched the house lit up as the dramatic story unfolded. Huge blown-up portraits were projected onto the façade. The highlight of the show was the appearance of Colin Scott, an accomplished piper, piping on the roof with his kilt and plaid swirling dramatically in the high wind. He was a slater by trade and had been able to climb through a skylight and perform this feat by balancing on the roof while two men clung on to his ankles.

Our duty in return for the sponsorship was for Catherine and I to entertain twenty Scottish Power guests to dinner three nights running after the performance. A row of plastic chairs was provided for them in the front row. On the first night the rain poured down. I have been through many uncomfortable moments at Traquair – knowing that there were 4,000 visitors in the grounds for a Fair and that the water had run out; hosting a lunch for a high-powered American group when a waitress spilt a glass of red wine on a designer-clad lady's pale lemon suit – and leading the guests through the rain to their chairs covered in an inch of water was definitely one of them. Scottish Power had provided large umbrellas and when Sir William Sutherland, the Chief Constable of Lothians and Borders Police, was among the guests, he managed to arrange them both above the heads and below the knees as if they were shields used in crowd control.

In spite of the weather and the short preparation time, the show attracted large audiences. With so much already recorded and the sound and lighting positions marked, we longed to make a few improvements and do it again. Perhaps one day this will happen.

While Catherine got to work on the daily administration and the brewery, I had to turn my attention towards the work on the house. Historic Scotland had finally decided that they would agree to give us a grant towards the estimated cost of repairing the gable wall only if we also carried out all the repairs that, in their opinion, would need doing over the next ten years. Our own architect backed them up and appeared to be just as eager to make the job as costly as possible. If you own a large house and an estate, it is impossible to make anyone believe that you do not have infinite resources behind you.

It was a ruinous policy for us. We simply could not afford to pay out such a huge sum all at once at that time. Apart from that, I did not like the idea of the house undergoing a big overhaul. It would be like a woman having a facelift. I much preferred the traditional way of keeping an old building in repair – to carry out work when it was needed.

It was obvious that we would have to sell something to raise capital. If we sold land it would reduce our income, so we decided on a silver tankard made for the fourth Earl of Traquair, the most interesting piece of silver in the house. Peter had always said it should be sold if we ever needed to raise capital, but it was a part of the history of the house and should have stayed there. My parents had given me a picture by Carlo Carlone, a moving painting of *The Descent from the Cross*, which I had hung at the back of the chapel. I decided to sell this for the cause. These sales, together with a few further items, all of which attracted capital gains tax, went towards raising the sum needed.

As the work could be carried out only in the summer, the front of the house would be covered in scaffolding over two seasons. I pointed out that it might deter visitors. I was told, 'Not at all. The public love to see a building being kept in good condition.' They do not know tourists.

Traquair, like many old Scottish buildings, was built of stone and then 'harled'. Harling is a mixture of sand and lime that is put over stone to keep out the cold and damp. In the fifties it was then covered with lime paint, and although it had lasted nearly fifty years damp had got in underneath and in a few places the harling was coming off. This was now to be rectified as well as the stonework round the windows and finally a coat of lime wash, mixed, we were told proudly, as it had been done in times gone by, would be applied to the whole building.

The work began. The scaffolding went up. The house looked like a ruin and the rooms became dark inside. Groups cancelled, and we had letters of complaint. Historic Scotland advised us to send out a begging letter and to put out a donations box. The guides generously worked for a day without wages to show their support, and we were grateful for other sums that were donated.

The cost of running Traquair and opening it to the public on top of the restoration was an eye-opener to me. If I found it hard to believe, I was sure the visitors had no idea either. Few people even realised, when they bought a ticket, that seventeen per cent of the ticket price was Value Added Tax. Although we kept being told how lucky we were to receive a grant from public money, we had in fact contributed to the public money in a big way and paid out more in tax then we ever got back. I decided to make a display of our 1990 accounts among our eighteenth-century ones that hung in the library: 'Cost of repairing drive, house and maintenance'. They were read with interest and particularly remarked upon in a *Which?* magazine report.

Although we had raised some money towards meeting the

cost of the repairs, we still had our overdraft to consider. The bank began to hassle us. They would not agree to accept the estate as collateral although it more than covered the overdraft. The local managers fed on gossip that they passed on to their superiors. Contrary to the Historic Scotland view, they apparently had the impression that the house was a wreck and past repair and only two incompetent women were left to deal with it. This led to a visit, when we were taken out to lunch at our local hotel, our affairs were discussed in public and they talked to us like children, explaining that it would be bad publicity for the bank if they had to call in the estate. I could not help remembering the deferential manner they had used when Peter was alive. They constantly compared us unfavourably to a 'successful' brewery that had been started up in the area, run by an ex-military gentleman who met with their approval. Within several years that brewery had been forced to sell out while we were flying high.

Now that we had a new lawyer, accountant and factor, all experienced in estate work, we lost no time in looking for a new bank. We were given a better rate on our overdraft although I still had to hand over some of my remaining share certificates as a 'comfort factor', but instead of being treated like naughty schoolgirls we were welcomed with open arms and continually entertained. They were priding themselves on upgrading their customer service and dealing with any queries or problems instantly. Five years later, the whole policy appeared to have changed. The capable man overseeing our account wrote to say that he had been made redundant, the girl who prided herself on always being at the other end of the telephone was transferred to Orkney and voicemail had taken the place of instant customer service.

They stood us in good stead when we needed them most, however, and we could concentrate on improving our business. We were being approached more often by agencies putting together entertainment for incentive groups, and official dinners in our dining room became popular. In the early days we could not afford to invest in new cutlery or china so we used my personal things and even the crested silver from the house. On one occasion we had to bring out a few eighteenth-century silver forks and spoons. One of the groups was so impressed that they wrote afterwards to ask if it had been a mistake.

That summer, Gian Carlo Menotti, the Italian composer who lived in Scotland for part of the year with his adopted son, Chip, and daughter-in-law, Melinda, invited me to stay with them in Spoleto for the music festival, 'Festival of Two Worlds', which he ran there. Catherine was happy to be left, and I accepted the invitation gratefully. I received every kindness from all the family. Spoleto is a charming Umbrian hill town that has been saved from disintegration by Gian Carlo's festival. I was put up in his beautiful house opposite the *duomo*, which contains exquisite Fra Filippo Lippi frescoes. Each day was filled with music, all in outstanding settings, including eighteenth-century theatres with the original backdrops and a Roman amphitheatre. It is a town that is small enough to give an intimacy to the festival, which centred on Gian Carlo and his family who entertained the artists. Everything was within walking distance. I was taken to operas, concerts, dinners and parties. The music and the warmth of the sun had a healing effect. I still felt as if I was in a trance and behaving mechanically, but my confidence, which had left me when Peter died, began to return.

The first evening we were having dinner in a restaurant and I did not catch the names of all the guests. Two of the house guests, I gathered, had just got married. From what he said the husband seemed to be an artist and there was something familiar about him. I suddenly caught sight of his profile and realised who he was – none other than Barry Humphries, also known as Dame Edna Everage. I had always been a fan of the middle-aged Australian lady whom I had taken for real the first time I heard her on the radio. Few people had heard of him in Spoleto so I was able to describe his act. I was told that Barry had a separate suite of rooms in his house where all his Dame Edna clothes and make-up were kept.

That summer Catherine decided to start up the Fair again. She had been working in theatre administration and I knew she would do it well. This time my philanthropic ideals had to be dropped and the profits put towards the house, but we still hoped to make it a happy affordable family day. We did decide to make the extra entrance fee to the house a donation to the Macmillan nurses, and over the years we have collected over £10,000 for them.

Catherine redesigned the layout and found new outstanding acts – aerial trapeze artists, stilt dancers and Russian Cossack dancers to perform on the Wine-Glass Lawn – as well as bringing back old friends from the past. She introduced 'Lady Cristobel', who played the Lady Bountiful, and with her butler, Scrotum, became a great favourite. She set up a small music stage in the old walled garden with the beer tent selling a special Festival Ale near by. Terry and Debbie, who now had the jewellery workshop, arranged for American Indian tepees to be put up at one end of the garden. We had classical music in the rose garden where I had at last managed to achieve a mainly white border. An alternative therapy tent and a children's theatre tent were set up on the avenue and a great mix of stall-holders took stands. The perpetual problem of the water running out in the lavatories was solved by Felicity, who produced a plan for 'green' earth closets. One was designed for mother and child and had a large seat with a small seat at the side. A bucket of earth was provided, and we hung dried herbs above them. I provided sphagnum moss to be used instead of paper but this did not prove so popular.

The first year we were interested in trying to have more serious theatre so we hired a blacked-out theatre tent. As it would be standing empty on the Saturday night, we decided to use it for a charity event and thought that the Edinburgh Aids Monitor needed most help. The year before he died, Peter and I had gone to an entertaining evening at the Edinburgh Festival with three stand-up comedians. A few days later we saw one of them, Simon Fanshawe, in the tearoom at Traquair. We got to know him, and he suggested an evening of stand-up comedy and a buffet supper. He would supply the comedians, and he persuaded Julian Clary, Nick Revel and Josie Lawrence to join him. Fay Presto, a flamboyant female conjurer who had had a sex change, also offered to take part. She was staying in the house and arrived in an ancient Rolls-Royce that she insisted on parking in front of the house with a man who spent most of the day polishing it. He also seemed to be her dresser and ran her bath water. One evening he asked me, as a great favour, whether I would like to take his place.

We had to sell the tickets at £25 each and wrote around to everyone on our list, which included friends and neighbours. The response was poor. Only a few booked. The county families in the Borders prefer excerpts from opera to alternative humour and the price was too high for the people who came to the Fair.

The evening was not a success. The entertainment was excellent but not sufficiently appreciated, and many of our friends who had kindly supported us were thoroughly shocked. The caterer, unknown to us, was in financial difficulties and cut down on the food. Fay Presto took a huff, departed in her Rolls for the fish and chip shop in Innerleithen and came back complaining that she had been stared at.

Simon Fanshawe had asked the Edinburgh Aids Monitor to bring down information boards describing the charity and the Aids virus and how to prevent it. This was hung in the supper tent where I saw the unusual sight of our charming Lord Lieutenant sitting beneath a blown-up photograph of a condom. The volunteers promised by the Aids Monitor to clear up never materialised, and our star, Simon, was left washing up until midnight.

The rest of the Fair went well and the four-year break did not affect the numbers. Catherine had managed to organise it on her own without any committee. It made a worthwhile financial contribution to the house, but we were always open to further suggestions.

A talented young man, Angus Farquhar, a friend of Catherine's who put on colourful events, suggested holding a

rave in a marquee on the avenue. He would sell tickets in
Glasgow and bus the partygoers down to a 'surprise destina-
tion'. He took every precaution, informing the police and
employing a security firm. He was also willing to pay for the
people who lived in the cottages nearby to go to a hotel for the
night if they wished. The police advised us that we should not
tell anyone else.

A chill-out marquee was erected in the garden, and we
were asked to keep the tearoom open for coffee and cold drinks
and to make sure there was plenty of drinking water on hand.
My friend Sara, who lives near by and is always open-minded
towards new experiences, volunteered to man the tearoom
with me for part of the night.

As we got the place ready, the security men rushed in like
a marauding force, told us that we had no idea what we were
in for and ordered us to put all glass bottles out of reach.
Feeling a little apprehensive, we waited for the coaches to
arrive. The security guards searched everyone at the gate.
Instead of the rioting mob we had been told to expect, a few
quiet shivering young men and women wandered in and
politely asked for coffee. When we poured it out, they looked
surprised. 'Real Nescafé,' they said appreciatively, 'we usually
only get instant.'

The band got going in the tent and although the music
was loud we could still hear ourselves speak. After a few hours
we looked in and saw everyone dancing wildly, and some
fantastically dressed characters were flaunting their costumes.
Sara and I then handed over to Rob and I retired to bed. In
spite of the music I was still able to go to sleep.

It was not until the next morning that the complaints
started to come in. Sound travels in a strange way. The music
had gone straight down to one side of Innerleithen where it
had been so loud that neighbours had been banging on each
other's doors all night asking them to turn down their music.
We received angry letters, and the local paper denounced the
menace from Traquair. It was some time before I dared show
my face in Innerleithen again. The ravers, on the other hand,

had caused no problems. It was the security men who were seen departing with cases of ale.

I had now been working on and off for several years on the biography of Lady Nithsdale. We had material in our own archive at Traquair but by far the most interesting letters were in the Stuart Papers at Windsor. After the death of Prince Charles Edward Stuart in 1788, his brother, Cardinal Henry Stuart, passed all the papers from the Jacobite court to the safekeeping of George IV, who placed them in the Royal Archive in the White Tower of the castle. It was a warm and luxurious archive to work in. I was given permission to spend ten days studying them and travelled down from London each day.

I had written a certain amount before Peter died, and I could have gone on researching for ever. When a publisher told me that it would be vital to get the book out in time for the 250th anniversary of the 1745, I had a deadline to work to. I often got up early and spent a few hours on the office computer before the staff came in.

Once the book was published I felt a great sense of relief. I had some good reviews, was interviewed on television, asked to lecture and received many complimentary letters. I had a call from an American television producer who was making a series on escapes. He was coming to London and wanted me to go down for a long interview on camera. I spent most of a day with him, going through the story, repeating bits over and over again.

Peter and I had always wanted to get our archives into order. The National Register of Archives had sorted some of the bundles. They farmed the work out to solicitors doing time in jail, but when there was a shortage of legal experts behind bars the work came to a halt. We were advised to lay the papers flat in cardboard boxes, which gave us a chance to glance through them.

Before Peter died, we had employed Margaret Fox, an archivist, once a week, but she found it too far to travel. One morning I received a letter to say that she had moved and would be willing to start again. The very next afternoon a group from a Catholic parish made a visit to the house and among the group was Robin Gard, the semi-retired Northumberland County Archivist, to whom I was introduced. By an amazing coincidence he had employed Margaret and knew her well. He generously volunteered to assess our needs, suggest sources of funding and help her from time to time if she started again.

I was successful in obtaining a grant from the Glenfiddich Living Scotland Awards to fit out a small room, once a priest's bedroom, next to the room where mass was said in the Penal times, and another grant from the British Library towards the archivist's wages, which enabled Margaret gradually to list all the papers on a computer. Registrar House in Edinburgh has a copy of the list and researchers can look through it and request which papers they wish to see. This cuts out all those who are not real researchers and just want a general rummage as well as the dealers who are more interested in their value.

I attended an interesting meeting on the future of archives. There were two points of view. Owners or curators of private archives could see the value of keeping the papers where they belong. The curators of national collections felt that they would be better preserved and of more use to the public if they were deposited in a national archive. I agreed with the former. Archives mean more when they are read in their own environment. They are the main source of history for the house to which they belong and bring the past inhabitants to life. When we had an exhibition of letters from fathers to their children over five generations, it was chosen in a visitors' questionnaire as one of the most interesting things in the house. We could all identify with the wayward child in one generation who would turn into the concerned parent in the next.

In 1651 the wife of the first earl wrote severely to her son: 'I cannot regret enough that you should have returned, John Stewart, without the least help for mine or your father's maintenance,' Fifteen years later, the same John Stewart, now the second earl, wrote a moving letter to his children from his death-bed: 'My time is running out and I have little enough to entertain myself in the thought of the mercies and love of my saviour towards me. My dearest children live together like one heart in diverse bodies. Be thankful to God for all his benefits bestowed on you and me; be faithful to him in all your ways.'

When the sixth earl heard that his son, Charles, was ruining the estate by prospecting for minerals and was considering taking his family to live abroad, he sent him the following broadside: 'What can you imagine or be induced to imagine that a proper scheme for retrieving your affairs is leaving your own country . . . This would indeed be plunging deeper in the mire in endeavouring to get out of it. I have often heard of people going to Rome or Naples – some out of curiosity and improvement and others for the benefit of their health but never heard of any that went for the health of their purse; that is so ridiculous a project for economy that I believe it was never thought of by any intelligent prudent person and therefore does not merit to be computed.'

His advice went unheeded. Twenty-two years later Charles was back at Traquair with his own rebellious son, described by his mother as 'a rude little boy who minds only his own will'. He was dispatched to boarding school and in answer to his first letter home, his father wrote with relief: 'I received your letter with infinite pleasure as it informed me of your being in good health and what is still more satisfactory to me that you are, my dear Child, sensible of your feelings. I most sincerely forgive and forget all the uneasiness you occasioned me for some time past before you left Traquair.'

The 'rude little boy' was later the eighth and last earl of Traquair. He was responsible for building houses in Innerleithen and planting many of the trees on the estate.

Mother and Daughter

~

I was in a curious position. Peter had left me everything, but the press insisted on calling Catherine 'the Laird' or, even worse, 'Lady' Catherine. I was financing the house and making the important decisions although I was always careful to involve her. I had done what I could to shield her from death duties and would make it all over to her when our finances improved and I could withdraw my own money. She was working hard and bringing publicity to the house, and I admired her for also studying for a Master of Business Administration degree in the evenings. Even so, I was getting tired of people consulting her over my head. We worked together in the office each day, not the easiest position for a mother and daughter. She had found it easier when I had lost my confidence but was finding it harder as I was steadily regaining it.

Basically we were being constantly undermined by the macho attitude to women. We had a few short-lived rows but on the whole we got on well. We had the same philosophy, the same sense of humour, and we loved and respected each other. We drank Rob's delicious soup together for lunch in the tearoom every day, and to prove their joint affection, Catherine's devoted King Charles spaniel decided to come down to the house and give birth to her puppies on my bed.

I found myself taking on Peter's role, adopting a firmer attitude to what was going on, while she became the liberal I had been. This was demonstrated when a few young men came to live in tepees on a bit of our land looking down on to a farm below. They managed to survive there through the winter and could sometimes be seen on the road in the mornings, walking down to the hotel in Innerleithen for breakfast. By paying no rent, their unemployment benefit went further. It seemed in some ways an admirable feat of endurance, but they were, of course, living on fish from our water and game from our land, not to mention magic mushrooms.

The farmer below was anxious to get rid of them as in good weather the tepee dwellers were visited by numerous friends, many of whom camped alongside and who had to walk across his land to get there. Catherine was all for letting them stay while I sympathised with the farmer. I was particularly annoyed when I heard that they criticised him for his farming methods. I told one of them, a young man who called himself Maynard, that as they seemed to have nothing to do all day, the least they could do in return for living there would be to offer to help either the farmer or us in some way. He seemed quite willing and said he liked painting so I suggested he painted some of our benches. Nothing happened and after a while I received a note which I have treasured: 'Dear Flo (a name I have never been called before or since), I am sorry I haven't been able to paint the benches but life has been choc a bloc.' Gradually, with a little encouragement, they left the site.

One day, I was walking with some friends over the hills and, looking down, I saw a horse-drawn caravan, except it had no horse. It was being pushed along the road. We watched to see where it was going and saw it turn in and park behind our old mill. A young couple settled down to live there. Again they seemed harmless enough, but I would have felt more kindly towards them if they had asked permission first. The inhabitants of the cottages nearby began to complain when they had late-night parties, so I went down to talk to them. They were unable to see how anyone could object to them being there. They were different from the original hippies, who were generally well-mannered and had some philosophy about the way they were living. This generation seemed more interested in saving money and looking after themselves, but perhaps I was just getting older. They, too, eventually moved on.

On the advice of our accountant, we had employed a book-keeper instead of a secretary. Mandi settled into the office and proved to be skilled in many spheres. Not only a wizard on the computer, she was soon able to deal with many of the day-to-day problems. We were both less tied to the office. In her spare time she turned out fantastic wedding cakes.

The repairs to the house were at last complete and there was only the final lime wash to be applied. I was flabbergasted to return from a day in Edinburgh to find the architect standing in the courtyard admiring a large patch of yellow ochre, Historic Scotland's flavour of the month, which had been painted on the front of the house. Catherine and I were horrified, as the house had always been a pale creamy white which changed its mood according to the weather. When it was damp it became dark and brooding, and in the sun it glowed with warmth.

'Just an experiment,' the architect told me hastily. We had begun to lose faith in the architects. The builders they employed were skilled men who had to listen to instructions from a professional trained in theory who knew little about the practicalities. Costing did not come within their orbit and clients had to pay for a quantity surveyor to do this for them. Many of their instructions, the workmen told me, were impossible to carry out, so as soon as they were left on their own they did it their way.

After an argument, the original colour, or as near as they could get to it, was used. At the back of the house, which was done over two years, the sample of the first colour was lost and they were unable to match it up. The massive rear of the building no longer looks like a whole as it is has been left in two different shades of cream. After a few years the 'authentic' lime wash began to grow an unattractive mould that gives the house a shabby appearance instead of the 'worn by time' look it had had before. No one accepted responsibility for it and we were left with the choice of living with it or paying to have the whole front done again.

Living in the house alone was a twenty-four hour duty seven days a week, and I was determined to get away for brief interludes. I have always enjoyed travelling and took every chance I had to go abroad. I went on a couple of expeditions led by the Edinburgh artist Richard Demarco. Richard lives in perpetual motion, travels from one country to another and is known by everyone in the art world all over Europe. He is interested in everyone he meets, boosts artists' confidence, tends to promise them the world and passes on. One of his friends has aptly described him as 'an artwork in himself'.

For the last forty years he has brought experimental art and theatre to Edinburgh, the most traditional of cities. Art is a spiritual experience for him. It is his life, and he can transmit his excitement to others. He is a Catholic by birth and, like myself, cannot come to terms with the changes in the Catholic liturgy which have reduced its aesthetic appeal. He comes from an Italian family who ran an art deco café in Portobello, a centre of social life in the twenties, and has inherited a special talent for bringing people together. Through him I have made some close friends. Occasionally he takes small groups on his travels, either to see art for its own sake or to bring it back to exhibit in Edinburgh.

The first time I accompanied him was with six or seven others when we went to the monastery of St Benedictus Berg in Germany. The modern church was designed by one of the Cistercian monks and is beautiful in its stark simplicity. As Richard pointed out to us, it has been designed to express spirituality rather than the ego of the architect. The monks live in silence and prayer. As we followed him into the church, he turned and said, 'If these people weren't here, *we* wouldn't exist.' I had never heard the value of prayer described so succinctly.

The next trip was to an art fair in Budapest. Richard had been given a stand to show paintings and sculptures. Some of the artists travelled with us and others from Eastern Europe joined us in Hungary. Our group grew as various artists joined us from Romania and Serbia. At night, we trailed after Richard through the streets of Budapest, looking for a restaurant for dinner, while he pointed out the details of the architecture and revelled in the beauty of the city. The fact that it was late and we had not eaten seemed far from his mind. He chatted to people we met on the way and asked them to join us. We became so many that no restaurant would take us in until an old haunt took pity on us, and we finally sat down at a huge banqueting table where dinner was enlivened by a speech from a female Serbian trade union leader.

Richard, who had recently developed an aptitude for holding auctions, had planned to auction off any of the art left on his stand at the end of the show. On the last day, the hall suddenly began to clear and the fair came to an end without any warning. Apart from our little group, there were few people left. Not discouraged, he held up a painting and started looking for bids. We looked at each other and realised that we were supposed to be bidding. It was painfully slow until an old friend, the curator of one of the Hungarian galleries, appeared. He bought a sculpture and saved the day.

The business part of our visit now over, we were led on a journey of discovery from Budapest to Vienna, visiting artists' studios and small theatres. It was impossible to return home without a head full of ideas and inspiration.

I made friends with one of the group, John Gruzelier, a professor of psychology who had an art gallery in his house in London and was interested in showing paintings at Traquair. He admired serious modern painters, as I did. I had shown paintings in the old Malt Loft for several years, but we decided to clear a larger unused room at the top of the house as well.

I had already experienced visitors' responses to modern art when we exhibited the abstract metal sculptures of the celebrated Romanian artist Paul Neagu in the courtyard. They stood in a circle and were a dynamic force. Paul had had to listen to visitors complaining that they were in the way when they wanted to take a photograph and they did not know what they were meant to be and how could they be called art.

I hoped that this attitude might have changed. During our first season we exhibited Norwegian artists who had formed a co-operative. Benthe Norheim had created a flock of semi-abstract shepherdesses which were slightly better received. They soon seemed to have taken up residence in the front of the house and I felt quite lonely when they left. The rest of the season we showed Norwegian paintings in the gallery. The artists were well thought of in Norway and Norwegian journalists came over to write about them.

The tourists who came to Traquair were generally well-educated and discerning people. Our main attraction was history and they obviously could not ally this with modern painting. It even seemed to upset them. Their annoyance was reflected in the visitors' book in the gallery. There was not only the 'could paint better with my feet' type of remark but also 'only the nepotism of the professional Artist keeps this rubbish on' and 'Ah, contemporary art! A practical way for many people without talent but looking for Arts Council money to make believe that they are more intelligent than the philistines who do not "understand their work".'

We were too far from Edinburgh for the critics, who seldom came, and we began to realise the location on the top floor of the house was inconvenient. Neither John nor I had the time or finance to get the gallery established, and although the sales just covered the costs, it did not seem fair to the artists. I enjoyed meeting and entertaining them, and it gave me the chance to buy some good paintings, but after eight years we decided to close the gallery.

The house still needed to increase its income. The Scottish Tourist Board had invented a correspondence course for American travel agents which ended up with the successful graduates coming over for a mock degree ceremony and a familiarisation tour. The Board also ran a scheme for tourist operators in Scotland to travel to the States to meet the agents on their home ground. I decided to go on one of these whistle-stop tours with four other tourist trade representatives – two luxury hotel owners, a coach company owner and a represen-

tative from Scottish Rail. We visited five cities on the west
coast, staying a night in each one.

We travelled in the evening and stayed in large hotels
where we gave a breakfast presentation in the morning. All
the travel agents in the area were invited and there were
usually about a hundred or so people present. A Tourist
Board official, based in the States, set up the event and
started the proceedings by showing slides and giving an
informative talk on Scotland. We were then allotted ten
minutes each to show our individual slides and give our own
spiel. I showed slides of Traquair and boosted the Freedom of
the Fairways, a golf course season ticket for the Scottish
Borders Tourist Board.

In San Francisco I fortunately remembered that I had
taken a coach-load of agents round the house the previous
season. When we were in the dining room I looked out of the
window that gives on to the rose garden and was horrified to
see my Vietnamese pig, which had always been perfectly
behaved, making huge furrows in the lawn. I had to leave the
agents on their own for a few minutes while I ran down and
put her into her sty. I introduced myself as the 'lady with the
pig' and received a round of applause.

At a lunch in Seattle, I met two men who had started an
agency to accommodate individuals in hotels or large private
houses in Britain. So far, historic houses that offered accommodation usually arranged it on the basis of renting the whole
house or hosting a shooting party. I decided that I would try to
let out two bedrooms at Traquair purely on a bed-and-breakfast basis. We had two large attractive rooms with half-tester
beds and private bathrooms, one of which had been Peter's and
mine. They could be reached without giving access to the
whole house.

I started by taking guests from the American agents. I
wanted to keep it on a personal level, and during the first years
I would give the guests a drink in the lower drawing room
before they went out to dinner and suggested places for them
to go. Only one French couple wanted a complete run-down

on all the menus and asked me to ring several restaurants to inquire how the lamb was being cooked.

In the mornings, if there was only one couple, I would cook the breakfast and ask whoever was cleaning the house to serve it in the Still Room. Inevitably, the guests would want the full breakfast, which was enough to keep them going for the rest of the day. I composed a menu that included kedgeree, smoked salmon and scrambled eggs, but fried eggs always seemed to be the most popular choice. They were something I rarely cooked and it seemed that, whatever I did, the yolk always broke. Even worse, one day I put out my hand to get an egg and found there were none in the rack. I rang Catherine in desperation and she rushed down to Innerleithen – a good ten minutes away. Fortunately, the guests were a honeymoon couple, and when I eventually took their breakfasts in, full of apologies, they were still gazing into each others eyes oblivious to the delay.

I found that bed-and-breakfasts were comparably easy to manage. The staff we already employed were able to clean the bedrooms and do the laundry. The guests did not hang around and were anxious to move on after they had been given a private tour of the house. Most of the visitors realised that it was not a hotel, but one Japanese family obviously did not. When I was lying in a hot bath late one evening, I was disturbed by a voice calling up the back stairs: 'Mrs Stuart – beer'.

When we became busier, I began to resent being tied to the house, waiting for guests to arrive. They were asked to come before six pm but often got lost on the way or their plane was late. One evening I was fed up with waiting. I had been asked out to dinner and decided not to delay any longer. I pinned a note to the front door, telling them to go to the cottage on the avenue where Laura, who helped in the house, lived. She had said she would see them in if I wasn't there.

As my guests drove up the avenue, they met Ian who, trying to be helpful, said he had a key. The following morning they gave me a lively description of being led around the dark castle, bumping into furniture before finally reaching the bedroom where they were to sleep. 'I was so scared I didn't want any dinner. I just jumped into bed and pulled the bedclothes over my face,' the wife told me. Luckily, her husband thought it a great experience and has no doubt enlivened many a dinner party with the story.

While the bed-and-breakfasts were starting to take off, Catherine was reorganising the brewery. While Ian and Frank were able to keep up the production and quality of the ale in the old brewery, she realised that brewing in the old vessels was extremely labour-intensive. After much thought, she decided to install a modern micro-brewery in the stable next door. The ale could be run through the adjoining wall and fermented in the same old oak fermenting vessel that was responsible for the unique flavour. The old brewery could be used less often. After months of disruption, the new brewery was installed. The first brew was bottled and we waited anxiously for anyone to detect any difference, but no one did. Production was increased immediately at a lower cost. We did not put the new brewery on view to the public. A young American beer journalist came to stay as a bed-and-breakfast guest. After he had spent some time in the Brew House, he asked if he could have a word with me. 'How is it,' he asked, 'that you have achieved such high production when it looks as if the old vessels have not been used recently?' I decided to tell him the truth and took him into the micro-brewery. He looked relieved and said, 'I thought you might be buying it in from somewhere else.' After that we decided to be quite open about our extended brewery.

On the recommendation of Henrietta Green, the celebrated food writer and journalist, the popular BBC *Food and Drink* programme was visiting specialist producers of food and drink as an extra item. At the end of the programme Jilly Goolden and Oz Clarke would have a tasting in the studio and give their verdicts. They could be very outspoken. When our ale's turn came, a television crew came up and shot the ale being made and the next day filmed a scene in our local bar, the Traquair Arms, where they asked the drinkers which of our ales they liked the best.

A few weeks later we watched the programme. I was in my bedroom in the house and Catherine in her cottage. We watched in trepidation as Jilly and Oz sampled our Jacobite ale. She took a sip, swilled it around in her mouth a little and then proclaimed in ecstasy, 'I think I'm a little bit in love – my kingdom has come.' She and Oz went on to extol its 'fruity richness'.

As soon as the programme ended, the telephone began to ring. Could I please tell them where their nearest supplier was or otherwise send bottles to such and such an address. I found odd bits of paper and a pencil and started to write down addresses. As soon as I put the receiver down, it rang again. There was never a pause to ring Catherine to ask her what to do or to get down to the office to put the answerphone on. It took at least an hour before I succeeded in doing this. The line was blocked for the next week, and we had to get extra help. A list was made of all the inquirers and they were put in touch with their nearest outlet. It gave the ale a long-lasting boost.

We were still being inveigled into helping at food-and-drink shows. Catherine was now creating a stylish stand that unfortunately always needed my bedside table and an old Turkish rug I had been given to complete the décor. When I saw her preparing for a show I knew they were soon likely to disappear. Now that the shows were farther afield – sometimes in London – I enjoyed them more. Friends from the past often appeared, and when I had time off I liked visiting the other stands and sampling the delicious food and drink.

Like farmers at this time, owners of historic houses were being forced to diversify. Although dinners for corporate groups were on the wane, it was now becoming the fashion to be married in an unusual setting. Traquair is a perfect place for a wedding. Our bishop has agreed to let all denominations use the chapel if they wish or, if it is a sunny day, the garden is a romantic setting. All the rooms can be used for the party afterwards and the bridal couple can spend the night in the honeymoon suite.

We have become professional through experience. At one

of the first weddings, the bride's mother insisted that she did all the flowers in the chapel herself. We waited for her anxiously all morning. We had almost given her up as the first guests began to arrive at the undecorated chapel, when she suddenly appeared, just before the bride, bearing huge bunches of gladioli. On another occasion, an American bride, flying in from Paris where she had ordered her dress, discovered only as she was dressing that she had collected the wrong one and it was three sizes too big. The wedding was delayed while Catherine managed to find a dressmaker to hastily tuck and hem. Since then we have had weddings of every description. Catherine has been asked to find a minister to perform the ceremony in the drawing room without mentioning God. Another couple made up their own ritual in the garden – the guests were divided into men and women and processed after the bride and groom towards an officiating woman in the centre. The wedding I most admired was planned by a young couple who seem to have taken Traquair to their hearts. It started with a straightforward marriage ceremony; the guests then changed into fancy dress. It was followed by a buffet lunch in the old walled garden, games on the lawn and finally a dinner-dance at night in the marquee.

Many of our wedding couples are Americans who have selected Traquair from the internet and have only a few friends and family present. It is the photographs that are important. These will be shown at a party when they return home so they dress as carefully as if they were to be married in a cathedral.

An Enchanted Summer

~

The season of 1995, which started wet and cold, ended in sunshine and happiness. It was an amazing summer with happenings all the way. Catherine was in love with a charming young man, John Grey. They had met at Glen, which was now owned by Colin and Anne's daughter-in-law, Tessa. She had chaired a green charity committee of which John was a member. For Catherine it was love at first sight.

John had set up his own design consultancy in London and Catherine persuaded him to redesign our beer labels. He would come up to Traquair most weekends and never complained that they were not the restful country weekends he might have expected. During the season there was usually an event of some kind going on and he was always roped in to help. One Saturday morning when I was in the office he knocked on the door. I asked what he wanted and he muttered that he was looking for Ella, Catherine's dog. I said I hadn't seen her and he left. About an hour later he returned and told me the real purpose of his visit – Catherine and he wanted to get married later in the year. I was absolutely delighted as I could see how right they were for each other.

Catherine had started another event, a Real Ale Festival. The early Festivals went relatively smoothly during the day. Ian and Frank, the two brewers, were willing to carry out all the extra work. It took place in a marquee in the old walled garden where real ale from every brewery in Scotland was available to sample. Real ale enthusiasts brought their families and sat in the sun sipping their beer while their children watched puppets or bounced on an inflatable castle. If the apple trees were thick with pink blossom and the bluebells were flowering below, it was a picturesque setting. The evenings were spoilt by a few local lads who were interested in alcohol but not in real ale. They often brought their own 'carry-outs' with them. The police had to be called in several times and they finally brought the event to an end.

That year it poured all the first day of the Ale Festival. The grass gradually turned into a quagmire and by the second day shoes were being sucked into the mud and abandoned. The atmosphere remained jolly, as is often the case in adversity, but when we looked at the lawns afterwards we feared that they would not recover in time for an international Indian bike rally that was booked for July. But in June the weather suddenly changed. It became hot and sunny and stayed like that for the next two months.

Richard Demarco had contacted me earlier in the year to talk about a joint project, with the artist Deryck Healey, to celebrate the millennium by creating an environmental art scheme. He envisaged community projects that would involve artists and creative individuals throughout Britain and encourage art to be made more accessible in our everyday lives. They also wanted to close the gap between art and science. It would take the form of a journey based on the constellations, starting in the south of England and ending under the celestial ceiling of the Scottish National Gallery. We would be part of the progression and artworks would be created in the grounds, inspired by the bear in our crest which would link it to Ursa Major and Ursa Minor, the Great Bear and Little Bear constellations.

Richard arranged for Deryck to come and visit us with Jeremy Wiltshire, his London agent. I had been a little dubious about the whole idea and our involvement in it, but as soon as we met, I was impressed by their sincerity and genuine inspiration. Once again Richard had introduced me to someone I immediately felt I could trust. Deryck had a magnetic personality and a belief in everyone's talent and wanted as many people as possible to take part and to create their own artworks in the grounds. Kevin and Ali, two young artists who had been working in the Demarco Gallery, volunteered to take part. As it was an unusually warm summer they were willing to camp by the Quair Burn while Deryck stayed in the house. Deryck got up early every morning and cleared the fallen branches from below the old yew trees in the walk by the Quair. He formed them into a long rounded serpent shape that twisted and turned through the wood.

They all collected dried grasses, ferns, ragwort, willowherb and ivy which they wove into the wire netting surrounding the old tennis court to form a huge tapestry that echoed the seventeenth-century needlework panels in the house. I would have liked to have spent all my time with them but was able to make only occasional visits. With Deryck's help I made a bird out of the dead heads of *Stachys lanata*. It was divided into sections and Deryck persuaded anyone who was interested to add to it. He also made designs in the ground with slates and stones while Kevin and Ali worked on separate sculptures. The visitors were intrigued. Some of them would add a bit and come back to see how it had grown. Every evening it was warm enough for us all to have supper out on the terrace, a magical occurrence in Scotland when hot summer days generally cool down quickly.

There were other diversions. Indian bikers from all over Europe arrived on their ancient bikes. They were attractive men, conscious of their image and dressed to enhance it. They camped at the end of the old walled garden which was no longer a quagmire and was covered by green grass again. During the day they had biking competitions on the avenue and at night there was a huge barbecue and fireworks display by the side of the Tweed.

It was such a busy summer that we scarcely had time to prepare for the wedding. Catherine and John had decided to get married in our small chapel. It had room enough for only family and close friends but afterwards we had a huge marquee on the lawn in front of the house. Besides friends and relatives whom Catherine had known since childhood, we invited everyone who worked for us and all those who lived on the estate or near by. John also had a large family and many friends.

Deryck transformed the whole event by offering to send for a friend, Graham, to help him decorate the marquee. The size made it a daunting task. He had young saplings brought in and placed uplighters on the ground to throw their shadows on the ceiling, creating a *Sylphide*-like setting to complement the white tulle Catherine had chosen for her dress. Everyone was involved. Debbie and Terry, who are imbued in American Indian culture, held an alternative stag night with sweat lodges in the garden. Tessa had a house party for John's friends at Glen. Jean made the bridesmaids' dresses. Mandi made one of her incredible wedding cakes. Sara arranged the flowers in the chapel. Felicity's daughter, Sylvia, and Joseph's daughter, Rebecca, as well as the children of parents who were connected with the house in some capacity, were bridesmaids and pages.

Inevitably, the weather broke, but Deryck and Graham worked on regardless, hanging garlands of flowers on the courtyard railings and around the chapel door. Our old friend Father Ronald Walls agreed to marry John and Catherine and turned the ceremony into a solemn and moving occasion. Catherine had asked me to give her away and her best friend, Francesca, was her 'best woman'. When we came out of the chapel, the sun had come out and the rest of the guests filled the courtyard. It seemed to be a portent of a joyful future. We danced all night in the marquee to bands and music played by friends living or working at Traquair. Elaine sang the blues, and at midnight John and Catherine left for a short honeymoon. The house had already taken over their lives – Catherine had agreed to return in ten days' time for a large Japanese wedding.

For the first time since Peter died, I felt completely at peace and happy. But happiness must never be taken for granted.

Tragedy

~

The year 1997 started well. A general election was to be held in the spring, and this time we had an able candidate, Keith Geddes, who had been Leader of Edinburgh City Council and whose family lived in the Borders. The Labour Party had been lent a room in the TGWU offices in Galashiels and I was free to canvass. I put leaflets through masses of letterboxes and knocked on lots of doors. I discovered all the narrow vennels and hidden patches of garden that Scottish towns conceal from the outside world. Both Catherine and John were Labour supporters, and we decided to get Ian to make a Blair's Brew. Keith arranged for Tony Blair to pull the first pint in the bar of the Edinburgh Sheraton Hotel when he came to Scotland for an election rally.

The ale was delivered to the deserted bar in mid-afternoon and Catherine and I sat and waited. Keith came in with his agent and told us that the campaign plane had arrived. Suddenly the place was overflowing with the Labour Party entourage followed by the world press who set up their cameras focused on our beer pump. Tony Blair and George Robertson went behind the bar and pulled the pints. It was shown for a few seconds at the end of the television news that day. Catherine and I went on to a rally in the Usher Hall where, it was said later, Blair made his best speech so far in the campaign, leaving his script and talking informally.

On election day I drove a small mini-bus taking voters to the polling station. We picked up a group from an old people's home who thanked us for the lift and told us, when they came out, that they had all voted Liberal! In the evening John and Catherine brought over another small keg of the Blair's Brew to the TWGU office. We had a party until the results began to come in and then started to watch the television. I kept my fingers crossed but could hardly believe what was happening. After so many disappointing election nights, it seemed like a dream as one Tory after another was toppled from his seat to be replaced by a Labour Member of Parliament. Our only disappointment was that Keith was just beaten by the Liberal.

In the autumn of that year all the joy went out of our lives. John was diagnosed with inoperable lung cancer. Their baby was due in two months' time. I do not wish to describe the private anguish of the months that followed, but I was full of admiration for the courageous way he faced his illness and of Catherine for the way she cared for him. John was just well enough to be present at the birth of his daughter, Isabella.

In the new year, as John's health deteriorated, I came home one evening to find a message on the answerphone to ring Nicholas Albery urgently. He was my brother Nicholas's best friend and they had shared many extraordinary and innovative schemes together, including the founding of the Institute of Social Inventions. He told me that Nicholas had been killed in a car accident in South Africa, where he had gone for a few days to research a book. I had been expecting him to come to stay the following weekend.

One of Nicholas Albery's most beneficial programmes was to start the Natural Death Centre, an organisation to encourage people to see death as a normal process and to take part in the burial of those you love yourself rather than handing everything over to an undertaker. Ironically, this was one scheme that my Nicholas could not bring himself to get involved in. He had always feared death. I was consoled by the thought that he had been killed instantly and would not have known that he was going to die, and also that he was more deeply in love with his latest girlfriend, Anya, and happier than he had ever been before, although for her it was a devastating blow. I was thankful, too, for the ten days we had spent together in Morocco when he took me to join a trekking group in the Ante Atlas for my sixtieth birthday. We shared a small tent and, totally relaxed after walking all day, lay side by side in the dark, talking and feeling closer than we had since our childhood.

Felicity, who always seemed to know when we needed her, offered to come and stay to look after John so Catherine and I and eight-week-old Isabella travelled down to London with Hilary, one of Nicholas's oldest friends. We talked and laughed for much of the journey, sharing stories about Nicholas and his extraordinary life. The reality that it had now come to an end had not sunk in.

Nicholas Albery supervised the burial. He had arranged for Nicholas's body to be flown back in a plain pinewood box. He and other friends fetched it from the airport in their own van. His burial was to take place in a clearing in an area of woodland outside London that Nicholas had fallen in love with and had managed to buy.

It was a mild February day as Catherine, holding Isabella, and I sat on hastily made benches around the coffin. A limited number of Nicholas's friends had been invited, which included a large number of his ex-girlfriends. Children played around happily. They were given felt-tip pens and sat on the coffin decorating it. Another friend had brought a huge hamper full of Nicholas's favourite food – chocolate biscuits and freshly made breads from the Neal's Yard Bakery and cheeses from the Dairy. It was passed round at intervals. People stood up spontaneously and told stories about him, including a friend who described volunteering to accompany him while he tried out his theory that if you bought a ticket to Hamburg and stayed on the plane you could end up in India without paying any more. Others recounted the ways that he had helped them, both personally and financially. A few younger people saw him as a guru. We laughed and ate and drank and almost felt he was there amongst us. When I watched the children on his coffin, I remembered how he used to lie down on the floor and let them crawl all over him.

Finally, we were all given bubble-blowing liquid (he had once set up a bubble machine that blew bubbles out into the street at intervals from a hole in his wall) and in a cloud of floating bubbles his coffin was carried to a grave that had been prepared a little way off. His son, Kristoffer, his eyes streaming, played his cello as the coffin was lowered. For the first time at a funeral, I felt that a body was really being returned to the earth. I read a poem by Helen Waddell that I had recently come across and had wanted to show him. I thought it described his love of nature and his search for spirituality:

> I shall not go to heaven when I die
> But if they let me be
> I think I'll take a road I used to know
> That goes by Slieve-ne-garagh and the sea.
> And all day breasting me the wind will blow,
> And I'll hear nothing but the pewit's cry
> And the sea talking in the caves below.
> I think it will be winter when I die
> (For no one from the North could die in spring)
> And all the heather will be dead and grey
> And the bog cotton will have blown away
> And there will be no yellow on the whin
> But I shall smell the peat,
> And when it's almost dark I will set my feet
> Where a white track goes glimmering to the hills,
> And see far up a light
> – Would you think heaven could be so small a thing
> As a window lit on the hills at night –
> And come stumbling from the gloom
> Half blinded by the firelit room.
> Turn and see you
> And there abide.
> If it were true,
> And if I thought they would let me be,
> I almost wish it were to-night I died.

Nicholas had given up being a Catholic. He had tried to believe but he was essentially a humanist by nature and he could not accept doctrine. I knew it was right for him not to have a church funeral. The coming together and love of friends with the burial in natural surroundings had a spiritual aspect that must have existed well before the ceremonies invented by the Church.

When John died peacefully at home with Catherine and his baby a few weeks later, she decided that he should have a funeral service in our chapel and be buried in the grounds with all the love and warmth of the many devoted friends he had made in his time at Traquair.

Happiness Regained

~

The house opening continued relentlessly. Easter was not far away and we were already spring-cleaning and getting ready for the new season. Catherine was invited to ski with her cousin Caroline for a few days and took Isabella with her. When she returned she was given huge support from friends and staff, and I was impressed by her fortitude. She continued to live in her cottage, leaving Isabella in the secure charge of her nanny, Fiona Bell, when she came down to work in the office each day.

Early in the season we were approached by the BBC to take part in a television series about cooking in country houses. We could talk about the house and we were each to cook one dish. We agreed to participate. Distractions were welcome, and we already knew Christopher Sykes, the presenter. I had hoped to cook beef, the Border speciality, with our own ale, but I was told that beef had already been 'done' and was asked to cook venison. I was still determined to use our ale so a new dish – 'carbonade of venison' – was invented. Catherine made her speciality, cranachan, a Scottish dessert of toasted oatmeal, honey and cream. After the filming was over, we ate the remains in the dining room with the crew, pretending to enjoy our creations.

The following month we were lucky enough to have another diversion. We were invited by old friends, the Wolfe Murrays, to go to the wedding of one of their sons in Romania. Rupert had been an aid worker there and had fallen in love with a lovely Romanian girl. Everything was arranged and Catherine, carrying Isabella in a sling, and I flew out with the other guests. We stayed in the hotel in Piatra Neamt where the wedding feast was held and dancing went on throughout the meal. We ate course after course and took it in turns to babysit, but neither of us managed to last out till the end, which must have been near dawn. 'Which course did you get to?' we all asked each other the next day as we were driven around the countryside visiting the richly decorated Orthodox convent chapels. The nuns could be seen kneeling in prayer, as still as statues in the garden.

Although Catherine had taken over most of the administration of Traquair, I would still find a note on my desk most evenings: 'Lights not working in King's Room'; 'One Ladies' toilet blocked'; 'Visitor reports damp marks in top passage'; and, worst of all, 'Dead cat reported by visitor outside Brew House'. They were all irritatingly small matters that made me long to get away.

Whenever I looked around the house and grounds, I was aware of the enormous amount of work and restoration that needed to be done. Although the increase in our income from weddings and accommodation was noticeable, it was obvious that we would not be able to carry out all the repairs and renovations that were needed. I felt I had done what I could. It would be up to Catherine to take over – it was time for me to leave Traquair. I thought of going to live in a flat in London but since Nicholas's death I had been put off that idea. London was a place I connected with both Peter and Nicholas and now its attraction had gone.

As Agnes had said to me, we had moved to the senior generation at Traquair. All the older couples I had been so fond of were no longer with us, but younger ones had become older and more responsible. The shop was now managed by Jean Vaughan, who had helped her husband with the silk-screen printing, and Rob, who had first come as a tapestry maker, was now an excellent chef and in charge of the tearoom, helped by

Elaine, who had once made hats. Terry had established a thriving jewellery business in one of the workshops, and Debbie was now training as a midwife.

Our new lawyer, an expert in the field, had suggested making Traquair a charitable trust. This would mean giving the main part of the house to the trust and it would be an irreversible decision. It was a big step and one that Catherine and I were reluctant to take. After much consideration, however, I began to realise the financial advantages. There were many points to talk over with Catherine, who was willing to sacrifice anything for Traquair. Gradually, changes had come into force. The whole relaxed concept of letting the public get enjoyment from your house in return for a contribution to its upkeep was not enough. In order to conserve Traquair we were now forced to be professional and to make the house work as a profitable business. A skill at procuring grants had become a necessity and once you received government grants you had already lost control of your building. If you wanted to attract enough tourists to make it worthwhile, you were in the hands of the Tourist Board, which had become a control freak. Stringent fire regulations were being brought in, which, although important, often tended to be out of keeping with an old building. All this required constant negotiation with the authorities. It was difficult to feel that you were living in a home of your own.

The Scottish Executive would be making land more accessible to the public. To relinquish ownership of the house would be a natural progression. As long as a family member could still live in it and be in control of its care, the charitable trust route seemed to be the sensible one to take.

One day I received a telephone call from Robin Crichton. Peter and I had known him and his wife, Trish, for many years but met only infrequently as they were film-makers and worked mainly abroad. The last time I had been to dinner at their house, his neighbour, the actor Robert Hardy, had brought his house guests. I arrived late and although I already knew Tim, as he liked friends to call him, I did not catch the other names. We chatted away all evening, and it was not until after they had gone that Robin asked me what I had thought of Emma Thompson and Greg Wise. With my inability to recognise people, I had had no idea who they were.

A few months later Robin rang me to ask advice about green funerals. Trish, who was a beautiful woman and still in her fifties, had been suffering from cancer for several years but had reached a terminal stage and there were only days to go. I put him in touch with Nicholas Albery.

When Trish died, Robin arranged his own theatrical version of her funeral. Her elegant pale panelled coffin, which he had made himself, stood on a podium in his film studio, guarded by six enormous candles. After a scripted programme, she was carried out by friends to the sound of music by Mozart which she had chosen and was buried in a grove of old beech trees near their house.

A couple of weeks later, Robin got in touch to ask whether I could sell some of his bric-a-brac in my antique shop. From that time on, we saw more and more of each other. We felt very comfortable together. We had shared similar experiences. We had both had long happy marriages and had worked closely with our partners. We both had daughters who we felt should be left to get on without us, and we had both come to a watershed. The film studio that Robin had built in the sixties, the first in Scotland, was too small for modern productions. He had formed a trust to turn the studio into a national studio and had already raised two million pounds and was waiting to hear if they would get a lottery grant to make up the shortfall. If this did not come off, he had made up his mind to sell his house and studio and do something else.

He decided to make his last film a follow-up of his first. When he was an anthropology student he spent two summers with the Meskwakie Indians in North America. He had taken a movie camera and been funded by the BBC to make a black and white 16-millimetre film. This had made him decide to become a film-maker. He took complete control of his films, finding the funding and producing and directing. His wife and daughters had all worked with him. Now, forty years later, he wanted to return to the Meskwakies to record the changes that had taken place and he asked me if I would go with him.

I was glad that I had already arranged to go to China with my Irish friend Maeve Hall. I felt that Robin was trying to fill the gap left by his wife and was not taking time to grieve. He told me that he had done all his grieving with his wife before she died as they had known for some time that she would not recover. I realised that his daughters, Miggy and Lou, were finding it hard to come to terms with their mother's death and thought that Robin was trying to get on with his life too quickly. Lou and her husband were living with him while their house was being built near by. She was about to have a baby but Robin seemed unconcerned. I did not know what to think; my emotions were frozen. I had always thought of him as an attractive flirtatious man and I did not know how serious he was. I had been living on my own for eight years and had become accustomed to it. I was sixty-four and he was six years younger. Peter had been twelve years older.

Whenever I travel abroad I live entirely in the present and forget about the rest of my life. I love the sensation of existing in a vacuum. Maeve is fun to travel with. She had already introduced me to Ireland, where I was overwhelmed by the hospitality and poetry of the people, and she had helped me to achieve my life-long ambition of visiting Nanny's village on the west coast.

Tuamgraney did not feature on many maps and few people had heard of it. By the time we reached the group of scattered houses looking out over the rocks towards America, we were already late for our next appointment. We found Nanny's niece, Mary, who kept the pub, a fact that Nanny had always felt obliged to keep from us, always giving her address as care of the Post Office. But her nephew, Jack, the American priest whom Peter and I had met in Kansas City, had stayed with her regularly. He had a great sense of fun and regaled us with stories of the life there. The pub was the centre of the village and the bar was part of the house. At closing time the front door was locked but everyone went in at the back. Mary looked so much like my memory of Nanny that I almost felt that it was her. She chatted about my family and relatives and seemed to know more about them than I did myself. Maeve sat at the bar, where she got the impression that there was a constant movement back and forth to the States and the inhabitants of Tuamgraney were well versed in American politics.

We had also travelled round southern India together and, being equally curious about ashrams, we stayed in two, where we slept on floors, and also visited Sai Baba's ashram. Maeve liked to travel with a large suitcase, which I found cumbersome, but someone (often a handsome young man) always seemed to pop up to carry it for her. She talked to everyone and asked them questions so I had only to listen.

For the trip to China, we flew to Moscow where we stayed a night before catching the Trans-Siberian Express. Moscow was full of glamorous young women, heavily made-up, flaunting their furs and designer clothes. We just had time to see a heavily guarded Lenin lying in his tomb and a shoe shop with the most expensive imported shoes I had ever seen before catching the train that would take us to China.

Once on the train we saw the other side of life in Russia. Wherever we stopped countrywomen were standing on the platform trying to sell their meagre possessions or bits of food. A Chinese woman on the train hopefully leant out of the window dangling a bunch of Chinese-sized brassières. Not only were they quite inadequate for the Russian bosom, but they were the last thing that anyone wanted. Our days passing through the Steppes and the Urals were of interest mainly for their association with Russian novels. The monotony was enlivened by meals in the restaurant cars. First, large solid meals in the dull Russian car followed by more interesting food in the drunken Mongolian car and finally inedible meals in the Chinese car where even the Chinese had to be given a free meal ticket to lure them in.

We continued across China by train to Hong Kong,

stopping off for a few days at a time. I was impressed by the size and structure of the Great Wall as we spent a day walking along it. At Xian I was stunned by the sight of the excavated massed terracotta warriors standing like the ghosts of a First World War battlefield. I spent a Saturday afternoon sketching in the town park and watched doting parents amusing their spoilt only sons. We sailed up the Yangtze river, strange pointed mountains rising steeply on either side. On the way I got into conversation with an elderly American. 'And what is waiting for you when you get home?' he asked. I found myself saying, 'I might be getting married again.' 'Make sure you really like the guy,' he said. 'Nothing else matters.'

In spite of language difficulties, Maeve was clever at finding good food. She would find out where the Chinese went for a treat so we had some excellent meals. On a Saturday night in Beijing we sat among families eating a set meal of numerous small courses. At another restaurant we were given an empty bowl and were served with bread. The Chinese couple at our table indicated that it must be crumbled. They looked at our first effort and shook their heads. Finer crumbs were indicated. When the delicious meat stew was finally served on top, the bread turned into a thick gravy.

I learnt to drink as little as possible before an overnight journey. In spite of there being an attendant in each carriage, the lavatories were never cleaned and often blocked. A trickle would start to run down the corridor, and the smell would get stronger the farther we went. We shared our sleeper with different Chinese couples, smiling and nodding at each other all the way. I wanted to ask them so many questions but we were totally unable to communicate. The language barrier must be one of the major obstacles to peace in the world.

We flew back from Hong Kong, and Robin was in touch with me as soon as I returned. He seemed to take it for granted that I would be going to the States with him. He has a strong personality, and it was a new and restful experience to have my mind made up for me.

He told me that before going to the States, we would have

to go to the Television Festival in Cannes to get backing for the film. He had a neighbour who used an aged taxicab to advertise his property company in Edinburgh. It had been taken to Nice for a property market, and Robin suggested that we pick it up and drive it home, casually mentioning that we would also be going through Germany, Austria and Italy to Slovenia where he had been asked to appear in a film.

We stayed with Robin's friends Norman and Maggie Hackett in Gallargues on the way to Cannes. I was conscious that they had both known Trish since they were all students together and were still shocked by her death and missing her. In spite of that, they were kind and welcoming. We then stayed with mutual friends in a château above Nice and from there went down to Cannes where Robin had set up meetings in advance with television executives to secure the necessary backing for the Meskwakie Indian film before we set off for Slovenia.

Robin is at home in Europe. He speaks French like a Frenchman and has a good stab at other languages. He also appeared to know the European continent like the back of his hand and scarcely needed to use a map. We stopped at Mantua for a night to pay tribute to the 'Admirable' Crichton, the brilliant young Scotsman who was tutor to the Duke of Mantua's son in the sixteenth century and was slain in the street at night by his jealous pupil.

In Ljubljana, where, at the start of the revolution that caused the break-up of Yugoslavia only eight years before, Robin was asked by the local television company, RTV Slovenia, to make a speech in the main square welcoming freedom, we were put up in a gloomy ex-communist hotel. The documentary Robin was to appear in was about an early photographer, a Slovenian priest, who discovered how to make negatives before the French photographer Louis Daguerre. Robin was playing the part of a learned Scotsman who was so impressed by the discovery that he came out to investigate. Scenes were shot in picturesque villages where a small white church sat on the top of every hill.

The crew worked to strict union hours, exasperating the director when, after time had already been lost sheltering from rain, they immediately announced that their time was up. I benefited from their insistence on having a good lunch every day and thoroughly enjoyed the home-made food in the country inns. We drove back through Austria, spending two nights in Unken, a romantic Alpine village where Robin had used the church for his film *Silent Mouse*. After a detour through Champagne, where we filled up with bottles as a thank-you for the owner of the taxi, we returned home.

It had been a wonderful journey and a successful one, as Robin had been promised the backing for the Meskwakie film he would be making later in the year. I was amazed that two people who had had their own way most of their lives could be so happy together. I realised we were in love.

On my return, Catherine told me that she had been seeing a lot of her old friend Mark Muller. They were students together at the LSE and he was one of the first of her student friends she brought home. He had become a good friend of John's and visited him constantly when he was ill. Now he was a brilliant barrister practising in London but since John's death he had still found time to come up to visit Catherine and Isabella most weekends. I felt I knew him well, and I had always liked him and admired his left-wing views and his defence of human rights. When she told me that they had decided to get married it seemed too good to be true. They agreed to move into the house while I was away and later, when I had altered the cottage, we would swap houses.

Robin and I flew to Edmonton in Canada and stayed with Robin's charming daughter Sian and her husband, Dave, and Robin proudly viewed his baby grandson for the first time. After an awe-inspiring visit to the Rocky Mountains, we flew down to Iowa where we stayed on the Meskwakie Settlement for a month.

The Meskwakies are the only American Indian tribe to have bought their land and therefore do not live on a reservation. They are a small tribe, with just over a thousand members, and a very private one, and they have retained their own culture, language and religion. When Robin filmed them forty years before, they were living in extreme poverty, but now they had opened a casino and the income was changing their lives. New houses were being built and health and welfare programmes were being carried out. Ironically, at the same time, the small white family farmers in this corn-and-soya country were going bankrupt. The Indians were now the biggest employers in the area.

Robin had told Jonathan Buffalo, the tribal archivist, that we would prefer not to live in the casino hotel but among the tribe in the woods behind. Jonathan took us to an empty house that was waiting to be demolished. It was filthy, but in spite of a temperature of ninety degrees Fahrenheit, we managed to clean it out and buy basic furniture. Jonathan's girlfriend, Suzanne, lent us more. She was a well-built dark-eyed young woman who could have been taken for an Italian or Spaniard. She had lived away from the settlement for a while and was trying to relearn Indian ways – to talk less and be still. 'Indians are different,' she told us, 'even physically different. Our teeth are not the same as white people and our hair is coarser.'

I was full of questions. 'What did the Indians eat?' I asked. 'We probably buy the same ingredients as white people, but we cook them differently,' she told me, 'and we grow our own Indian corn, which is sweeter. The men hunt in the woods, and we consider squirrel a delicacy.' I asked her what the white Canadians thought about the casino. 'They keep asking us what we are doing with all the money,' she said, 'and they like to tell us that we have been cheated and don't understand business. Even though we are no longer underprivileged and have a standard of living equal to theirs, it makes no difference to their attitude. We don't want to be like them, but we would like some respect.'

Each day we went out to interview members of the tribe. Robin concentrated on the Johnson family, with whom he had stayed on his first visit. Then they were a young couple with three children. Now they had nine children and thirty-eight grandchildren. Barbara Jean was a true earth mother, always looking after at least four or five little ones while their mothers were out at work.

Robin looked round the small modern house with the built-in kitchen at one end and commented, 'This is a nice change from your old kitchen when you had to cook out of doors and got your water from a pump.' 'Aw, Robin, cooking and washing up are not all that much different wherever you do it,' she answered calmly. Her comment reminded me of the Buddhist monk at Samye Ling who, when someone congratulated him on the magnificent temple that had just been completed, he only shrugged his shoulders and said, 'It's all right.'

Underneath what appeared to be almost an American way of life there was a very different awareness. The Meskwakies are less interested in material things. They exist as a tribe and not as individuals. Everything they own is shared. Competition and self-aggrandisement are looked down upon. They consider that their land is God-given and held in trust by the tribe.

The Meskwakie belief has been handed down through the years: 'I am a Meskwakie, my creator made me in his own likeness and he made this country for me. My creator placed me on this earth and laid down laws by which I should live. He gave me my religion so that I might worship him so that I might dwell for ever in the Hereafter that has been prepared for me.' It seemed to echo the first line of the catechism that I had learnt in my convent school: 'Why did God make you?' was the question and, 'To know him and love him and serve him in this world and be happy with him for ever in the next,' was the answer.

As a Catholic I felt deeply ashamed of the treatment that the Indians had received from the Spanish and French missionaries in the sixteenth century. They had encouraged violence to subject them to the 'yoke and obedience of the church'. The similarities in their worship had gone unrecognised. Fasting and meditation have always been an important part of their religion and are still practised for days at a time by many of the Meskwakie men.

The Meskwakies had had a lasting influence on Robin, and I now realised why he gave away all his wife's clothes as soon as she died, an action that had puzzled some of his friends. When a member of the tribe dies, all his or her clothes and belongings must be removed from the house or the spirit of the dead person cannot leave. The Spirit World is not far away, and ghost feasts are regularly held for those who have died. Food is prepared for the living and the dead. The ancestors are not far away, and if you go home feeling hungry you know that the spirits have shared your food.

Our neighbour in the settlement, Alec, who lived next to a disused farm building, had a social science degree and had fought in Vietnam. He was a member of the Tribal Council and was a religious man who kept a tepee in his garden for daily meditation. He warned us about an owl that sat on a post near his house. He said it was a witch in disguise, and he and his wife took their child into bed at night in case it harmed her.

In spite of the new houses and higher standard of living that the tribe are now enjoying, many members hanker after their old way of life, when they had fewer material things to look after and more time for carrying our their ceremonies and for socialising and neighbourliness.

At the end of our visit the Pow Wow was held. It is the time that friends and relatives return. Indian costumes are worn, and music and dancing carry on over three days. Stalls are set up, and many of the families build a wickiup and move down to the Pow Wow ground while it is on. The wickiup is an igloo-shaped tent made of bent poles and originally covered by woven reed matting but now covered by any kind of old fabric. At our Pow Wow, Barbara Johnson cooked 'fry-bread' non-stop, a favourite Indian food made from self-raising flour mixed with water to form a dough that is then kneaded and flattened and dropped into a pan of hot fat.

My month with the Meskwakies left a great impression. I had at last met a truly democratic society and one that realises that spirituality is more important than materialism. I worried about their future. The tribe is no longer in danger of dying out through poverty. The danger now is the allure of the Canadian way of life. Every house already has a huge television set. It is up to the young Meskwakies to decide whether to stay with the tribe or whether to become Canadian.

We flew home laden with presents. On the plane Robin started scribbling on the back of an envelope. 'What are you doing?' I asked. 'I am drawing up plans for our new house,' he replied.

Mark and Catherine were married in October 1999 in St Etheldreda's Church in London, where I had married Peter and where a memorial service had been held for John. A splendid dinner-dance was held afterwards in his chambers at Gray's Inn.

Robin and I were married quietly in the Traquair chapel on 28 December 1999 by one of my favourite priests, Father John Robertson. Robin's father-in-law showed his generous spirit and goodwill by travelling up from England to be present with all our children and grandchildren. The service started with a verse that Robin had written for our wedding day:

We've loved before, both deep and strong,
And part of our hearts will always belong
To our previous lives with Peter and Trish.
That's right and natural and as we would wish.
With them we learned what it meant to love,
And as we believe they are watching above
Will show their love in the love *we* build
In our years together – our lives fulfil.

Life's a gift – *a gift of time*
And combining our lives – yours with mine,
Will make our time both richer and broader.
We cannot arrange our future to order,
Nor can we foretell what our span may be,
But finding each other is destiny.

May we love and share for the rest of our life
And be blessed and happy as man and wife.

It would be the start of a new millennium and a new life. I had learnt that when someone dies they are not forgotten but remain a part of us and help to shape our future. With their influence, we mellow and enjoy our 'gift of time'.